CONDUCTING A CULTURALLY INFORMED NEUROPSYCHOLOGICAL EVALUATION

CONDUCTING A CULTURALLY INFORMED NEUROPSYCHOLOGICAL EVALUATION

Daryl Fujii

American Psychological Association • Washington, DC

Published by
American Psychological Association
750 First Street, NE
Washington, DC 20002
www.apa.org

To order
APA Order Department
P.O. Box 92984
Washington, DC 20090-2984
Tel: (800) 374-2721; Direct: (202) 336-5510
Fax: (202) 336-5502; TDD/TTY: (202) 336-6123
Online: www.apa.org/pubs/books
E-mail: order@apa.org

In the U.K., Europe, Africa, and the Middle East, copies may be ordered from
American Psychological Association
3 Henrietta Street
Covent Garden, London
WC2E 8LU England

Typeset in Goudy by Circle Graphics, Inc., Columbia, MD

Printer: United Book Press, Baltimore, MD
Cover Designer: Mercury Publishing Services, Inc., Rockville, MD

The opinions and statements published are the responsibility of the authors, and such opinions and statements do not necessarily represent the policies of the American Psychological Association.

Library of Congress Cataloging-in-Publication Data

Names: Fujii, Daryl, 1961- author.
Title: Conducting a culturally informed neuropsychological evaluation / Daryl Fujii.
Description: First edition. | Washington, DC : American Psychological Association, [2017] | Includes bibliographical references and index.
Identifiers: LCCN 2016004355 | ISBN 9781433822940 | ISBN 1433822946
Subjects: LCSH: Neuropsychological tests—Evaluation. | Neuropsychological tests—Cross-cultural studies.
Classification: LCC RC386.6.N48 F85 2017 | DDC 616.8/0475—dc23
LC record available at https://lccn.loc.gov/2016004355

British Library Cataloguing-in-Publication Data
A CIP record is available from the British Library.

Printed in the United States of America
First Edition

http://dx.doi.org/10.1037/15958-000

CONTENTS

ACKNOWLEDGMENTS

First of all, I thank Raul Gonzalez for directing my mental energies to this topic in 2012 when he invited me to give a continuing education workshop on cross-cultural neuropsychology at the 2013 International Neuropsychological Society Conference, held in Waikoloa, Hawaii. It was there that I met Gary VandenBos, who invited me to write this book for APA Books. Serendipity.

Thanks to members of the Society for Indian Psychologists (SIP)—Mark Powless, Daniel Foster, Dennis Norman, and Wendy Peters—for sharing their insight on Native Indian Alaskan Native culture and to Joseph Gone for directing me to the SIP listserv. Thanks to the many cultural consultants for sharing their expertise: Sam Yoon Fujii (Korean), Alia Ammar (Arabic), Mariana Strutt (Latino), Ia Xiong (Hmong), Guy Vingerhoets (Belgian), Michael Nestor (Saudi Arabia), Neal Palafox (Marshallese), Roselin Naryboy and Deirdre Piotrowski (Navajo), and Laith Enani (Jordanian). Thanks to APA Books Development Editor, David Becker, and the reviewers for providing such wonderful feedback to improve the content of the book. June Paultzer, Tedd Judd, Paul Craig, Marc Norman, Lawrence Pick, Alia Ammar, and Adrian Strutt are acknowledged for their support and understanding.

Finally, I would not be a good Asian if I did not acknowledge my family. Thanks to my dad, Earl Fujii, who quietly taught me the keys to success in life: find your passion, work hard, always do your best, and, most of all, stay humble. I know you continue to watch over us. Thanks to my mom, Judy Fujii, who always encouraged and fostered my creativity, and my brother Jay, my musical partner in crime. Thanks to my lovely wife and lifelong partner, Sam, who has continually supported me for the past 24 years, including the past 4 years working on this project. Thanks to my eggies Dylan Eden and Daniel Cody, who have been my pride and joy, and Barry and Sachi, who always greet me with smiling faces and wagging tails. Doomo arigato gozaimasu.

CONDUCTING A CULTURALLY INFORMED NEUROPSYCHOLOGICAL EVALUATION

INTRODUCTION

It is difficult to understand the universe if you only study one planet.
—Miyamoto Musashi

Clinical neuropsychologists are well versed in the technical, rote processes of conducting a neuropsychological evaluation. However, neuropsychology is not simply reporting test scores. To be a good neuropsychologist, one must first be a good psychologist, part of which entails making context-dependent clinical judgments. Understanding a client's background is imperative for collecting accurate data and interpreting it to make useful recommendations. This can be challenging with any client, but especially so with a client from a cultural background different from that of the neuropsychologist.

The following example illustrates a scenario that a neuropsychologist might encounter when evaluating a culturally different client (CDC). Maria is a 34-year-old Mexican American woman who sustained a seizure of unknown origin while riding the bus on her way home from her job as a seamstress. She was referred to Dr. Neil for neuropsychological testing to clear her for return to work. Maria is highly motivated to return to work

http://dx.doi.org/10.1037/15958-001
Conducting a Culturally Informed Neuropsychological Evaluation, by D. Fujii

because she has three children to support. She does not speak English well and has only a second-grade education; thus, testing was conducted through an interpreter. Maria failed two of four performance validity tests and scored in the impaired range for almost all tests, including attention, visuospatial skills, processing speed, and memory. Inconsistent with her test performance was her self-report of catching the bus to the office, which entailed transferring twice and walking several blocks without the aid of a GPS. She also does all the grocery shopping for the family and was reported to be one of the best workers at her company. Dr. Neil was certain that there were cultural, language, and educational factors affecting testing; however, on the basis of her test results, he could not determine if her seizure disorder significantly impacted her cognitive functioning.

Although a neuropsychologist's primary concern may be with English-language proficiency, many other elements of a CDC's personal history play important parts in an effective neuropsychological evaluation. Language comprehension is just one piece of a very complex puzzle. The neuropsychologist must develop a more detailed understanding of the client's educational background, cultural values, communication style, comfort with the testing process, and conception of intelligence, which may not conform with Western conceptualizations of those issues. Without knowledge of these and other important cultural factors, the neuropsychologist risks using tests that are not validated for the client's culture and country of origin, interpreting results incorrectly, and making improper diagnoses and recommendations that could cause the client distress or harm.

Thus, the goal of this book is to provide clinical neuropsychologists with a broad framework for conducting culturally informed neuropsychological evaluations. However, this is not a step-by-step manual that provides "answers" or specifics for working with a client from a given cultural background. Instead, my intent with this book was to help clinical neuropsychologists understand and identify their potentially biased perceptions of CDCs and minimize biased assessment methodologies through careful preparation. Preparation is the most important aspect of a culturally informed neuropsychological evaluation. The book provides a detailed description of this process by familiarizing the reader with the disparate literature on cultural characteristics that can affect a neuropsychological assessment. These elements are then organized into a systematic approach for evaluating a CDC. Although it is imperfect, I hope that the framework introduced in this book will point neuropsychologists of all cultures in the right direction toward more culturally informed neuropsychological assessments. The clinician can then find his or her own answers to challenges associated with specific CDCs.

OVERVIEW OF CLINICAL NEUROPSYCHOLOGY
AND CROSS-CULTURAL NEUROPSYCHOLOGY

Clinical neuropsychology is the subspecialty of clinical psychology that focuses on the evaluation of brain functioning and associated cognitive, behavioral, and emotional sequelae of neurological disorders; the goals of neuropsychological assessment include diagnosis, reaching data-driven opinions of functionality and treatment, and gaining a basic understanding of brain–behavior relationships. As with clinical psychology, neuropsychology was developed in Western countries with both quantitative and qualitative approaches to assessment. Thus, there is a strong Western bias in assessment techniques. The quantitative tradition emphasizes assessment through psychometrically sound tests in which performances are interpreted in relation to the distribution of scores in a given sample or population. Proponents of this approach include Ward Halstead, Ralph Reitan, and Arthur Benton. Qualitative approaches, espoused by Norman Geshwind, Edith Kaplan, and Russian Alexander Luria, are more dynamic and use hypothesis testing to determine the processes that underlie complex behaviors. Contemporary neuropsychological approaches can be conceived as a hybrid of both traditions, with the majority of clinicians using a flexible battery of validated tests for different neurological conditions (Sweet, Meyer, Nelson, & Moberg, 2011).

Cross-cultural neuropsychology is the assessment of cognitive functioning and the examination of brain–behavior relationships across people of different cultures or ethnicities. One of the earliest cross-cultural neuropsychological studies was conducted by Luria (1979) in the 1930s, when he examined the impact of culture and education on the cognition of Uzbekistan villagers undergoing accelerated social change secondary to government efforts for modernization. However, the importance of cultural issues in neuropsychological assessment has really gained traction only within the past 20 years. A number of clinical and scientific factors have contributed to this growing interest.

In the United States, the growing ethnic diversity of the population, culminating in projections of ethnic minorities overtaking White Americans as the majority population around 2044 (Colby & Ortman, 2015), and the 2001 U.S. Surgeon General's Report (Satcher, 2001) on mental health disparities between Whites and ethnic minority populations, have been instrumental forces for incorporating culturally fair psychological assessments in health care services.

Internationally, the growing affluence of countries with developing economies has resulted in better access to Western-influenced health care and mental health services; increased access to information via the Internet, Western training, and other electronic data sources; and growing public health concerns, such as aging populations. These factors have contributed to the development of neuropsychology across the globe (Fujii, 2011). In addition, many researchers have studied the neuropsychological functioning of people living in a range of countries to better understand how experiences and behaviors affect brain–behavior relationships (Agranovich & Puente, 2007) and the impact of diseases, such as malaria, on brain functioning (Boivin & Giordani, 2013).

The growth of cross-cultural neuropsychology is reflected in expanding neuropsychological literature. including contributions of non-Western researchers in academic journals (Matsuoka, Uno, Kasai, Koyama, & Kim, 2006; Senanarong et al., 2005; Yang et al., 2012), the publication of cross-cultural neuropsychology books (Fletcher-Janzen, Strickland, & Reynolds, 2000; Fujii, 2011; Nell, 2000; Uzzell, Ponton, & Ardila, 2007), coverage of cultural issues in newer editions of classic texts (Lezak, Howieson, Bigler, & Tranel, 2012; Strauss, Sherman, & Spreen, 2006), cultural chapters in neuropsychology books (Artiola i Fortuny, 2008), and association guidelines for addressing multicultural issues in assessment (American Psychological Association [APA], 2003; American Academy of Clinical Neuropsychology [AACN] Board of Directors, 2007), as well as growth in international membership in the International Neuropsychological Society.

Numerous clinicians and researchers have identified and addressed specific issues pertinent for using Western neuropsychological tests with CDCs, including test validity (Mungas, Reed, Farias, & DeCarli, 2005), English as a second language (Artiola i Fortuny, 2008), acculturation (Greenfield, 1997), conception of intelligence (Sternberg et al., 2001), test translations (International Test Commission, 2010), bilingualism (Rivera-Mindt et al., 2008), illiteracy and low education level (Ardila et al., 2010), quality of education (Manly, Jacobs, Touradji, Small, & Stern, 2002), novelty of task (Nell, 2000), cultural and demographic variables (Judd & Beggs, 2005), perceived meaning of testing situation (Ardila, 2007), heterogeneity within a race (Fujii, 2011), selection biases in immigration for country of origin (Fujii, 2011), race norms (Heaton, Miller, Taylor, & Grant, 2004), effort testing (Salazar, Lu, Wen, & Boone, 2007), and test development and adaptation (Y. H. Chen & Chen, 2002; Ostrosky-Solís, Ardila, & Rosselli, 1997).

OVERVIEW OF THE BOOK

Despite an emerging cross-cultural neuropsychological literature, thus far there has not been a comprehensive integrated resource that describes how to conduct a neuropsychological evaluation with a CDC. This is the goal of the present book: the application of multiculturalism to neuropsychology via practical guidelines to produce a culturally informed evaluation. It should be emphasized that the goal is not a "culturally fair" or even a "culturally neutral" evaluation because most neuropsychological assessments are grounded in Western culture and values and based on adaptations, translations, or indigenous emulations of Western technology. Thus, it is argued that neuropsychological assessments would hold different levels of inherent biases to the spectrum of CDCs. Moreover, given my background, the process described in this book is inherently "United States–centric."

Although the primary audience for this book is clinical neuropsychologists, given the importance and ubiquity of the topic, the content would be of interest to any psychologist or psychology trainee who performs cognitive psychological assessments or works with CDCs.

The book is divided into three parts. Part I is foundational and focuses on the clinician's attitude and perspective. I argue that before learning how to conduct a culturally informed neuropsychological evaluation, the neuropsychologist must have a respectful, open-minded attitude toward the CDC and an appreciation of how culture affects the neuropsychological process. Without these cornerstones, the neuropsychologist's conduct, conceptualizations, and conclusions may be clouded with biases and a lack of respect and appreciation of the client's culture. Chapter 1 thus describes how an ethnorelative perspective is a prerequisite for a culturally informed neuropsychological evaluation. First, it introduces Bennett's developmental model of intercultural sensitivity (1993) and illustrates how assessment biases can result from a clinician's stage of cultural awareness. Categories of behaviors and values are then introduced to assist the clinician in developing an awareness of assumptions in his or her own culture and thereby allow for comparison and contrast with a CDC's culture. In this regard, it provides categorical tools for meeting APA's (2010) Ethical Principles of Psychologists and Code of Conduct, hereafter referred to as the APA Ethics Code, and Revised Competency Benchmarks for Professional Psychology (APA, 2011) for working with CDCs.

Chapter 2 provides an overview of how culture affects the neuropsychological process based on a summary of APA's (2010) Ethics Code and Guidelines on Multicultural Education, Training, Research, Practice, and Organizational Change for Psychologists (APA, 2003) and the AACN Practice Guidelines concerning Underserved Populations/Cultural Issues, as well as American Educational Research Association (AERA) 2014 standards for fairness in testing. A "big-picture" conceptualization of how culture specifically affects the neuropsychological assessment process is then introduced. Together, these principles guide the culturally informed neuropsychological process.

Part II provides an overview of the preparation a neuropsychologist must undertake before conducting a neuropsychological evaluation. Chapter 3 describes how to create a context for understanding a CDC through three preparatory tasks: (a) contextualizing behaviors and presentation, (b) maximizing cooperation during testing, and (c) facilitating communication. The chapter uses a comprehensive review of Native Indian and Alaskan Native cultures to illustrate the importance of societal structures, religious beliefs, family structures, concepts of intelligence, beliefs about illness, and other cultural factors that will have an impact on the neuropsychologist's hypothesis development and test selection. Chapter 4 distills the inherent goals of the evaluation; breaks down components of moderating factors, including acculturation and communication/language, to identify potential threats to validity; and offers strategies for addressing these threats, working with interpreters, and interpreting test results, the latter to meet International Test Commission recommendations. Chapter 5 introduces strategies and formulas for estimating CDCs' premorbid functioning in general and on Western neuropsychological tests. In that chapter, I argue that intelligence testing and estimating premorbid IQ give neuropsychologists a general understanding of how well a CDC has acculturated to Western norms, thus providing a benchmark to predict and interpret test scores. Chapter 6 describes psychometric considerations for test selection and recommendations for test translation. It then identifies specific approaches recommended by the AACN for data collection helping neuropsychologists determine which strategies may be most appropriate for a particular CDC. Chapter 7 follows up this discussion and closes Part II with a list of neuropsychological tests that have demonstrated cross-cultural validity along with references for validation studies describing norms from different countries.

Part III demonstrates how all this preparation is put into action through a comprehensive case sample[1] of Jae Song Kim, a 66-year-old Korean American man who sustained a right-sided basal ganglia stroke. This case runs through the final three chapters and illustrates what a culturally informed neuropsychological process entails in actual practice. The case is introduced in Chapter 8 and exemplifies the process of developing a cultural context with a specific client, demonstrating how knowledge about a client's cultural background and values can inform the evaluation process. It also illustrates methods for overcoming common challenges when working with a CDC. The chapter closes with the neuropsychologist interviewing Mr. Kim and his family with the aid of an interpreter, showing how this can be valuable in developing a context and aligning the neuropsychologist's goals with those of the CDC and the CDC's family. Chapter 9 breaks down the process for interpreting interview and test data and integrating them into a coherent case formulation.

---

[1]All case examples are composites, and proper steps were taken to maintain the confidentiality of the individuals in these examples.

The case example follows the five essential steps of this process: (a) scoring tests with appropriate norms, (b) identifying potential threats to validity, (c) determining effort through performance validity tests, (d) reviewing the pertinent neuropsychological literature, and (e) interpreting the data. Chapter 10 provides guidelines for writing a report, which is illustrated by a full case report for Mr. Kim. It also details how to conduct a feedback session with a CDC and his or her family. Mr. Kim's session demonstrates how careful preparation and developing a context result in culturally useful treatment recommendations that promote positive outcomes for the CDC.

I

FOUNDATIONS: ATTITUDES, PERSPECTIVE, AND CONCEPTUAL OVERVIEW

1

A RESPECT FOR CULTURE

Knowing others is wisdom . . . knowing yourself is enlightenment.

—Lao Tzu

According to cognitive behavioral therapy (Beck, 1979), an individual's attitude or underlying belief system has a profound influence on his or her interactions with the world. In other words, positive beliefs typically beget positive interactions, and negative beliefs beget negative ones. This principle also applies to cross-cultural neuropsychology: A clinician's attitude toward the client can permeate all aspects of the assessment process and influence his or her clinical opinion. Thus, I argue that having the right attitude or mind-set is essential for performing a culturally informed neuropsychological assessment.

In the preamble to the American Psychological Association's (APA; 2010) *Ethical Principles of Psychologists and Code of Conduct*, Ethical Guidelines Principle E: Respect for People's Rights and Dignity, highlights two important elements when working with a culturally different client (CDC): (a) the need for self-awareness in how one's attitudes and beliefs can negatively affect beliefs, perceptions, and overall interaction with persons different

http://dx.doi.org/10.1037/15958-002
Conducting a Culturally Informed Neuropsychological Evaluation, by D. Fujii

from oneself and (b) the importance of understanding, knowledge, and sensitivity to the needs of others. These two qualities are the cornerstones for cultural competency, and, when combined, equate to respect for the CDC.

Guidelines for working with a CDC are further elaborated in APA's (2011) *Revised Competency Benchmarks for Professional Psychology*, which include the following key benchmark:

> 2. Individual and Cultural Diversity: Awareness, sensitivity and skills in working professionally with diverse individuals, groups and communities who represent various cultural and personal background and characteristics defined broadly and consistent with APA policy. (p. 2)

This is further broken down into other benchmarks of competency:

2.A. Self as Shaped by Individual and Cultural Diversity and Context
2.B. Others as Shaped by Individual and Cultural Diversity and Context
2.C. Interaction of Self and Others as Shaped by Individual and Cultural Diversity and Context
2.D. Applications based on Individual and Cultural Context

For conceptualization in each sub-competency, clinicians should consider the impact of age, gender, gender identity, race, ethnicity, culture, national origin, religion, sexual orientation, disability, language, and socioeconomic status on self and client.

This chapter elaborates on the importance of APA guiding principles for ethical treatment and cultural competency by introducing Bennett's (1993) developmental model of intercultural sensitivity (1993) and illustrating how the degree of a clinician's intercultural sensitivity can have a significant impact on his or her approach to neuropsychological assessment, with ethnocentric attitudes resulting in biased assessments and ethnorelative attitudes facilitating culturally accurate assessments (Adeponle, Thombs, Groleau, Jarvis, & Kirmayer, 2012). Next, a taxonomy of behavioral dimensions is introduced to elucidate potential cultural differences between the clinician and CDC. The chapter closes with a brief description of how an awareness of behavioral dimensions can facilitate development of cultural competency as it pertains to a neuropsychological evaluation.

BENNETT'S DEVELOPMENTAL MODEL
OF INTERCULTURAL SENSITIVITY

According to Bennett (1993), the clinician's sensitivity to and acceptance of a CDC falls along a developmental continuum of six stages. The first three stages fall within the ethnocentric category where the behaviors of CDCs are interpreted within one's own cultural lenses and values with the assumption of superiority. In the *Denial* stage, the individual does not acknowledge the existence of cultural differences. Everyone is viewed as the same, although not because of an assumption of equality. Instead, differences are experienced as overwhelmingly threatening to one's worldview because, if differences exist, then one's own perspective could be wrong or inferior. *Defense* is the second stage, in which cultural differences are acknowledged but perceived as threatening. Thus, the individual denigrates the other's culture or holds one's own culture as superior to reduce the threat of an inferior or incorrect worldview. A variation is *reversal*, in which the individual identifies with the other culture as being superior. In all cases, the individuals and other cultures are perceived in simplified stereotypes or black-and-white categories, and therefore inaccurately. The highest level of ethnocentrism is *Minimization*. In this stage, there is a superficial acceptance of the culturally different as equal; however, the assumption of commonality is defined ethnocentrically, using one's own culture as the standard to judge behaviors. Again, this perspective will frequently result in inaccurate perceptions because behaviors of the other are taken out of context.

The final three stages of Bennett's (1993) model fall within the *Ethnorelative* category in which the other culture is perceived as having a viable alternative worldview, with the assumption that it is different but equal. The transition from ethnocentricism to ethnorelativism can be difficult.

Cognitively, the two categories are analogous to Piaget's (1929) concepts of assimilation and accommodation. In *assimilation*, complex new information from the environment is interpreted within preexisting cognitive categories or schemas. When applied to cultures, this cognitive operation could easily result in stereotypes because behaviors of the CDC are perceived with one's own cultural lens and thus out of context. This operation is the default mode; no other schemas for interpreting behaviors exist. *Accommodation* is the creation of new categories, thoughts, or perceptions to process information to fit the realities of the external world. Accommodation is associated with new learning and growth, which are necessary to understand and appreciative a foreign worldview.

The greater challenge, however, is an emotional one because the process is frequently associated with feeling threatened. Transitioning from an ethnocentric to an ethnorelative perspective is akin to an epiphany of moving from a geocentric model of the universe, in which the earth is the center of the universe, to a heliocentric model, in which the earth is just one planet revolving around what is one among many suns. This transition is not an easy one because it is generally difficult for a person to lose stature or accept a lesser role from what one is used to. In contrast to ethnocentric stages, individuals in ethnorelative stages of intercultural sensitivity demonstrate respect through active learning and adapting behaviors to culturally different others.

- In the *Acceptance* stage, the individual recognizes and values cultural differences without judging them as positive or negative. Differences are merely differences. There is an understanding that members of another culture have unique behaviors that make sense within their cultural context. Furthermore, there are good and bad aspects of every culture. Individuals in this stage are often active in developing a knowledge base of the other culture.
- The next step beyond understanding is *Adaptation*. In this stage, the individual applies knowledge and adapts his or her behaviors to accommodate cultural differences.
- The final stage is *Integration*, in which the individual can interact comfortably with a variety of cultures and still maintain a sense of self. The person is a virtuoso or what I like to refer to as a *cultural bodhisattva*, a person who sees reality for what it is without judging.

Bennett's (1993) developmental model of intercultural sensitivity embodies both of APA's ethical guidelines for working with a CDC and all four factors for cultural competency. A description of how a neuropsychologist at each stage of Bennett's model might approach a neuropsychological evaluation for a CDC is provided to illustrate types of assessment biases associated with each ethnocentric level of intercultural sensitivity cultural and how these compare to ethnorelative approaches.

Denial

Because neuropsychologists at this stage do not acknowledge differences between themselves and CDCs, there would be no preparation to learn about a client's culture. Administration of neuropsychological testing would be standard without any accommodations. The neuropsychologist may obtain the services of an interpreter if there are obvious language comprehension weaknesses. However, data are interpreted as an accurate estimate of abilities.

Defense

In this stage, differences between cultures are acknowledged, thus the neuropsychologist would make accommodations, such as using an interpreter and possibly selecting tests with normative data. The neuropsychologist may adhere to standardized test administration with a client whose second language is English or who has little testing experience to prevent an unfair advantage. Other preparation is unlikely, however. A significant impact at this stage is in the neuropsychologist's attitudes toward findings: CDCs who perform poorly would provide support for an inherent belief in the intellectual superiority of the neuropsychologist's culture, whereas CDCs who perform exceptionally may be denigrated as overachievers who have authoritarian, even abusive, parents. If the neuropsychologist is prone to reversal, poor scores for any culturally different person would be totally invalidated because of the insensitivity of the dominant culture.

Minimization

Because of the neuropsychologist's increased respect for the CDC at this stage, more accommodations would be made to ensure validity of findings. Literature-based test selection for quality translations and applicability, and possibly nonstandardized instructions to ensure understanding, would be incorporated with the underlying assumption that tests have universal validity if adjusted for item content and language. However, the basic dynamic of the test-taking situation for the CDC (e.g., motivation, comfort level, or meaning of the situation) are believed to be experienced similarly to the dominant culture. Caveats for test interpretation are also made out of respect; however, these are typically generalized statements because of a lack of substantive knowledge of the experiences, values, and behaviors of the client's culture.

Acceptance

Neuropsychologists in this stage appreciate the importance of cultural context and life experiences when conceptualizing and interpreting behaviors. They actively pursue knowledge about the culture of the client before an evaluation to understand the impact of culture on behavior and cognition— not only for test interpretation, but for the entire assessment process because there is an appreciation that the client's experience of this process differs from the neuropsychologist's experience in many ways. There is also an appreciation that Western tests and scores are not absolute or equivalent and hold different meanings across cultures. Caveats for test interpretation are specific and based on a nuanced understanding of the other culture.

Adaptation and Integration

In these stages, neuropsychologists apply acquired cultural knowledge by strategizing methods for developing rapport, maximizing communication, minimizing test biases, and maximizing the accuracy of test interpretation.

From this illustration, it should be apparent that an ethnorelative perspective is the embodiment of both APA's Ethical Principle of respecting one's client and also the APA Revised Competency Benchmarks for working with CDCs. A reassuring aspect of Bennett's (1993) model is its developmental nature because an individual is not fated to remain at one stage forever but can progress through stages over time. Exposure to other cultures, motivation to interact effectively with other cultures (Ng, van Dyne, & Ang, 2012), and Big Five personality traits (Costa & McCrae, 1992) of Openness to Experience (intellectual curiosity and appreciation for adventure and variety of experiences) and Conscientiousness (self-discipline and the tendency to act dutifully) have been found to be predictive of cultural intelligence (Moody, 2007). Similar to acquisition of any knowledge base or skill, development is directly associated with the amount of concerted time and effort put into learning.

BEHAVIORAL DIMENSIONS AND DIVERSITIES FOR UNDERSTANDING CULTURES

To facilitate an ethnorelative perspective and skill development in the APA Benchmarks for Cultural Competency, cultural dimensions which have been proposed and studied by psychologists, cultural anthropologists, and business researchers (Gelfand et al., 2011; E. Hall, 1969; Hofstede, 1980; House, Hanges, Javidan, Dorfman, & Gupta, 2004) are presented here to elucidate similarities and differences between one's culture and the culture of other ethnicities. Cultural dimensions, which are continuums of specific behaviors or values in which cultures may differ, are described with a brief discussion of where the United States and other countries fall within each dimension. It should be emphasized that cultural dimensions are not mutually exclusive, and there is overlap between different dimensional concepts. In addition, wide individual variability for each dimension occur within each ethnic group.

GLOBE STUDY

The following behavioral dimensions were described and researched in the Global Leadership and Organizational Behavior Effectiveness (GLOBE) study of culture leadership and organizations (House et al., 2004). In this study, middle managers from 62 countries were surveyed on nine cultural dimensions: (a) individualism versus collectivism (institutions), (b) individualism versus collectivism (in group), (c) power distance, (d) uncertainty avoidance, (e) performance orientation, (f) future orientation, (g) assertiveness,

(h) gender egalitarianism, and (i) humane orientation. Data were analyzed by country and country clusters, the latter of which comprised the following 10 subdivisions of culturally similar regions:

- Nordic Europe (Finland, Sweden, Denmark)
- Eastern Europe (Albania, Kazakhstan, Hungary, Poland, Russia, Slovenia, Greece, Georgia)
- Latin America (Argentina, Bolivia, Brazil, Colombia, Costa Rica, Ecuador, El Salvador, Venezuela, Mexico)
- Middle East (Qatar, Morocco, Turkey, Egypt, Kuwait)
- Latin Europe (Italy, Portugal, Spain, France, Switzerland [French speaking], Israel)
- Germanic Europe (Austria, Germany, Netherlands, Switzerland)
- Confucian Asia (Taiwan, Singapore, Hong Kong, South Korea, China, Japan)
- Southern Asia (India, Indonesia, Philippines, Malaysia, Thailand, Iran)
- Sub-Saharan Africa (Namibia, Zambia, Zimbabwe, South Africa [Black sample], Nigeria)
- Anglo (Australia, Canada, New Zealand, United States, South Africa [White sample], England, Ireland)

Findings of the GLOBE study are summarized in Table 1.1, which also includes scores from the United States as a separate category.

Individualist Versus Collectivist (In Group): This dimension describes a person's sense of self and the degree to which the self is defined in terms of individual characteristics versus in relation to others (Hofstede, 1980). This characteristic is particularly influential in the context of decision making, where the assumption in individualistic cultures is that the person makes his or her own decisions. By contrast, in collectivist cultures, the impact a decision has on the group, such as the family or peers, is an essential consideration (Livermore, 2013). In individualistic societies, laws are based on protecting the rights of the individual, whereas collectivist cultures organize laws on what is best for the group (Livermore, 2013).

Individualist Versus Collectivist (Institutional): This dimension applies the collectivist versus individualist dichotomy within institutions. Collectivist institutional cultures have members who identify strongly with the organization to which they belong. Members focus on duty to the organization; they are willing to make personal sacrifices for the organization with the expectation that the organization would stand by them in difficult times. There is an assumption of a long-term relationship. In individualist institutional cultures, members do not identify with the organization but assume that they are hired for their unique skills and that they will be compensated appropriately for

TABLE 1.1

Summary of Findings From the GLOBE Study

	Collectivist vs. individual (in group)	Collectivist vs. individual (institution)	Power distance	Uncertainty avoidance	Performance orientation	Future orientation	Assertiveness	Gender egalitarian	Humane orientation
United States	4.25L	4.20	4.88	4.15	4.49H	4.15	4.55HH	3.34	4.17
Anglo	4.30L	4.46	4.99	4.42	4.37	4.08	4.14	3.40	4.20
Nordic Europe	3.75L	4.88H	4.54	5.19H	3.92	4.36H	3.66L	3.71	4.17
Germanic Europe	4.21L	4.03L	4.95	5.12H	4.41	4.40HH	4.55HH	3.14	3.55LL
Eastern Europe	5.53H	4.10	5.26	3.56L	3.73L	3.38	4.33	3.84	3.85
Latin Europe	4.80	4.01L	5.21	4.18	3.94	3.68	3.99	3.36	3.71LL
Latin America	5.52H	3.86L	5.32	3.62L	3.85	3.54LL	4.15	3.41	4.03
Sub-Saharan Africa	5.31	4.28	5.24	4.27	4.13	3.92	4.24	3.29	4.42H
Middle East	5.58H	4.28	5.29	3.91L	3.90	3.58L	4.14	2.95	4.36
Southern Asia	5.87H	4.35	5.39	4.10	4.33	3.98	3.86	3.28	4.71HH
Confucian Asia	5.42H	4.80H	5.15	4.42	4.58H	4.18	4.09	3.18	3.99

Note. All scores are based on a 7-point scale. H = significantly high at $p < .05$; HH = significantly high at $p < .01$; L = significantly low at $p < .05$; LL = significantly low $p < .01$.

those skills. There is no assumption of the individual's loyalty to the organization or the organization's to the individual.

Power Distance: This concept pertains to a culture's comfort with inequity in power, influence, and wealth (Hofstede, 1980). Societies with high power distance assume that formal hierarchy and inequities are appropriate, whereas low power distance societies believe in more equality, even among persons of different statuses (Livermore, 2013). In low-power-distance cultures, people of different statuses frequently address each other by first names, children are treated more equally, and they encouraged to be active participants in learning and question teachers. In high-power-distance cultures, people are addressed by formal titles and surnames, learning is based more on rote memory, and children may still consult parents for big decisions.

Uncertainty Avoidance: This behavior entails the comfort level a culture has for tolerating and dealing with uncertain or ambiguous circumstances (Hofstede, 1980). Cultures high in uncertainty avoidance will have strict laws, rituals, and social norms to foster routine and predictability in their environment. Cultures low in uncertainty avoidance have less structured systems. In the classroom, low uncertainty avoidance students will attempt to answer questions even if they are not sure and are open to feedback and discussion; students in high uncertainty avoidance cultures will only answer a question if they are certain of the answer (Livermore, 2013).

Performance Orientation: This is the degree to which a culture values achievement and is exemplified by encouraging and rewarding members for excellence, innovation, and performance improvement. Cultures high in performance orientation value initiative, reward individual achievement, and have a high sense of urgency. Cultures low in performance orientation value harmony with nature and cooperation in social relationships over competition, emphasize loyalty and tradition, and have a low sense of urgency (Javidan, 2004).

Future Orientation: Cultures differ in their perspective of time, and the impact that past, present, and future have on behaviors. Future orientation is the extent to which behaviors are organized towards the future. Cultures high in this value engage in future-oriented behaviors such as delaying gratification, planning, and investing in the future and place a high priority on long-term success. Cultures low in future orientation value instant gratification and focus on the recent past for making decisions that lead to quick results (House & Javidan, 2004).

Assertiveness: This behavior describes assertive, confrontational, and aggressive actions in social relationships. Highly assertive cultures value initiative, competition, control, and outcomes more than relationships. Cultures low in assertiveness value cooperation and harmony, and perceive the individual nature of assertiveness as socially unacceptable (House & Javidan, 2004).

Gender-Egalitarianism: This concept pertains to the extent to which a culture promotes gender equality and minimizes gender-based role differences.

Cultures high in gender egalitarianism have more women in the labor force and in positions of authority, and literacy rates and educational achievement are similar for both males and females. The converse is true in cultures with low gender egalitarianism (House & Javidan, 2004).

Humane Orientation: This describes the degree to which a society values, fairness, altruism, generosity, friendliness, and kindness towards others. Cultures high in this trait are motivated by affiliation and have strong social support networks. Cultures low in humane orientation are motivated by power, material possessions, and self-enhancement (House & Javidan, 2004).

Other Cultural Dimensions: Ratings of cultural dimensions from non-GLOBE studies are presented in Table 1.2.

Monochronic Versus Polychronic Time Orientation: Monochronic cultures are task oriented and typically focus on one thing at a time. Events are organized around clock time, and meeting deadlines is a priority. Activities are scheduled to begin and end at precise times, and promptness is the expectation (Hall, 1969). In *polychronic* cultures, activities are not tied to strict time deadlines and "things get done when they get done." The focus is on the outcome. Human relationships take precedence over time and material things and are the basis for coordinating activities. This priority can significantly influence scheduling because commitments to personal relationships trump established appointments with acquaintances.

Low- Versus High-Context Communication: In low-context communication cultures, communication is based primarily on the content of what is said; thus, effective communication is direct and explicit. Nonverbal aspects of communication, such as body language, inflections, and facial expressions, are deemphasized. Because content is emphasized, when miscommunication occurs, it is assumed that the speaker did not communicate clearly. By contrast, in high-context communication cultures, meanings are often stated indirectly, and content is deemphasized. Thus, it is not automatically assumed that people will state what they want, and what is not said may be just as important as what is said. The context of the communication, such as who speaks to whom, where meetings take place, and delays in communication, often provide important meaning. It is presumed that the listener understands the unwritten rules or context of the communication because she or he is constantly evaluating the contexts of communication. In high-context cultures, misunderstandings are attributed to failure of the listener (Hall & Hall, 2001; Livermore, 2013).

Being Versus Doing Lifestyle: Cultures differ in how they value and prioritize time spent in work versus pleasure or activities valued by the person (Kluckhohn & Strodtbeck, 1961). Being cultures emphasize relationships and quality of life over work and strive for a balance between work and play. For doing cultures work, results and material rewards are highly valued and people strongly identify with their job (Livermore, 2013).

TABLE 1.2
Summary of Findings From Non-GLOBE Studies

	Time orientation	Contextual communication	Lifestyle	Rules	Affective expression	Social norms
United States	Monochronic	Low	Doing	Universal	African American-High	Loose
Anglo	Monochronic	Low		Universal		
Nordic Europe	Monochronic	Low	Being	Universal		
Germanic Europe	Monochronic	Low		Universal		
Eastern Europe		High		Particular	High	
Latin Europe	Polychronic	High	Being		High	
Latin America		High		Particular	High	Varies
Sub-Saharan Africa	Polychronic	High	Being			
Middle East	Polychronic	High			High	
Southern Asia		High	Varies		Low	Tight
Confucian Asia		High		Particular	Low	Tight

Particularist Versus Universalist Rules: Particularist cultures value inter-personal relationships with situational enforcement of rules, laws, and treat-ment. In these cultures, there are many exceptions to the rules, and decisions are dependent on the person involved and his or her relationship to the deci-sion maker. For example, when prioritizing engagements, close relatives have priority and nonrelatives can be left waiting despite scheduled appointments. In universal cultures, rules are assumed to apply to everyone and all situations (Trompenaars & Hampden-Turner, 1997).

Neutral Versus Affective Expressiveness: This dimension pertains to how emotions are expressed, not how emotions are experienced. In neutral expressive cultures, control over one's emotions is associated with respect and dignity. Behaviors are highly influenced by reason, and people do not reveal their thoughts or feelings. Silences are often welcome and are also a sign of respect. Emotional displays are associated with loss of control (Livermore, 2013). Affective cultures believe that emotions should be expressed sponta-neously and that doing so is a sign of warmth, openness, and honesty. There is a wide range of facial expression and physical gestures, and argument and debate are welcome; interruptions are acceptable. Emotions or intuition are frequently incorporated into decision making. Silences are awkward, and quiet people may be viewed as hiding something (Livermore, 2013).

Tight Versus Loose Social Norms: Cultures differ in their adherence to societal norms. *Tight* cultures have strong social norms with low tolerance for deviant behaviors; *loose* cultures are more tolerant of variability in behavior (Gelfand et al., 2011). Tight cultures have fewer civil liberties; more laws, regulations, and political pressure to control media; more police; and lower crime and murder rates. They are more religious, have greater personal con-straint, and are more dutiful (Gelfand et al., 2011). Tight cultures are char-acterized by cultural homogeneity and religious purity, whereas loose cultures place high value on free speech (Livermore, 2013).

RELATIONSHIP BETWEEN CULTURAL DIMENSIONS

According to Livermore (2013), certain cultural dimensions tend to clus-ter together, particularly in relation to individualistic versus collectivist cul-tures. In *individualistic* cultures that emphasize the rights and autonomy of the individual, time is organized around precise schedules that are based on consen-sual agreement (monochronic) to facilitate task completion. Communication is direct to promote the message of the individual (low context), and laws are developed to protect the rights of all (universal). By contrast, in *collec-tivist* cultures where relationships and obligations take precedence over the needs of the individual, time is organized around relationships, which can influence when things get done or when a person shows up to an appointment (polychronic). In communication, relationship harmony is valued over self-expression; thus, communication is indirect to avoid conflict or embarrassing others (high context). Relationships and obligations to others also have an impact on how rules and laws are enacted, and decisions are more likely to be influenced by unique circumstances (particularism).

APPLICATION TO APA COMPETENCY BENCHMARKS AND NEUROPSYCHOLOGICAL ASSESSMENT

The preceding taxonomy of cultural dimensions is a useful tool for conducting a culturally informed neuropsychological assessment with a CDC that would meet APA (2011) standards for cultural competency. Understanding one's own behaviors (Principle 2.A) and the behaviors of the CDC (Principle 2.B) can be determined by mapping cultural characteristics onto the taxonomy of different cultural dimensions. For a clinician of majority background in the United States, this analysis could reveal that behaviors and values he or she took for granted are not universal and that other cultures differ on numerous dimensions, such as the collectivist orientations that predominate around the world outside of Europe and Anglo cultures. Interestingly, significant differences are even found between the United States and other countries in the Anglo cluster to which the United States belongs, for example in performance orientation and assertiveness (see Table 1.1).

Dimensional differences between the clinician and CDC can also provide hypotheses on how the CDC's cultural background may affect components of the neuropsychological evaluation (Principle 2.C). For example, females from low gender egalitarian societies would not have the same educational and occupational opportunities as males. CDCs who come from cultures low in future orientation may be less motivated for higher education. Thus, this cultural knowledge would be useful for putting a CDC's cognitive abilities and performances into perspective.

In terms of communication and rapport, a female American clinician could unintentionally insult a male CDC from a society with high power differential and low gender egalitarianism if she does not address him in the proper manner. Similarly, if he or she is unaware of cultural differences, a clinician may be uncomfortable with a CDC who comes from a highly affective expressive culture or perplexed in interviewing a CDC from a high-context-communication culture.

Cultural dimensions could also affect test-taking style or performance. For example, CDCs from a culture low in performance orientation may be less motivated to perform well on tests. A CDC from a society with a polychronic time orientation may perform slower on timed tasks. A client from a culture high in uncertainty avoidance may refuse to guess on items, which could significantly affect test scores. In these cases, noncognitive cultural factors could reduce performances, thereby having an impact on test validity.

Finally, an awareness in cultural differences between the clinicians and the CDC can inform strategies for working with CDCs (Principle 2.D). Thus, a culturally informed clinician could plan to ask more specific questions of a CDC from a less assertive or high-power-distance culture who may be reticent to disclose; use more self-disclosure to build rapport with a CDC from a collectivist culture; or familiarize oneself with communication styles and tune in to nonverbals when working with a CDC from a high-context-communication culture. In later chapters, more specific examples of how cultural differences can affect a neuropsychological evaluation are provided.

2

CONCEPTUAL GUIDELINES: APA, AACN, AERA, AND NCMA

In order to carry a positive action we must develop here a positive vision.
—Dalai Lama

With an ethnorelative attitude of respect, the next essential ingredient for conducting a culturally informed neuropsychological evaluation is a good appreciation for how culture affects the evaluation process and what a competent cross-cultural evaluation entails. Such a "big-picture" conceptualization is important for facilitating a deeper understanding of the task through simplification. Neuropsychologists unfamiliar with the client's culture or without a good conceptualization of how culture affects all aspects of a neuropsychological evaluation can easily miss relevant information by not approaching the client in the right manner, not communicating the right way, not asking the right questions, or not attending to the right nonverbal behaviors. Moreover, the clinician may not appreciate the limitations or make sense of the data that are collected.

The purpose of this chapter is twofold: (a) to provide a broad conceptual framework for how culture affects a neuropsychological evaluation and

http://dx.doi.org/10.1037/15958-003
Conducting a Culturally Informed Neuropsychological Evaluation, by D. Fujii

(b) to provide a description of elements that a culturally informed neuropsychological should possess. To attain this culturally informed blueprint, we first review recommendations from several sources including the American Psychological Association's (APA's; 2010) *Ethical Principles of Psychologists and Code of Conduct* and its *Guidelines on Multicultural Education, Training, Research, Practice, and Organizational Change for Psychologists* (APA, 2003) for assessments, the American Academy of Clinical Neuropsychology (AACN; 2007) Practice Guidelines concerning underserved populations and cultural issues, and American Educational Research Association (AERA; 2014) *Standards for Educational and Psychological Testing*. Next, a conceptualization of how culture affects the neuropsychological evaluation process with implications for essential knowledge bases is introduced. It is believed that a combination of a big-picture approach and a detailed description of important elements provides a strong blueprint for conceptualizing and conducting a culturally informed neuropsychological evaluation.

APA ETHICAL AND MULTICULTURAL GUIDELINES

A key issue that the APA Ethics Code (2010) addresses is whether a psychologist practices within his or her boundary of competence (APA Standards 2.01 and 2.02). According to the guidelines, a psychologist can only provide services to populations for which she or he is adequately trained and should make appropriate referrals to psychologists competent to work with the specific characteristics of a particular client. If a competent psychologist is not available, a psychologist who is not adequately trained to work with a specific population may still provide services if she or he has training or experience that is closely related to the specific population and has made reasonable efforts to attain competence by reviewing the relevant research, through consultation, or through additional studying to ensure that services are not denied. A psychologist can also provide services in an emergency situation to ensure services are not denied; however, services should be discontinued once the emergency situation is over or a more competent provider can be found.

Results of a recent survey of North American neuropsychologists found that 35.5% of clinicians surveyed reported difficulties finding a colleague to refer to or consult when receiving a referral for a culturally different client (CDC) and estimated that 34.3% of the surveyed clinicians' clientele are persons of color (Elbulok-Charcape, Rabin, Spadaccini, & Barr, 2014). Thus, a significant percentage of neuropsychologists' practices typically involve working with CDCs.

In what follows, I synthesize key portions of the APA Ethics Code (2010) and Multicultural Guidelines for Assessments (2003) into a set of 10 general strategies that address issues for evaluating with CDCs.

1. Tests need to be in client's language. (APA Standard 9.02, Use of Instruments)
2. Tests need to be validated with the client's population. (APA Standard 9.02, Use of Instruments)
3. Psychologists should be aware of test's reference population. (Multicultural Assessment)
4. Psychologists should be aware of limitations of assessment practices and tests for a culture, including test bias, test fairness, and cultural equivalence. (Multicultural Assessment)
5. Neuropsychologists should avoid using interpreters who have a dual relationship with the client (e.g., a family member), which could lead to either exploitation or loss of objectivity. Neuropsychologists ensure that interpreters are adequately trained and supervised to provide competent services. (APA Standard 2.05, Delegation of Work to Others)
6. If procedures are not explained, a client may feel disrespected and perceive that the therapist does not value their relationship and thus may not follow recommendations. (Multicultural Assessment)
7. Informed consent must be understandable to the client and include consent to use an interpreter. (APA Standard 9.03, Informed Consent in Assessments)
8. When interpreting tests, exercise critical judgment because situational, personal, linguistic, and cultural difference may affect judgments or accuracy of interpretations. (APA Standard 9.06, Bases for Scientific Judgment; Multicultural Assessment)
9. Data need to be sufficient to justify findings. (APA Standard 9.01, Bases of Assessments)
10. Limitations of data need to be documented, especially if using an interpreter. (APA Standard 9.01, Bases of Assessments; Standard 9.02, Use of Instruments; Standard 9.06, Bases for Scientific Judgment)

About half of the preceding recommendations (1–4) concern test selection. Specifically, selected tests should be in the client's language and validated with his or her population. Knowledge of the test's reference population and cultural biases are important considerations for test selection. Three recommendations (5–7) address issues in conducting the neuropsychological evaluation. If the need arises, neuropsychologists need to ensure adequately trained interpreters and avoid family members who have dual relationships that can have a negative impact on this role. Neuropsychologists should provide careful explanation of procedures and obtain informed consent, the latter of which should include the use of an interpreter. These recommendations not only ensure understanding of test procedures but foster a good relationship and ensure that the client feels respected. If a trusting relationship is not established, the client may not follow recommendations. Two recommendations (8 and 9) address issues of accurate test interpretation. Clinicians need to be aware of possible threats to validity, including cultural, linguistic, personal, or situational biases, and be cautious that data are adequate to justify clinical opinions. The final recommendation (10) concerns the documentation of data limitations within the report.

AACN PRACTICE GUIDELINES: UNDERSERVED POPULATIONS AND CULTURAL ISSUES

The AACN, the specialty board certification group for psychologists who have received board certification in neuropsychology from the American Board of Professional Psychology, provides three additional guidelines specific to neuropsychological assessments. First, AACN warns clinicians that cultural, linguistic, disability, other demographic or socioeconomic factors can influence participation in the assessment process, and thus the meaning of the data collected. Second, to address the lack of standardized and normed tests for a particular client, AACN recommends alternative assessment strategies, such as relying on direct observation and relevant supplementary information about adaptive functioning within the community, charting behavioral changes over time, criterion-referenced testing, or using norms of demographically similar groups in published research. Finally, limitations in communication should be detailed in the report, for example, concerns regarding the clinician's fluency in the client's language; uncertainties about the fidelity of translation; the quality of interpersonal communication, including literal content and meaning communicated by prosody and body language; culturally mediated meanings; and the impact of using an interpreter on the validity of interview data and test results.

AERA STANDARDS FOR EDUCATIONAL AND PSYCHOLOGICAL TESTING: FAIRNESS IN TESTING

AERA, APA, and the National Council on Measurement in Education jointly authored standards to guide the development and evaluation of educational and psychological tests. Cross-cultural issues are addressed in a foundational chapter that describes four essential elements of fairness in testing. First, test takers must be treated fairly during the testing process. This element entails the importance of feeling comfortable in the testing situation and with the testers, particularly for communication purposes. In addition, testers may need to maintain flexibility in administration to ensure that all test takers have equivalent opportunities to demonstrate understanding of the construct being tested.

Second, tests need to be free of or minimize measurement *bias*, which is defined as characteristics of the test that are not related to the construct being measured. Biases can occur at the item and test levels. Predictive bias occurs when differences exist between groups in the association of test scores and other variables. An essential issue for measurement bias is whether the construct has equivalent meaning across individuals or subgroups of test takers.

Third, tests must be fair in *accessibility*, which is the ability to demonstrate one's knowledge of the construct being measured. A common method to increase accessibility is to use interpreters for test takers who are not fluent in English. Thus, testers need to consider individual characteristics of the test taker and how these interact with the contextual features of the testing situation.

The fourth aspect of fairness concerns the *validity* of the test taker's score interpretations for the intended use. When drawing inferences from a test, it is important to consider individual characteristics of the test taker and how his or her characteristics interact with the contextual aspects of the testing situation. In this regard, inferences of scores can differ between subgroups as well as for members within a subgroup. Thus, testers need to be cognizant of heterogeneity within a specified group. Threats to fair and valid interpretation of test scores include differential advantages associated with test content, test context or administration biases, test response requirements or rubrics for scoring that are not construct related, and differential opportunities to learn the content and skills measured by the test.

To address threats to fairness in testing, the joint committee recommended minimizing construct-irrelevant components of tests through test design and testing adaptations. *Universal test design* is an approach that seeks to maximize accessibility to all test takers. This approach aims to avoid items or formats with construct-irrelevant characteristics that could bias scores for individuals or subgroups. To achieve this goal, it is imperative that test designers be precise in defining constructs to be measured, purposes for how scores will be used, inferences made from scores, and characteristics of the entire examination population that could influence accessibility. In this manner, test designers can maximize measurement of the intended construct and minimize construct-irrelevant characteristics of the test, thereby maximizing accessibility for all intended test takers.

For existing tests, when construct-irrelevant test characteristics impede accessibility, the solution is adaptation. An *adaptation* is defined as any change to the original test design or administration to increase accessibility for a test taker. There are two types of adaptations. *Accommodations* are minor changes that specifically address construct-irrelevant barriers to test performance. Changes do not provide an unfair advantage over those who do not receive accommodations, and thus comparability of scores is retained. Examples include test translations and the appropriate use of interpreters. With *modifications*, changes to design or administration are more pronounced, and thus the construct being measured is actually altered. The rationale for a modification is to provide the tester some access to the construct being measured. Using categorical and multiple-choice cuing for recall items on the Mini-Mental State Examination is an example of a modification to evaluate for retrieval memory deficits associated with subcortical neuropathology. Modifications invalidate both norm-based and criterion-based test interpretations.

IMPACT OF CULTURE ON NEUROPSYCHOLOGICAL ASSESSMENT PROCESS

The impact of culture on a neuropsychological evaluation is illustrated in four parts. First, the impact of culture on the assessment process is distilled into two components. Next, cultural moderating factors are identified and described. Third, a description of the processes in a typical psychological evaluation is provided. The chapter closes with a discussion on cultural effects on the neuropsychological assessment process.

It is argued that the impact of culture on assessments can be distilled into two components: (a) obtaining accurate data and the meaning of data, and (b) providing a context for understanding and interpreting the data and making useful treatment recommendations.

Obtaining Accurate Data

Culture can significantly affect the clinician's ability to obtain accurate data in many ways. First, the interview process itself can have different meanings for CDCs that have an impact on self-disclosure. For example, Native American clients may respectfully agree with a doctor due to the power dynamic, but this response may not reflect their true feelings (Substance Abuse and Mental Health Services Administration [SAMHSA], 2009). For Alaskan Natives, the specific questioning process in interviews can be offensive (Hays, 2006).

Communication can be another significant obstacle to obtaining accurate data. Persons for whom English is a second language will have varying levels of competency with comprehension or expressive fluency, and thus meanings can easily be "lost in translation" even with an interpreter (Artiola i Fortuny, 2008). The clinician may not be familiar with a CDC's gestures; for example, for some Alaskan Natives tribes, raising or widening one's eyebrows means "yes" (Hays, 2006). Communication styles may also differ; for example, Native Americans tend to communicate information indirectly by telling stories that may be characterized by long pauses (SAMHSA, 2009).

Even when language and a willingness to disclose are not issues, there can still be challenges in obtaining accurate data from CDCs or collateral sources such as family. If a clinician is not familiar with a culture, he or she may not ask pertinent questions (Judd & Beggs, 2005). For example, in Thailand, the most common cause of traumatic brain injuries are bicycle and motor bike accidents; thus, a prior head injury may be missed if the clinician does not specifically ask about this type of accident (Ratanadilok, 2011). Less acculturated clients may suffer from "culture-bound" syndromes; for example, bouffée délirante, nervios, or dhat syndrome (American Psychiatric Association, 2013), would be missed if symptoms are not asked about directly. Knowledge of Western medicine may also affect a client's ability to provide specific information. Among less acculturated Asians, for example, memory loss is often perceived to be a normal part of aging; thus, a clinician may not suspect a client has an early stage of dementia, if basing memory problems on family reports of unusual behaviors (McBride, 2006).

It may be more difficult to obtain accurate information from records for CDCs for several reasons. Clients from non-Western cultures are less likely to see a medical or mental health professional (U.S. Department of Health and Human Services, 1999), and thus there may be fewer records available. If records are available, there may a greater likelihood that information is inaccurate because the previous clinician may have experienced similar difficulties in obtaining accurate information. Cultural differences between clinicians and clients are also often associated with misdiagnosis, as in cases in which African Americans have been incorrectly diagnosed with paranoid schizophrenia (Barnes, 2004). Similarly, clinicians who are unfamiliar with Asians' tendency to somaticize stress may not suspect possible depression in a client reporting vague physical complaints (Nakao, Yamanaka, & Kuboki, 2001).

In terms of behavioral observations, differences in norms for affective expressiveness can influence interpretation of mood, affect, or honesty (Livermore, 2013). For example, culturally different therapists may misinterpret the emotional expressiveness and nonstandard language of African American clients as an inability to regulate emotions and communicate effectively (Kelly & Boyd-Franklin, 2004).

As emphasized in the APA and AACN guidelines, culture is an essential consideration for test selection because tests may need to be translated and validated to reduce potential biases.

Providing a Context

The second major impact of culture on neuropsychological assessment is providing a context for interpreting the data and making recommendations. In Chapter 1 of this volume, the dangers of an ethnocentric perspective on conceptualizing behaviors or assessment were described. Thus, to appreciate the impact of a neurological event on cognition and behavior and family system, we need to understand who the individual is within the context of his or her culture. We need to understand common experiences and norms for behavior or presentation of an individual's culture to understand how behavior has changed and how experiences interface with testing. Cultural knowledge is essential to provide a context for appreciating who the person is—how history, beliefs, acculturation, and values organize behaviors and experiences. As described in the previous section, many CDCs do not have the educational opportunities or experiences that the dominant culture has, have varying levels of English comprehension or speaking skills, and have different levels of familiarity and comfort with testing situations or help seeking from psychologists. Thus, behaviors and test performance must be interpreted within these contexts.

The following is an example of how an ethnocentric perspective can have a negative impact on clinical formulation. Let's say you have to estimate the premorbid abilities of a 36-year-old female client with a sixth-grade education and a fourth-grade reading level and who is a grandmother. Within the context of American society, a clinician may likely hypothesize that the client comes from a family in the low socioeconomic class, maybe from a broken home, and has a below average IQ. This conceptualization, however, radically changes when placed within the context of traditional Hmong culture. Hmong have no written language, and most women have no formal schooling because of the lack of educational opportunities for Hmong within the dominant, strongly patriarchal Lao society. Hmong who do attend schools learn to read Lao, which has a written language. Hmong typically marry in their early teens and thus are more likely to become grandparents before age 30 (Fujii & Vang, 2011). Thus, within the context of her culture, this client is actually better educated than the typical Hmong woman and is late in starting a family compared with her peers.[1]

---

[1]It should be emphasized that despite educational and literacy disadvantages of their parents, many second-generation Hmong have excelled academically, have earned doctorates, or are enrolled in psychology graduate programs. In fact, 70.1% of Hmong between the ages of 18 and 21 are enrolled in college (Xiong, 2013). Thus, the presentation in this example would also have different implications for the next generation.

The importance of cultural context for conceptualizing behaviors is also illustrated in a study by Adeponle, Thombs, Groleau, Jarvis, and Kirmayer (2012) that examined the accuracy of psychiatric and neurological diagnosis in ethnic minorities. Ethnic minority subjects were diagnosed by dominant-culture clinicians and then rediagnosed after consultation with a cultural broker. Clinicians changed diagnoses in 49% of subjects who were initially misdiagnosed with psychotic disorders and 50% with neurological disorders.

Similarly, for recommendations to be useful, they must be made within the context of the culture. For example, it is not unheard of for affluent Saudi parents to send their child to the United States for a neuropsychological evaluation to determine whether he or she has a learning disorder. Unfortunately, recommendations often include a referral for special services that are common in the United States but unavailable in Saudi Arabia, significantly affecting the usefulness of the evaluation (Michael Nestor, personal communication, August 4, 2015).

Moderating Factors

The impact of culture on a neuropsychological evaluation is not absolute but varies on two primary dimensions: (a) proficiency in the language of the dominant culture and (b) acculturation. As the preceding examples illustrate, English proficiency can have a significant impact on the neuropsychologist's ability to collect accurate data. This effect on Western test performance, particularly for verbal tests, varies on a continuum: Test results for ethnic minorities who are native English speakers (e.g., the majority of African Americans) are more valid than results from clients for whom English is a second language (e.g., Burmese immigrants). Similarly, test results on verbal tests of immigrants in countries where English is routinely taught in school (e.g., the Philippines) would typically be more valid than immigrants of countries where English is not taught in schools (e.g., Ukraine). Level of English proficiency is also a contextual factor, and thus has an impact on the interpretation of test results. For example, an average-level vocabulary score would have different meaning for a client born and raised in the United States than for a Kenyan immigrant for whom English is a fourth language.

Acculturation, which for our purposes is broadly defined as the similarity of a client's culture and experiences to, and adoption of mainstream culture, is the other moderating factor. The more similar the cultural values and range of experiences, the more comfortable and familiar with testing situation, and more similar conceptualization of intelligent behavior of a culturally different client, the more performances on western tests will accurately reflect intellectual abilities. For example, performances on western tests should be more valid for a student from a highly industrialized country like Finland than for a student from a poorer country like Mali with much different experiences and less educational opportunities. Level of acculturation is also a contextual factor; for example, a below average score on the Block Design test would have different interpretive meaning for the Finnish and Malian students.

Impact of Culture on Components of the Neuropsychological Evaluation

A typical neuropsychological evaluation has five components. First is receiving and accepting the referral. In this step, the neuropsychologist determines the referral question(s), which typically involves diagnosis, impact of a neurological condition on cognition and functionality, or legal and capacity issues. The second component is estimating premorbid functioning and abilities, particularly as they relate to intelligence. Estimates of intelligence are typically based on client history and demographics as well as test data—for example, word recognition reading tests such as the Wechsler Test of Adult Reading (Psychological Corporation, 2001). Demographics such as education and occupation can be informally factored into the neuropsychologist's estimate or used in formulas such as the Oklahoma Premorbid Intelligence Estimate (OPIE; Schoenberg, Duff, Scott, Patton, & Adams, 2006). Once premorbid intellectual functioning is estimated, the third step is data collection to determine current functional abilities. Selecting and administering appropriate tests and behavioral observations, as well as collecting descriptions of current functioning and presentation or changes from premorbid levels are primary sources of data. In this step, rapport with the client is important for obtaining accurate self-reporting. The fourth component is answering the referral question based on the fit between neurological presentation and diagnostic criteria, discrepancy between premorbid estimates and current tests scores, or consistency of current estimated abilities with diagnostic or capacity criteria. The final component is making recommendations based on test results and the client's living situation, including life goals and support system.

Given the previous discussion on data and context, it is apparent that all aspects of the neuropsychological assessment process are potentially affected by culture, including estimating intellectual/cognitive abilities, identifying behaviors consistent with neurological symptoms, identifying test biases and interpreting results, and understanding family systems and typical daily functioning and activities to base recommendations. Culture also has impact on receiving a referral because the clinician must determine whether she or he is qualified to perform the evaluation (APA, 2010), and there may be culturally associated clues for diagnosis with mental health referrals. For example, Arab Americans may initially present with somatic complaints to physicians (El-Islam, 1982), and less acculturated Asian Americans may only seek mental health services when the symptom or distress level is severe (Abe-Kim et al., 2007).

CONCLUSION

In summary, the first section of this book has described attitudinal and conceptual foundations for conducting a culturally informed neuropsychological evaluation. At the attitudinal heart of the evaluation is respect for the CDC, which equates to an acceptance of the other as different but equal, with behaviors viewed through an ethnorelative perspective. Conceptual foundations discussed in this chapter include the appreciation that culture affects accurate data collection and contextual interpretation of data that permeates all aspects of a neuropsychological assessment. Ethical considerations for competent assessments involves determining and addressing issues of fairness in testing, minimizing biases of language and acculturation to facilitate accuracy of findings, and identifying limitations of the process to determine strength of evidence for conclusions.

A comprehensive method for addressing these issues described in this chapter is introduced in the next two parts of the book, which describe preparations and a step-by-step method for conducting a culturally informed neuropsychological assessment. Practice guidelines and issues of fairness in testing are discussed and applied to different aspects of a culturally informed neuropsychological evaluation.

II

PREPARATION

3

CREATING A CULTURAL CONTEXT

Give me knowledge, so I may have kindness for all.

—Plains Indian

The first step in conducting a culturally informed neuropsychological assessment is to acquire a contextual knowledge base for developing an ethnorelative—as opposed to an ethnocentric—conceptualization of the culturally different client (CDC). This aim focuses on the "psychology" of neuropsychology. Two questions arise when researching information for understanding a CDC: (a) what information is important and (b) why is it important (in other words, what are the functional implications of this information for a neuropsychological evaluation)?

This chapter illustrates the process for obtaining pertinent targeted information through a comprehensive literature review of Native Indian and Alaskan Native (NI/AN) cultures. I selected NI/AN culture as a representative example from which general principles can be extrapolated for the following reasons:

1. NI/ANs are highly heterogeneous, and although this review generally refers to a pan-NI/AN culture, it emphasizes the concept

http://dx.doi.org/10.1037/15958-004

Conducting a Culturally Informed Neuropsychological Evaluation, by D. Fujii

of specificities within an ethnicity and how one size does not fit all for a given ethnic group.

2. The differences between NI/AN versus Western values and beliefs are profound, and thus the comparison provides a good study in contrast.

3. NI/ANs have historically been perceived negatively by the majority culture largely because of an ethnocentric viewpoint. Thus, by placing NI/AN behaviors properly within a cultural context, it is hoped that neuropsychologists will gain a greater understanding, respect for, and appreciation of the indigenous people of America, and thereby facilitate the provision of culturally informed services that are useful for them. In turn, this same process can be applied to culturally different clients (CDCs) of other cultures to provide a contextual understanding, appreciation, and respect for their culture, which can guide assessment through culturally sophisticated hypotheses generation, targeted data collection, culturally informed data interpretation, and culturally relevant recommendations.

This chapter covers the following preparatory tasks: (a) contextualizing behaviors and presentation, (b) maximizing cooperation during testing, and (c) facilitating communication. Each section is organized by listing subcategories of behaviors and questions to elicit information pertinent for the area that can guide the clinician's data collection. Many of these demographic characteristics were proposed by Judd and Beggs (2005). A literature review targeting pertinent information for understanding the CDC is then presented, followed by clinical implications for the neuropsychological evaluation, including issues of fairness in testing. Later chapters demonstrate how this knowledge base can assist the neuropsychologist in addressing the individual components of a neuropsychological evaluation. The Appendix provides a list of resources to learn about different cultures.

CONTEXTUALIZING BEHAVIORS AND PRESENTATION

Macrosocietal Structures

The first step in understanding a culture or ethnicity is to review the macrosocietal structures such as geography, population, economics, government, general history, and languages spoken; these provide a broad context for how cognition, values, attitudes, and behaviors are shaped.

The following list of structures includes pertinent questions to guide the literature review.

- *Geography:* Is the country large or small? What is the climate and topography? What are the surrounding countries?
- *Population:* What is the population number? How is the population distributed (e.g., what and where are the major cities)? What is the ethnic distribution?
- *Economics:* Where does the country rank in gross national income (GNI) per capita? What type of economy (e.g., low, low-middle, upper-middle, or high; World Bank, 2013) does it have? What are the major industries (e.g., industrial, oil and minerals, agricultural, technology)? What social classes exist, and are they associated with different ethnicities or locations?
- *Government:* What type of government? Is the government stable (e.g., a new country or regime)?
- *General history:* What are important historical events for the country? Was there a "golden age," and if so, when was it? Was the country ever colonized? When and by whom? When did the country modernize?
- *Languages spoken:* How many major languages are spoken, and what are they? How are the languages distributed among the population? Is there a written language? What foreign language, if any, is emphasized in formal schooling? What is the general population's exposure to English?
- *Educational system:* What is the level of compulsory education? What is the quality of education? What are the qualifications of the teachers? What are typical school facilities like? What is the curriculum? Where does the country rank on international testing? What are the top universities, and where do they rank among regional and world universities?

Macrosocietal Structures of NI/AN Cultures

The United States covers approximately 9,692,091 square kilometers, making it the third-largest country in the world, after Russia and Canada and just ahead of China and Brazil. The terrain, topography, and temperatures in the United States are highly diverse, including mountain ranges, flat plains, forests, coastal areas, and deserts. Hundreds of individual NI/AN tribes (currently 566 are federally recognized; Federal Register, 2016) inhabited and shared this diverse land for about 28,000 years before the arrival of European settlers in the 16th century. According to McDonald and Gonzalez (2006), early NI/AN relationships with Europeans were generally cooperative until they discovered that the Europeans were exploitive, coveting and, for the most part, stealing their land, often through brute force. Tribes had three choices in response to this invasion: (a) retreat to unknown and often inhospitable land, (b) stay and fight, or (c) stay and submit to total domination.

With the Dawes or Land Allotment Act of 1887, all NI/ANs were relocated to reservations and expected to subsist by farming primarily infertile land. Once relocated, the U.S. government attempted to assimilate NI/ANs through several mechanisms, including (a) prohibiting them from speaking their languages and participating in cultural ceremonies; (b) separating children from parents and sending them away to boarding schools that were often abusive; (c) removing children and adopting them into White families; and (d) relocating NI/ANs from reservations and providing job training and housing to urban areas such as Chicago, Denver, Albuquerque, Los Angeles, Oakland, San Francisco, and San Jose. These government policies and programs were developed without NI/AN input and diametrically opposed to traditional cultural values of inclusiveness with family and harmony with the land. Governmental policies were not rescinded until the 1970s with the Indian Self-Determination and Education Assistance Act (1975), the Freedom of Religion Act (1977), and Indian Child Welfare Act (1978). Unfortunately, these early polices had serious negative long-term psychological impact on NI/ANs, causing identity confusion and cultural alienation, as well as anger and mistrust of the government and White majority (for a review, see Gone & Trimble, 2012).

Today, there are approximately 5.2 million NI/ANs living in the United States, including 2.3 million, or about 44% who are bi- or multiracial (Norris, Vines, & Hoeffel, 2012). About 22% reside on the 334 federally and state-recognized NI/AN reservations, off-reservation trust lands, or state-designated American Indian statistical areas. The states with the largest NI/AN population are California (723,225), Oklahoma (482,760), and Arizona (353,386). The largest NI/AN tribes include Cherokee (819,105), Navajo (332,129), Choctaw (195,764), Mexican American Indian (175,494), Chippewa (170,742), Sioux (170,110), Apache (111,810), and Blackfeet (105,304). The median income of NI/ANs ($37,227) is far below that for the U.S. population as a whole ($53,657), and almost twice as many live in poverty (28.3%) compared with the general population (15.5%; Infoplease, n.d.).

According to the National Indian Education Study 2011 (U.S. Department of Education, Institute of Education Sciences, National Center for Education Statistics [NCES], 2012), NI/AN fourth-graders are evenly divided between low-density (LD) and high-density (HD) schools, with 89% attending public schools and about 7% attending Board of Indian Education (BIE) schools. The overwhelming majority of BIE schools are rural (91%), with a high percentage of students who are learning English as a second language (40%). As a whole, NI/AN families have much fewer resources than White families; only 50% have more than 25 books in their household (compared with 79% of Whites), and 78% have computers at home (compared with 93% of Whites; NCES, 2012). Scores on the National Assessment of Educational Progress (NAEP) for 2011 were low compared with national standards (reading = 202, math = 225 [mean = 500]; NCES, 2012).

Academic achievement of NI/AN fourth-graders varied by region and tribes. For example, NAEP reading scores from 2011 were highest for NI/AN students living in Oregon (213) and lowest for those living in Alaska (175), whereas math scores were highest in Oklahoma (234) and lowest for those in Alaska (213; NCES, 2012). In terms of educational attainment, 78.4% of NI/ANs have earned at least high school degree compared with 88.6% of non-NI/ANs, whereas 14.9% have earned a bachelor's degree compared with 29.4% non-NI/ANs (Aud, Fox, & KewalRamani, 2010).

Despite earlier government attempts to eradicate native languages, 28% of NI/ANs age 5 years and older spoke a language other than English at home compared with 21% for the general population. Bilingualism is particularly pronounced for residents of the Navajo Nation Reservation and Off-Reservation Trust Land, where 73% of persons older than age 5 spoke a language other than English at home (Seibens & Julian, 2011).

Neuropsychological Implications of NI/AN Macrosocietal Structures

The unique history of NI/ANs reveals several themes that are relevant to contextualizing behaviors. First is the diversity in the NI/AN population, which, as noted earlier, includes 566 recognized tribes spread across the continent, most with different cultures, histories, and degrees of interaction with dominant American society. Thus, behavioral and test norms for one NI/AN tribe will not necessarily be applicable to another. Second, a related issue is acculturation and racial identity. Experiences such as living situation on or off the reservation attending boarding schools, reasons for and generation of assimilating into mainstream society, and characteristics such as bi- and multi-racialism, languages spoken, and quality of education are pertinent areas for evaluation.

To better understand the potential cultural identities of NI/ANs, Garrett and Pichette (2000) formulated a five-stage model for conceptualizing Indian ethnic identity:

1. *Traditional*—These individuals adhere closely to traditional cultures. They may speak little English, think in the native language, and practice traditional tribal customs and methods of worship.

2. *Marginal*—These NI/ANs are often bilingual, speaking both traditional languages and English but have lost touch with Native culture and are not fully accepted in mainstream society.
3. *Bicultural*—These individuals are conversant with both sets of values and can communicate in a variety of contexts.
4. *Assimilated*—These individuals embrace only the mainstream culture's values, behaviors, and expectations.
5. *Pantraditional*—Although these individuals have only been exposed to or adopted mainstream values, they have made a conscious effort to return to traditional customs.

Underlying this model is how a NI/AN broaches, adapts to, and accepts life in both traditional and mainstream cultures. It is important to remember that given the heterogeneity, traditional identity is tribe specific. Age and location of residence, for example, on the reservation versus in a city, are important considerations for acculturation.

Third, a high percentage of NI/ANs are of low socioeconomic status, which has significant implications for health and cognition. Fourth, because of the long history of atrocities against NI/ANs by the U.S. government, NI/AN clients may not trust persons associated with mainstream society. This mistrust may influence the ability of clinicians to develop rapport with these clients and can result in *passive collaboration*, which is the appearance of being cooperative without disclosing or fully engaging in the evaluation (Dennis Norman, personal communication, May 6, 2015). This behavior developed from decades of "outsiders" studying or classifying NI/AN without disclosing how the data would be used—or misused. Issues of trust with clinicians could have an impact on comfort level in the testing process, which is important for communication with the tester (American Educational Research Association, American Psychological Association, & National Council on Measurement in Education [AERA, APA, & NCME], 2014). Fifth, although NI/AN students tend to demonstrate lower academic achievement than non-NI/ANs, their scores appear to be associated with command of English, environmental variables such and household educational resources, density of schools, rural versus urban schools, and cultural values and conceptualization of intelligent behaviors (discussed in the next section). Awareness of academic contextual variables is important to conceptualize issues associated with validity of test score interpretations and opportunities for learning (AERA, APA, & NCME, 2014).

The vast heterogeneity between and within of NI/AN has potential implications for all elements of fairness in testing including fair treatment, measurement bias, accessibility, and valid test interpretations. However, the clinician must analyze how specific characteristics of the individual client interact with the contextual aspects of testing to determine the specific impact of culture for each client (AERA, APA, & NCME, 2014).

VALUES, BELIEFS, AND SOCIAL STRUCTURES

The next group of characteristics describe more specific aspects of culture that can affect general beliefs and behaviors.

- *Worldview:* What are cultural beliefs about why things occur? What is the perceived control one has over life and life events? What is the purpose of life (Judd & Beggs, 2005)?
- *Values:* What do people value (e.g., includes concepts of honor, shame, justice, family expectations, time sense; Judd & Beggs, 2005)?
- *Religion and beliefs:* What are formal theological beliefs, rituals, and the function of religion in everyday life? How does it affect social structures (Judd & Beggs, 2005)?
- *Family structures:* What is the family structure, and what are the roles of family members? What are behavioral expectations for each member toward the others? What are the boundaries of family? How is kinship described (Judd & Beggs, 2005)?
- *Social roles and expectation for interactions:* What are expectations for behavior and interactions based on age, gender, position of authority (Judd & Beggs, 2005)?
- *Boundary issues:* How do cultures interact with other ethnic groups (Judd & Beggs, 2005)?
- *Learning styles:* How do people learn best (Van Hamme, 1996)?
- *Concepts of intelligence:* What do people consider intelligent behavior (Sternberg, 2004)?

In general, NI/ANs are highly spiritual people whose spirituality is intertwined with everyday life. The traditional core belief is that the person is an interdependent and equal part of nature. All objects in nature, such as animals and plants, as well as inanimate forces and objects such as mountains, rocks, the wind, and bodies of water, are imbued with life, sacred, and should be honored and respected. The good life is being connected to and living in harmony with nature and mother earth (Sutton & Broken Nose, 1996). Specific spiritual beliefs and ceremonies vary by tribe, but most are community rather than individual oriented. These beliefs and rituals are often considered sacred and not to be shared with outsiders. For many NI/ANs, traditional and mainstream faiths coexist (Substance Abuse and Mental Health Services Administration [SAMHSA], 2009).

Given their worldview of interdependence, it is not surprising that NI/ANs are a highly collectivist culture. Emphasis is placed on the group and maintaining group harmony, and thus the needs of the group are placed above those of the individual (Prescott, 1991). To maintain harmony, behaviors such as patience, placidity, careful listening, observation, moderation in speech, and respect for everyone's dignity and personal autonomy are highly valued. Economically, group orientation is reflected in valuing generosity toward others and indifference to ownership (Prescott, 1991).

The core support system is the extended family, in which there is sharing of roles and few relational terms. Cousins or close friends can be referred to as brothers and sisters. Aunts and uncles can be referred to as parents. Many tribes do not have terms for in-laws because families are blended through marriage. The primary relationship is with grandparents, who provide training and discipline, as well as with other elders, including great uncles and aunts. Elders are venerated because it is believed that with age comes wisdom (Sutton & Broken Nose, 1996).

Within this communal family organization are four core values (L. D. Harris & Wasilewski, 1992): (a) *being a good relative*, which involves mutual reciprocal exchange obligations; (b) *inclusive sharing*, in which resources are shared and redistributed throughout the community; (c) *contributing*, in which each person can participate and contribute to the community; and (d) *noncoercive leadership*, in which the driving value of leaders and persons in authority is a responsibility for others.

The naturalistic worldview of NI/ANs also influences their conceptualization of time. Time is perceived as cyclical versus linear and is based on personal and seasonal rhythms versus specific hours and days. Things happen when they happen and are not bound by specific hours, days, or scheduled appointments. Ceremonies start and end when everyone arrives and everything is completed versus being bound by scheduled 1-hour time slots (Sutton & Broken Nose, 1996). NI/ANs also tend to be present oriented. They live in the here and now rather than focusing on future goals (Sutton & Broken Nose, 1996). Nature provides sustenance, and thus work for the sake of working or storing for the future are foreign concepts and can be perceived as hoarding or being greedy (Prescott, 1991).

A comparison and contrast of NI/AN versus Western values, adapted from Prescott (1991), is summarized in Table 3.1.

Values and experiences also have an impact on learning styles. NI/ANs tend to be visual learners, relying heavily on observation and use of visual imagery. They perceive things globally and holistically with an intuitive learning style. Being intuitive, if something does not fit into their worldview or understanding, then little effort will be put into it (Mark Powless, personal communication, May 8, 2015). Dyc and Milligan (2000) argued that NI/ANs

TABLE 3.1
Comparison of Native Indian/Alaskan Native and Western Values

Native Indian and Alaskan Native	Western
Group allegiance	Individualistic
Present oriented	Future oriented
Things happen when they happen	Time is precious
Work ethic to meet needs of the group	Strong work ethic
Ownership is a foreign concept	Ownership
Elders valued for wisdom	Young is beautiful
Cooperation	Competitive
Modesty	Attention seeking
Silence	Uncomfortable with silence
Patience	Aggressiveness
Listening	Speaking up
Sharing	Taking
Harmony with nature	Conquering nature
Intuitive	Logical
Caution	Risk taking
Careful observation	Doing
Humility	Self-attention
Life is spiritual	Religion is a part of life

have a visual intelligence in which multiple levels of meaning can be discerned from native graphic designs and icons. In addition, use of storytelling, which has layers of meaning, has been the primary mode of passing down the wisdom of a tribe through generations (Dyc & Milligan, 2000). Reflection is another important aspect of learning that allows for certainty before attempting to perform or communicate and is related to values of silence and an unhurried time orientation (for a review, see Van Hamme, 1996).

Neuropsychological Implications of NI/AN Values, Beliefs, and Social Structures

The stark contrast in worldview and values between NI/ANs and mainstream Western culture has several important implications for neuropsychologists. First, cultural self-awareness (e.g., assumptions and personal biases) is "absolutely mandatory" when working with NI/ANs to prevent ethnocentric interpretation, judgments, and recommendations for treatment (Gone, 2004, p. 15). With this awareness, the clinician can truly appreciate how devastating Western oppression and attempts at assimilation have been on NI/ANs and, it is hoped, prevent repetition of this type of tragedy on an individual basis.

Second, given the potential for significant cultural differences in treatment, a collaborative approach is recommended in which clinicians strive to respect and incorporate the client's treatment preferences and goals (Gone, 2004). When conceptualizing recommendations for NI/AN clients, SAMHSA (2009) suggests that a number of cultural strengths should be considered, including the following: (a) natural support systems that include extended family and kinship ties and community with a collective obligation and sense of responsibility toward each member, (b) indigenous knowledge and wisdom, (c) natural resources (e.g., food, animals, plants, water, land), (d) resiliency and survival skills when faced with adversity, (e) reclamation and retention of traditional cultural practices and languages, (f) ability to live and adapt to different cultures (e.g., mainstream and NI/AN), and (g) community pride. However, when considering strengths, it is important to remember that cultural identity and experiences differ for each individual.

Third, contrasting values and learning styles indicate that NI/AN conceptualization of intelligence would differ from that of Western culture. Gottfredson's (1997) prototypical Western definition of *intelligence* is the "ability to reason, plan, solve problems, think abstractly, comprehend complex ideas, learn quickly and learn from experience" (p. 1). By contrast, a NI/AN would perceive an intelligent person as a good listener and observer who uses cautious reflection and intuition for formulating holistic conceptualizations before responding to everyday situations with overriding goals of maintaining harmony within human relationships and relationship to nature. Although there are overlapping qualities, such as an ability to reason and problem solve, Western cultures emphasizes abstract thinking and learning quickly, whereas NI/AN culture values slower reflective processes focusing on relationships (emotional, intellectual, physical spiritual, intra- and interpersonal), respect for all things, peace, and keeping harmony. Unlike Western culture, in which breadth of vocabulary is associated with intelligence, an ability to engage in appropriate storytelling targeted toward the specific listener would be the NI/AN equivalent (Teacher Certification, n.d.).

There are two implications for the contrasting perceptions. In terms of academic learning, NI/ANs who are visual learners may not excel in Western classrooms where instructions and information are primarily imparted verbally. Introducing abstract material in a sequential manner for detailed analysis is antithetical to their holistic and intuitive ways of learning. Being reflective listeners who only respond after a certainty of skill level, they would be uncomfortable in discussing topics in trial-and-error manner such as in brainstorming. Abstract material would be unimportant to students whose concerns are everyday relationships and harmony with nature. Finally, competitive environments would be a source of stress (Van Hamme, 1996).

Similarly, NI/ANs would be at a disadvantage in Western testing situations, including IQ or neuropsychological tests in which questions typically ask about abstract or impersonal topics that may be unimportant to them. The irrelevance of the material could certainly affect motivation. On IQ tests, the Western equation of speed with intelligence is demonstrated on tests such as the Block Design, which assigns bonus points for quick completion. NI/ANs who value caution and reflection would be penalized for their natural style of problem solving. Also, some IQ tasks may look as if they are set up to be tricks, which would influence trust and motivation for performance (Mark Powless, personal communication, May 8, 2015). In general, the issues of trust and significant cultural differences could potentially have an impact on all facets of fair testing and ultimately the validity of test score interpretations (AERA, APA, & NCME, 2014).

Fourth, the mismatch of values and beliefs between NI/AN and Western cultures is a major reason for the economic and educational challenges of NI/ANs "within" Western society. Unlike members of many other ethnicities who immigrated here to find a better life and thus were often motivated to assimilate, Western culture imposed itself on the indigenous NI/ANs. To deal with this imposition, NI/ANs could either maintain their own cultural values or attempt to assimilate into Western culture. Those who opted to maintain their identity rejected Western culture, with its societal values of individual economic attainment and participation in an educational system that promotes this ideology. Although content with their lifestyle, these NI/ANs may appear to lead an austere existence when viewed through a Western cultural perspective. Those who attempted to assimilate into Western culture met significant challenges because their diametrically opposed values and beliefs made it difficult to fit in.

MEDICAL CONDITIONS AND BELIEFS ABOUT ILLNESS

The next group of characteristics pertain specifically to the etiology of medical and neurological disorders that affect cognition and treatment. Information from these categories can provide a context for receiving referrals, making a diagnosis, and tailoring recommendations to the client's culture.

- *Epidemiology:* What are common neurological and psychological disorders (Judd & Beggs, 2005)?
- *Attitudes and beliefs regarding health and illness:* What are the beliefs regarding the causes of medical and mental illnesses, including culture-specific mental disorders? What are beliefs regarding interventions, including both traditional healing practices and Western medicine (Judd & Beggs, 2005)?

- *Recent history:* Are there life-shaping events, such as wars, famines, natural disasters, or epidemics, that may be associated with brain injury (Judd & Beggs, 2005)?
- *Responses to psychotropic medications:* Are there ethnicity-specific responses to medications or dosing recommendations (Judd & Beggs, 2005)?

NI/ANs experience a disproportionate amount of health disparities compared with the general U.S. population, including increased risk for stroke (5.9% vs. 2.6%), prostate cancer (9.3% vs. 2.4%), diabetes (16.3% vs. 8.8%) liver failure (2.6% vs. 1.4%), and obesity (39.6% vs. 27.6%). NI/ANs are more likely to suffer from hearing (20.7% vs. 15.7%) and vision (15.1% vs. 9.1%) problems (Schiller, Lucas, Ward, & Peregoy, & the National Center for Health Statistics, 2012).

In terms of mood, they are more likely to experience feelings of sadness (14.3% vs. 8.8%), hopelessness (7.3% vs. 4.6%), and restlessness (10.1% vs. 6.2%; Schiller et al., 2012). NI/ANs also have higher rates of smoking than the general population (42.2% vs. 26.9%; Centers for Disease Control and Prevention, 2011). Prevalence of psychological disorders vary by tribe. For example, Northern Plains males were found to have lower rates of any type of depressive disorder versus a national sample (8.2% vs. 14.4%), whereas Southwestern (9.4%) and Northern Plains males (11.5%) demonstrated higher levels of posttraumatic stress disorder (PTSD) than the general population (4.3%; Beals et al., 2005). Similar to males, Southwestern (14.3%) and Northern Plains (10.3%) females have lower rates of major depression than the general female population (21.3%), but report higher levels of PTSD (Southwestern 22.5%; Northern Plains 22.2%; general female population 9.1%; Beals et al., 2005). Rates of PTSD are particularly high among NI/AN Vietnam veterans, with one study reporting 45% to 57% lifetime prevalence for two reservations (Beals et al., 2002).

Alcohol abuse is a significant problem with NI/ANs, affecting not only the individual but also their families and the community. Although their rate of regular drinking (44.1% vs. 54.9%) and binge drinking (15.4% vs. 17.5%) is less than rates for Whites, their frequency of binge drinking is higher (6.7% vs. 3.9% per previous 30 days), they drink more per sitting (8.4% vs. 6.7%; Centers for Disease Control and Prevention, 2011), and rates of alcoholism are higher (4.1% for Southwestern tribes and 6.6% for Northwestern Plains tribes vs. 3.1% for Whites; Beals et al., 2005). Perhaps more significant are the health ramifications of drinking. NI/ANs die at higher rates than other Americans from alcoholism, including death from liver disease (55.2%; Indian Health Service [IHS], 2013) and have the highest alcohol-related motor vehicle mortality rates in the nation (Naimi et al., 2008). It has been estimated that 65% of motor vehicle accidents occurring on the reservation are associated with alcohol-impaired driving versus 47% nationwide (U.S. Department of Transportation, 2004).

Another comorbidity is fetal alcohol syndrome, which is associated with developmental delays in speech and motor development, attention-deficit disorder, and global neuropsychological deficits including intelligence, attention, learning and memory, visual spatial functions, and executive functioning (for a review, see Mattson, Crocker, & Nguyen, 2011). National prevalence rates range between 0.2 and 1.0 cases per 1,000 live births, whereas NI/ANs have some of the highest rates of this disorder at 1.5 to 2.5 per 1,000 (Centers for Disease Control and Prevention, 2002; May, McCloskey, & Gossage, 2002) Prevalence varies among tribes, with Navajo and Pueblo tribes reporting rates similar to the overall U.S. population, whereas Alaskan Natives (5.6), Plains (9.0), and Southwest Plains Indians (9.8) report much higher prevalence rates per 1,000 live births (May, McCloskey, & Gossage, 2002).

Environmental factors may contribute to poor health, as NI/ANs are more likely to live in inadequate housing (31.9% vs. 22.7%) and unhealthy housing, the latter associated with exposure to toxins and evidence of rodents (53% vs. 33%; Centers for Disease Control and Prevention, 2011). Unfortunately, health care is inadequate for many because NI/ANs are less likely to have health insurance than Whites (14.6%/33.7%; Centers for Disease Control and Prevention, 2011), whereas those living on the reservation have their health care provided by the IHS, which is chronically underfunded and understaffed. For example, one estimate reports that there are two psychiatrists and four psychologists on IHS staff per 100,000 people (Gone, 2004).

Consistent with their worldview, NI/ANs generally conceptualize health and wellness as a harmony or balance among mind, body, spirit, and the environment. Thus, both medical illnesses and emotional disorders such as depression or anxiety, which are perceived as weakness of the mind, will burden the spirit (Cross, 2003; SAMHSA, 2009). According to Vogel (1970), NI/ANs attributed diseases to three causes: human agency, supernatural agency, and natural causes. Human agency pertains to wounds inflicted by self or others, emotional reactions to loss, or the result of breaking cultural taboos. Natural causes include water accidents, fire, and wind. Supernatural causes involve intrusion into the body by outside agencies. Object intrusion is similar to germ theory and occurs when small animals, such as a worm or insect, enter the body and causes a disease. Diseases can also result from intrusions from the spirits of animals or nature, taking revenge for being disrespected, and spirit intrusion, which refers to charms or spells cast by others or souls of the dead (Vogel, 1970). Traditional Indian NI/AN medicine is holistic in nature and can include herbal medicines, "sweats" ceremonies for cleansing, and healing ceremonies that can involve prayers, songs, dances, feasts, and community participation (Thompson, Walker, & Silk-Walker, 1993). Depending on where the person lives and the level of acculturation, both traditional and Western medicines can be used to treat the same illness.

According to several NI/AN mental health professionals, the oppressive history of NI/ANs is a significant contributor to the high rates of suicide, alcoholism, domestic violence, child abuse, and other social problems (Duran & Duran, 1995). Heart, Chase, Elkins, and Altschul (2011) described these experiences as *historical trauma*, which they defined as the "cumulative emotional and psychological wounding across generations, including the lifespan, which emanates from massive group trauma" (p. 283). Historical trauma has been associated with depression and anger and poses a risk for alcohol abuse.

A review of the epidemiology of physical and mental health morbidity, attitudes toward health, and recent history reveals several themes for neuropsychologists to consider before conducting a neuropsychological evaluation. First, higher rates of cardiovascular disease, tobacco use, and alcohol-related physical disorders that include involvement in motor vehicle accidents should alert the clinician to these conditions when gathering history. A history of maternal drinking that may be associated with fetal alcohol syndrome would be particularly pertinent among certain tribes. Second, neuropsychologists should be aware of comorbid psychiatric conditions such as depression and PTSD that can also affect performance on testing. Third, the etiology of dementia appear to be more multifaceted than it is in the general population. Fourth, conceptualization of health and healing among NI/ANs tends to be more holistic than in Western culture and should be respected with considerations of systemic interventions when developing recommendations. Fifth, health and mental health disparities should be understood within the context of the traumatic history of NI/ANs and the significant challenges of existing in a society with diametrically opposed values and beliefs that it attempts to impose on them.

MAXIMIZING COOPERATION

Many CDCs are uncomfortable with mental health professionals and psychological testing due to unfamiliarity with and differing assumptions of the situation. Unbeknownst to the neuropsychologist, this discomfort may affect not only what is disclosed during the examination but also how a person responds to tests and ultimately to test performance and validity of interpreting test scores (AERA, APA, & NCME, 2014). Thus, it is imperative that the neuropsychologist be aware of expectations of the CDC and tailor evaluation processes to establish and maximize rapport and obtain an accurate representation of abilities and results (Judd & Beggs, 2005).

As discussed in the previous sections, developing rapport with NI/ANs can be highly challenging because of (a) the inherent distrust of persons representing mainstream culture and (b) significant differing worldviews and values between NI/ANs and mainstream Western culture. In addition, NI/ANs may be reluctant to attend sessions with a mental health professional because of stigma, fear of being judged, or fear of racial discrimination (Thomason, 2011). The following are recommendations to facilitate rapport with NI/ANs (SAMHSA, 2009; Thomason, 2011):

- Be professional and respectful.
- Be warm and friendly.
- Sharing food is a way of welcoming visitors; thus, offering water, coffee, or tea is an inviting gesture. This gesture should be done in moderation.
- Engage in casual conversation with some self-disclosure (e.g., where you are from, personal interests, general information about your family) to build a relationship.
- Do not talk about distant NI/AN relatives in your genealogy as an attempt to establish rapport unless you have maintained a connection to those relatives and the NI/AN community.
- Use the community self-reference for tribal name.
- Do not impose your personal values, morals, or beliefs.
- Be transparent about the purpose of the evaluation, the evaluation process, and your role in the evaluation (e.g., who referred you, what the information will be used for). Provide a simple explanation for your note taking.
- During the formal interview process, invite the client to tell his or her story before engaging in a specific line of questioning.
- Do not interrupt the client during disclosure, and avoid interjecting during pauses or long silences. Learn to be comfortable with silence or long pauses in conversation. Listen and observe more than you speak.
- Avoid intrusive questions early in the interview.
- Use good mirroring skills done in moderation (e.g., adapt tone of voice, volume, pace of speech, and posture to match communication style of client).
- Body language, posture, and personal space depend on tribal norms and the nature of the personal relationship. Observe and allow the client to create space and initiate or ask for any physical contact.
- Gender roles can vary significantly between NI/AN communities. Males and females typically have distinct social rules for conduct

in everyday interactions. Neuropsychologists should be aware of norms for eye contact, style of dress, physical touch, personal space, and decision making for males and females and interactions between genders.

■ Be open to proceed according to the principle that "things happen when they are supposed to happen." Avoid frequently looking at your watch.

When working with NI/ANs, it should be emphasized that the importance of rapport building cannot be underestimated because of their inherent mistrust of Western authority figures and the collectivist NI/AN culture, which places a high value on relationships. Initial mistrust should not be taken personally. In addition, because of the slower pace of rapport building and disclosure, clinicians should plan for a longer session or schedule multiple sessions to allot for more time to interview the client.

FACILITATING COMMUNICATION

Once rapport is established and the CDC is comfortable disclosing information, the next step for the neuropsychologist is to ensure that he or she is able to receive this information accurately. This process can be highly challenging for the neuropsychologist who is unfamiliar with communication styles that are much different from his or her own. A lack of awareness could have a significant impact on accessibility or the ability of the client to demonstrate his or her knowledge about the construct being measured. Without adequate communication of knowledge, the validity of score interpretation would be significantly affected (AERA, APA, & NCME, 2014). Judd and Beggs (2005) identified several aspects of the communication process that the neuropsychologist should be aware of to maximize listening skills during the evaluation.

■ *Language:* What is the client's primary language? Is English a second language, and if so, what is the client's proficiency in comprehending, speaking, reading, and writing English (tonal languages, nature of writing system, use of an alphabet)?

■ *Norms for personal disclosure:* What information is considered appropriate to disclose to others and in what contexts? How is information disclosed?

■ *Nonverbal conventions:* What are norms for interpersonal distance, eye contact, and pace of exchange? What are common nonverbal gestures?

- *Expression of pain:* How are physical and emotional pain communicated? What are common idioms of distress?

NI/ANs may vary in their English proficiency. As mentioned previously, 66% of Navajo living on the reservation older than 5 years spoke a language other than English at home (Norris et al., 2012; Seibens & Julian, 2011). By contrast, NI/ANs raised and living in urban areas would most likely speak English as a primary language. Because of the wide range of experiences, assessing for English proficiency is particularly important for certain tribes, older clients, and those residing on the reservation. English as a second language and bilingualism are discussed in more depth in Chapter 10.

Even if rapport is established, obtaining information from NI/ANs can be challenging due to norms for personal disclosures and unique communication styles. NI/ANs are typically cautious when encountering others and do not freely share personal and family problems because they do not want to embarrass or cause others to think negatively about them (Prescott, 1991). This reticence extends to others because it is considered disrespectful or disloyal to speak negatively about another person—and unacceptable to criticize another person directly (SAMHSA, 2009). Similar to other collectivist cultures, NI/ANs do not want to offend or openly disagree with others, particularly authority figures; thus, they may nod their head politely even if they do not understand what the person is saying or agree with recommendations (Prescott, 1991).

When disclosing about oneself, it is not unusual for NI/ANs to use self-deprecating comments to demonstrate humbleness and humility, which does not necessarily connote low self-esteem. Another unique manner of communicating is storytelling (both traditional and personal) to make a point. This style can appear cryptic and is in contrast to the "get to the point" style characterized by Western communication. Finally, humor or teasing is often an indirect way of correcting inappropriate behavior (SAMHSA, 2009).

Because of NI/ANs' reticence in self-disclosure and their indirect style of communication, neuropsychologists need to pay careful attention to nonverbal aspects of communication when evaluating a NI/AN client. Clinicians should be aware of the following gestures that have unique meaning in NI/AN culture: (a) looking down is a manner of showing respect or deference to elders; (b) ignoring a person indicates disagreement or displeasure; (c) a gentle handshake is a sign of respect, not weakness; and (d) pointing with one's finger is considered rude (SAMHSA, 2009).

NI/ANs typically convey difficult messages through humor. Painful disclosures are frequently made as part of a joke or covered by smiles (SAMHSA, 2009). If a NI/AN should cry during an interview, provide support without further questions until the client composes himself or herself and is ready to continue (SAMHSA, 2009).

Given the communication style of NI/ANs, neuropsychologists should attend to the following:

- Avoid using jargon; a likely response from NI/ANs is a polite nod even if they do not understand what has been said.
- Be careful when probing for negative characteristics of a person or family members (e.g., substance abuse, physical abuse, mental illness) because NI/ANs are reticent to talk badly about self and others. Attempt to use euphemisms or positive reframes of negative behaviors. Use local cultural idioms if possible.
- Problems that are disclosed are likely much more distressing than what is expressed
- Reasons for coming to the evaluation can be an important source of information and signify distress of the family system.
- Clinicians need to pay close attention to humor because it may be invasive to ask for clarification of sensitive topics contained in these disclosures.
- Approaches to maximize rapport building are inefficient for gathering specific data. Clinicians will have to find a balance between the two.
- Listen carefully for the point of a story or joke, or else you risk losing respect and rapport (likely without even knowing it). (M. Powless, personal communication, May 8, 2015)

4

CONCEPTUALIZING GOALS
AND CULTURAL CONSIDERATIONS

Right view, right aspiration, right speech, right action, right livelihood,
right effort, right mindfulness, right concentration.

—Siddhartha Gautama

The next three chapters detail a preparatory process for neuropsychological evaluations with culturally different clients (CDCs). First, underlying goals of the neuropsychological evaluation and their implications for assessment are described. Second, cultural characteristics pertinent for, and their impact on, elements of data collection are identified, along with guidelines to address cultural influences. Strategies for data collection, their associated strengths and weaknesses, and appropriate applications are described in upcoming chapters, including strategies for estimating premorbid functioning on Western testing.

GOALS OF NEUROPSYCHOLOGICAL TESTING

The goals of a neuropsychological evaluation typically involve differential diagnosis (if a diagnosis has not already been identified by referral sources), the impact of a neurological condition on cognition and functionality, legal and capacity issues, and treatment recommendations.

http://dx.doi.org/10.1037/15958-005
Conducting a Culturally Informed Neuropsychological Evaluation, by D. Fujii

Differential Diagnosis

Differential diagnosis is a common reason for referral for a neuropsychological evaluation. Although measurement of cognitive skills is important for the diagnosis of neurological disorders, according to criteria from the two major taxonomies of medical and mental illnesses, the *Diagnostic and Statistical Manual of Mental Disorders, Fifth Edition* (DSM–5; American Psychiatric Association, 2013) and the *International Statistical Classification of Diseases and Related Health Problems, 10th Revision* (ICD–10; World Health Organization, 2015) these data are not essential. In fact, for many disorders, other types of data, such as emotional and behavioral symptoms, age of onset, family history, history and progression of symptoms, and severity of functional impairment, are equally important. In this section, synopses of DSM–5 and ICD–10 diagnostic criteria for several neurological disorders are described to illustrate various types of data that are needed to determine diagnoses.

Dementia (ICD–10)/Major Neurocognitive Disorder (MaND; DSM–5)

Dementia and MaND require a decline or disturbance in cognitive functioning from premorbid levels in at least one cognitive domain which is not due to delirium. The *ICD–10* describes the course as chronic or progressive and as commonly preceded by deterioration in behaviors, emotional controls, or motivation, but it does not describe the severity of deficits required for diagnosis or how severity is determined. The *DSM–5* provides a general benchmark (deficits are significant enough to interfere with functional independence) as well as modifiers for levels of severity. For example, persons with mild MaND experiences difficulties in instrumental activities of daily living, moderate levels are associated with challenges in activities of daily living, whereas persons with severe MaND are fully dependent. Although cognitive impairment is preferably supported by standardized neuropsychological testing, it can also be based on concerns from a collateral source in addition to substantial impairment. Both nomenclatures have codes to identify etiology.

Mild Cognitive Disorder (MCD; ICD–10)/Minor Neurocognitive Disorder (MND; DSM–5)

These comparable disorders parallel dementia and MaND; however, the cognitive deficits are modest: Mental tasks are more difficult to perform but do not interfere with everyday functioning. Deficits should not be attributed to another mental disorder. The *ICD–10* criteria specifically state that MCD is associated with physical disorder or infections that can have an impact on the brain or others systems, although evidence for cerebral involvement is not required. Similar to MaND, *DSM–5* criteria state that cognitive impairment in MND is preferably supported by standardized neuropsychological testing, but testing is not required for diagnosis.

Dementia in Pick's Disease (DPD; ICD–10)/Frontotemporal Etiology (FTE; DSM–5)

DPD and FTE describe a specific etiology of dementia/MaND. Both the *ICD–10* and *DSM–5* nomenclature report an insidious onset and slow progressive behavioral changes associated with early prominent deficits in frontal lobe functioning, such as character changes, deteriorating social functioning, apathy, and disinhibition, followed by cognitive changes. The *ICD–10* states that the progression begins during middle age. The *DSM–5* identifies two variants. The behavioral variant, which is comparable to DPD, also lists symptoms of a loss of empathy, perseveration, and hyperorality. The language variant is characterized by a decline in speech production, word finding, object naming, comprehension, or grammar. *DSM–5* uses qualifiers of *probable* if genetic or imaging evidence is available and *possible* if supporting evidence is lacking.

Mental Retardation (MR; ICD–10)/Intellectual Disability (ID; DSM–5)

In contrast to the aforementioned disorders, MR and ID describe a neurocognitive disorder with onset during childhood and adolescence. The condition is characterized by significant intellectual impairment and concomitant deficits in adaptive functioning within the contexts of the person's environment and age-related expectations. According to *DSM–5* criteria, intellectual deficits must be confirmed by standardized testing normed for the person's sociocultural background and native language with maximum scores ranging between 65 and 75. Clinical judgment is required for interpreting test results, and clinicians must factor in the impact of culture. Intellectual limitations are associated with impairments in adaptive functioning in at least one of the following areas: conceptual, social, or practical. Levels of severity include mild, moderate, severe, and profound and are based on adaptive functioning within the contexts of the person's culture and environment. When standardized tests are unavailable, the individual can still be diagnosed with an unspecified ID.

For *ICD–10* criteria, intelligence is also estimated by standardized intelligence tests; however, the overall level is determined through clinical judgment. Nomenclature for severity is similar to that of the *DSM–5* but is more heavily weighted for IQ ranges, for example, mild (50–69), moderate (35–49), severe (20–34), and profound (under 20), although there are brief descriptors of functioning. The *ICD–10* comments on the dynamic nature of intelligence and functioning, which can improve with training and rehabilitation, and thus diagnosis should be based on a current assessment.

The following recommendations, based on the sample diagnostic criteria, may assist the clinician in preparing to conduct a neuropsychological evaluation:

- Important data for making diagnoses include premorbid history, neuropsychological test data, knowledge of expected functioning, information about current functioning, and accurate interpretations of behaviors.
- Neuropsychological data are important for determining areas of cognitive strengths and weaknesses that can aid in differential diagnosis through pattern analysis of test data and observations. It is also important to quantify cognitive skills that are needed for diagnosis based on discrepancy measures or thresholds.
- Although preferred, neuropsychological testing is not essential for diagnosing a neurological disorder, nor determining severity. *ICD–10* criteria for dementia, MCD, and DPD do not specifically state the need for cognitive testing, whereas *DSM–5* criteria for MaND, MND, behavioral variant of FTE, and unspecified ID can be made based on history, behaviors, and functionality. Thus, such diagnoses can be made in CDCs where valid quantifiable data are difficult to obtain.
- For diagnostic categories such as IDs, which require quantifiable measures of cognitive skills, there are limitations in what a neuropsychologist can conclude when culture and language have an impact on test data. The stronger the impact, the less confidence one can have in clinical conclusions, particularly for milder forms of a neurological disorder.
- Challenges in meeting diagnostic criteria are culture specific. For example, when trying to diagnose ID, it would be easier to obtain accurate IQ scores in the lower ranges for an immigrant from Japan, a culture that has IQs comparable to those of the United States and validated tests, compared with a client from Mozambique, where there are no indigenous tests developed to measure IQ, there are no translated tests, and the mean IQ score on Western tests in a limited sample was reported to be approximately 64 (Lynn & Meisenberg, 2010).
- In general, accurate quantifiable measures of cognition are more important for milder forms of a disorder or when there are strict cutoff scores or discrepancy criteria for diagnosis.
- When formulating a diagnosis, cultural knowledge is crucial for developing a contextual understanding of normative expectations for general functioning in everyday life.

- Cultural knowledge is also important for conceptualizing how behaviors associated with diagnoses present in a specific culture. For example, in the FTE for MaND, a clinician must be familiar with the client's culture to determine how disinhibition, apathy, loss of empathy, or perseverative behavior would present in a culturally different person.
- Clinicians should be aware of cultural clinical presentations of psychiatric disorders or culture-bound syndromes that are specific manifestations of mood, anxiety, or psychotic disorders. Such awareness is particularly important because specific questions may need to be asked to obtain information.
- Foundational knowledge of brain–behavior relationships in behavioral symptoms (see Heilman & Valenstein, 2012; Mesulam, 2000), psychiatric presentations (see Cummings & Mega, 2003), and cognition (see Mesulam, 2000) is especially important when working with CDCs because using behavioral and psychiatric indicators becomes more diagnostically salient when neuropsychological test data are limited or unavailable.

Determining Functionality

Another common goal of neuropsychological assessment is determining functionality. Here, the clinician must determine diagnosis and cognitive strengths and weaknesses and then extrapolate their impact on everyday functioning. This analysis can be as simple as making sense of what cognitive deficits underlie current presentation or difficulties that the client has in performing a specific task. Functionality can also involve legal criteria, such as decision-making capacity. For example, according to the Uniform Health-Care Decisions Act (National Conference of Commissioners on Uniform States Laws, 1994), *health care decision-making capacity* is defined as "the ability to understand significant benefits, risks, and alternatives to proposed health care and to make and communicate a health-care decision" (p. 3).

Four decisional elements based on case law are evaluated to determine capacity (American Bar Association & American Psychological Association [APA], 2008):

- *Expressing a choice* is the ability to communicate decisions. In this element, vacillation of decision is interpreted as reflecting decisional impairment.
- *Understanding* refers to the ability to comprehend information concerning diagnosis and treatment.

- *Appreciation* refers to the ability to relate treatment information to one's own situation. Components include the ability to believe the diagnosis and infer risks and benefits of treatment.
- *Reasoning* that is rationale and consistent needs to be demonstrated in decision making.

In evaluating for capacity, clinicians must determine whether cognitive or psychiatric factors affect capacity. Specifically, clinicians should evaluate for impairment in key cognitive abilities and determine how the client's cognitive profile translates to strengths and weaknesses in specific decisional elements. There are several important cultural considerations when determining capacity issues:

- To determine functionality, the clinician needs to be cognizant of the CDC's behavioral repertoire and normal routines. If there are limitations in functioning, to what extent is this due to lack of cultural experiences, differences in values and beliefs that affect motivation, different styles in performing a task, language proficiency, or cognitive deficits.
- For legal criteria, clinicians need to ensure that the CDC understands the questions asked; how values, experiences, and beliefs can affect decisions; and how communication styles can affect disclosure.
- Clinicians need to respect culturally congruent decision making even if it runs counter to Western values or those held by the medical staff.

Treatment Recommendations

Treatment recommendations are at the heart of clinically referred neuropsychological evaluations. No matter how accurate the conceptualization and diagnosis of an assessment, without sound recommendations, the client will still experience the same problems and challenges. Recommendations can be targeted toward the referral source or the client and support network, or they can be empirically based.

Referral Source

Reason for referrals differ widely and are not always straightforward. Referrals differ on the specificity of the referral questions and the amount of background information provided. Referring clinicians differ in their awareness of what information neuropsychological testing can provide; knowledge of neurological disorders and associated clinical issues and interventions, and knowledge, appreciation; and respect for a CDC's culture. Thus, to ensure that the intent of the referral is fully met, it is recommended that the neuropsychologist consider asking the referring clinician the following questions to clarify the motivation for the evaluation:

1. What observations or events piqued your interest or motivated the referral for a neuropsychological evaluation?
2. How familiar are you with the culture of this client? or How many clients of your current client's heritage have you worked with?
3. What two to three specific questions do you want this evaluation to answer?

One aspect of answering the referral question is to determine whether cultural confusion is a possible impetus for the referral. *Cultural confusion* can occur when there appears to be discrepancies between what the CDC says versus what she or he does, or if the CDC appears inflexibly to demonstrate behaviors that do not make treatment sense for the clinician. For example, Eduardo, a Filipino man suffering from excruciating pain secondary to bone cancer in a hospice unit, appeared to be depressed and slept most of the day. When asked about any medical decision making, he told the team to ask his daughter Virginia, who is a nurse, and his son Robert. They refused to consent to do not resuscitate (DNR) status until Robert's son Ernie, who was away for college, finished his semester so he could visit. Medical staff suspected that Eduardo could not make a decision for himself and Virginia and Robert had undue influence over their father. Thus, Eduardo was referred for a medical decision-making capacity evaluation. Unbeknownst to the physician, it is culturally consistent for Filipinos to have family involved in decision making, particularly if there is a professional in the family. Eduardo was both lucid and consistent in his wishes, and thus he was deemed to have capacity to grant decision making to his children.

Clients

For neuropsychological examinations in which the overarching goal is to maximize functioning, questioning clients or family about their goals for the evaluation can not only facilitate usefulness of the evaluation for the client and family but also assist in attaining buy-in from them and help in developing a working relationship. The following are sample questions for clients and family:

- What specific information do you want from this evaluation?
- What are your (or the family's) biggest concerns after the (neurological event)?
- What would you like help with?

- Are there disagreements between you and your family about your recovery?
- What are your recovery goals? or What is the family's recovery goals for the client?

Empirically Based Recommendations

Finally, goals can also be empirically based. This category is the purview of the neuropsychologist because referral sources or clients are seldom experts in implications for neuropsychological testing or treatment issues for specific disorders. An example of comes from Marcopulos and Fujii's (2012) evaluation for persons with schizophrenia. Their neuropsychological test battery consists of tests that have predictive validity for important functional outcome measures such as fitness to stand trial, social cognition and problem solving, community functioning, and learning in rehabilitation modules. Treatment recommendations are then targeted toward these empirically based clinical issues.

CULTURAL CHARACTERISTICS PERTINENT FOR NEUROPSYCHOLOGICAL EVALUATIONS

This section continues the previous chapter's focus on preparatory work for understanding culture. I begin by describing preassessment questions that clinicians can use to commence researching pertinent aspects of culture. This initial conceptual context can be used to generate preliminary hypotheses about the client's premorbid functioning. Next, I discuss pertinent moderating variables associated with acculturation and language proficiency to assist with conceptualization, identify challenges for the evaluation, and guide strategies for developing rapport with and interviewing CDCs. Recommendations to evaluate for acculturation and English proficiency follow. I close the section, and the chapter, with recommendations for selecting and working with interpreters. Different strategies for data collection and test selection strategy are described in Chapter 6.

Questions for Commencing Hypotheses Generation

Information about the client can be obtained from the referral source when asking for clarification or from the client and family when scheduling the appointment. Basic preassessment questions include the following:

- What is the client's ethnicity(s)?
- Is the client an immigrant? If so, what is his or her country of origin (if known)? What city or province did he or she come

from? How long has he or she lived in the United States? At what age did he or she immigrate?

- Employment in country of origin (if known)? Employment in the United States (if known)?
- Is English the client's first language? If not, how strong are his or her English skills? In your opinion, is there a need for an interpreter? Why or why not?

Once these demographics are obtained, the clinician can begin researching background on the client's culture as outlined in Chapters 3 and 5. An initial task would be to construct a general context for understanding the CDC. Macrostructures of the country of origin, such as geography, population, economics, government, general history, languages spoken, and educational system, are especially salient for immigrants but less so for later generations with increased acculturation into mainstream society. Values, beliefs, and social structures, which include worldview, religion, family structures, social roles and expectations for interactions, boundary issues, learning styles, and concepts of intelligence, can provide important contextual information for more specific behaviors.

When formulating a contextual conceptualization and data collection strategy, the clinician should develop hypotheses about the impact of acculturation and English proficiency on the evaluation process.

Moderating Factors

Acculturation

Acculturation, broadly defined, is the similarity of a client's culture and experiences to, and adoption of, mainstream culture. Research indicates that level of acculturation significantly affects test performance on standard neuropsychological tests in various cultures, including African American (Manly et al., 1998), Hispanic (Coffey, Marmol, Schock, & Adams, 2005; Razani, Burciaga, Madore, & Wong, 2007), mixed Asian, Middle Eastern, and non-Hispanic Whites (Touradji, Manly, Jacobs, & Stern, 2001).

According to cross-cultural psychologist Patricia Greenfield (1997), intellectual and cognitive tests are cultural genres that reflect the values, knowledge, and experiences of the society in which they developed. Each domain is associated with various underlying assumptions germane to that particular culture. Thus, for Western tests to be valid for a CDC, she or he must share the Western foundational assumptions underlying all of these domains. Greenfield further argued that test items must mean the same thing to people in different cultures, and there must be agreement on the value or merit of particular responses to a test question. The universal unit for knowledge must be the individual as opposed to the group, and there must be a distinction between the process of knowing and the object of knowledge. Finally, aspects of the testing situation, such as the purpose of asking questions, definitions of relevant information, decontextualized communication (i.e., talking about something that is not present), and conversing with strangers, must be universally accepted. If conventions of the test are not congruent with the test taker's culture, then test performance will be affected by his or her deficiencies in these conventions, and thus the test will not accurately measure the intended abilities.

To prevent the inappropriate use of Western tests with CDCs, clinicians must attain knowledge of clients' culture to determine congruence with Western culture. Cultural knowledge can aid in interpreting reasons for discrepant performances on Western tests and determining alternative strategies for assessing specific abilities (Greenfield, 1997). The next subsections discuss the most salient cultural moderating factors for neuropsychological assessment, including education and literacy, conceptualization of intelligence, poverty and low socioeconomic status (SES), familiarity and comfort with the evaluation process, and communication. Included in each discussion is how these cultural variables can affect fairness in testing. The section closes with recommendations on how to measure acculturation.

Education and Literacy

The positive association of educational level and performance on Western neuropsychological tests is one of the most robust findings in the literature (Heaton, Miller, Taylor, & Grant, 2004; Mitrushina, Boone, Razani, & D'Elia, 2005). Quality of education—for example, as measured by expenditure per student—has also demonstrated a significant impact on cognition (Manly, Jacobs, Touradji, Small, & Stern, 2002). The impact of education on test performance is most pronounced at the lowest educational levels (for a review, see Ardila et al., 2010). For example, Ostrosky-Solís (2007) reported that performances of normals with no education on the Mini Mental State Examination are comparable to those of subjects with severe dementia, whereas scores for normals with 1 to 4 years of education are commensurate with those of persons with mild dementia. Similarly, illiteracy, which is generally associated with low education in low-resource countries, has been associated with global deficits, specifically in digit span (backward more than forward), verbal abstractions, long-term semantic memory, calculation, phonemic verbal fluency, visuoconstruction, visuoperception, ideomotor apraxia, and executive functioning (Reis, Guerreiro, & Petersson, 2003).

There are numerous reasons why formal education and literacy significantly affect performance on Western neuropsychological tests. Formal education exposes individuals to basic cognitive and motor skills required to perform tasks on Western tests, such as the use of a writing tool (e.g., pen or pencil) needed for simple drawing, use of taxonomic classification, familiarity with two-dimensional drawings of real-life objects, multiple-choice testing, and use of computers. It facilitates the development of formal operational thinking and improves semantic processing and size of lexical storage (for a review, see Ardila et al., 2010). Attending school also reinforces attitudes and values that facilitate the learning process, for example, memorizing information and acquiring knowledge, appreciating that learning is a step-by-step process that moves from simple to complex, and applying rules to new situations (Ardila et al., 2010; Laboratory of Comparative Human Cognition, 1983).

Ardila et al. (2010) described school as a *transnational culture* because of its impact on training-specific skills and its reinforcement of certain values. The theorists, however, are careful to emphasize that with the exception of focus on literacy and numeracy in primary education, schools vary considerably between and within countries. Examples of the ways schools differ include curriculum of study; length of school year; teacher qualifications; student-to-teacher ratio; learning expectations; values instilled; availability of books, desks, and computers; facilities of the learning environment, such as the availability of air-conditioning, running water, and bathrooms; extracurricular field trips; and availability of ancillary personnel such as counselors and special education teachers.

Likewise, literacy is also transformational, affecting verbal and visual memory, phonological awareness, executive functioning, visuospatial and visuomotor abilities, and effectiveness of phonological processing (for a review, see Ardila et al., 2010). Perhaps more important, Ardila et al. (2010) argued that literacy provides another avenue to acquire information. Instead of relying on oral communication, information can be attained by reading, which increases access to a larger and potentially unlimited source of knowledge. In addition, writing can facilitate memorization by recording information in a notebook, like an "auxiliary hippocampus."

On a more basic level, Greenfield (1997) argued that formal schooling changes a person's epistemology. On the basis of her studies on cultures without formal education, Greenfield found that her subjects did not make a distinction between thoughts or statements and an object; attempts to explain that thoughts and object are different entities were futile. For example, when performing a Piagetian conservation of quantity task with Senegalese children in which water was transferred from a shorter, fatter beaker into a taller, thinner one, the children did not respond when asked why they "thought" the water was the same or different. However, they were able to accurately respond when the question was posed more concretely: "Why is the water the same or more or less?" Greenfield called this state of knowing *cognitive realism*. With exposure to written language, in which thoughts about the world written on a page are visibly distinct from the world itself, individuals begin to appreciate that thoughts about the world are distinct from objects in the real world. This experience leads to the realization that people can have different thoughts about a given object and that different people can have different thoughts about the same thing. Greenfield refers to this epistemology as *cognitive relativism*.

A significant implication of this epistemology for performance on Western tests is familiarity with decontextualized communication, such as asking questions about something that is not present. Persons without formal education are at a disadvantage because most questions on Western tests ask about abstract ideas or intangible things (Uribe, LeVine, & LeVine, 1994). This contention is supported by studies comparing people who are illiterate versus literate while controlling for socioeconomic status. In one study, participants who were illiterate performed more poorly on most cognitive measures, but no differences were found in naming and identification of real objects, verbal fluency using ecologically relevant semantic criteria (e.g., items from a supermarket), verbal memory, or orientation (Reis et al., 2003). In a related study qualitatively analyzing responses on animal fluency, participants who were illiterate named only animals existing in the immediate environment, such as dogs, cats, or horses, whereas participants who were literate were able to name dinosaurs and animals from foreign countries that they have never seen in person before (da Silva, Petersson, Faísca, Ingvar, & Reis, 2004).

It should be emphasized that persons without formal education, particularly in low-resource countries, function well within their own environment despite what can appear to be impairment on Western neuropsychological tests. For example, in a study comparing knowledge of semiurban and rural Yup'ik Eskimos (Grigorenko et al., 2004), The researchers found that the semiurban children outperformed the rural children on crystallized intelligence, whereas the rural children performed better on indigenous practical intelligence tests evaluating for skills such as hunting, fishing, dealing with weather conditions, and picking and preserving plants. Similarly, a study with elderly persons living in the United States reported that education attainment was significantly related to performance on verbal tests but not systematically related to everyday problem solving (Cornelius & Caspi, 1987). These findings led Ardila et al. (2010) to argue that people who are illiterate develop different types of learning that are more procedural, pragmatic, and sensory based compared with those who are literate.

There are several methods for determining educational levels and education quality in CDCs. For those educated in the United States, knowledge of the schools and districts that the client attended can provide information about education quality, because schools in low-income districts typically have fewer resources than schools located in high-income neighborhoods.

For clients educated in foreign countries, the Programme for Individual Student Assessment or similar international test scores, a country's gross domestic product, a country's test scores on IQ tests, and IQ scores of neighboring countries can provide clues to educational quality and resources for that country (these indicators are discussed more in depth in Chapter 5). Similar to the United States, countries have regional differences in education quality, thus information about rural versus urban upbringing, quality of specific schools, and immigration selection biases for country of origin are also important sources of information.

Given the ubiquitous impact of education on experience, skill development, and epistemology, the potential impact of low educational attainment and illiteracy on fair testing is profound. CDCs with low educational levels would be unfamiliar with testing situations, which would be experienced as uncomfortable and even strange, and this may hinder communication. With a contrasting epistemology, constructs measured on Western tests would likely not apply to CDCs; thus, Western tests would be biased and nonequivalent. CDCs with low educational levels may not have pencil skills or the basic literacy required to respond to test items, thereby affecting accessibility. Finally, in addition to the aforementioned threats to fairness, CDCs with low levels of education would lack the opportunities to learn much of the content and skills measured by Western tests, thereby affecting valid interpretations of test scores (American Educational Research Association [AERA], APA, & National Council on Measurement in Education [NCME], 2014).

Conceptualization of Intelligence

According Sternberg (2004), *intelligence* is a culturally defined construct and thus cannot be understood outside one's context. For many cultures, concepts of intelligence differ radically from Western conceptions. For example, African conceptions of intelligence emphasize skills to facilitate and maintain harmonious and stable intergroup relationships. Specifically, Kenyan parents perceive children as intelligent if they are able to perform what is needed to be done around the homestead without being asked (Sternberg, 2004).

An important implication of how intelligence is conceived is its impact on skills that members of a society develop. For example, in a study of Kenyan children, Sternberg et al. (2001) developed a measure of practical knowledge that included skills such as identifying where medicines come from, what they are used for, and proper doses to determine a child's ability to adapt to his or her environment. Interestingly, a significant negative relationship was found between scores on this measure and Western tests of fluid and crystallized abilities. Sternberg interpreted these findings as reflecting an interaction between abilities and cultural patterns of schooling within the Kenyan society. For many poor rural Kenyan families, formal schooling does not have intrinsic value. Thus, children from these families will forgo school to learn about important indigenous knowledge that can assist family around the home. In comparison, children who attend formal schooling will not learn about these practices. When applied to principles of fair testing, the rural Kenyan children's construct of intelligent behaviors differed from Western tests, resulting in differential opportunities to learn the content and skills measured by these tests. Thus, the equivalency of testing and the validity of these scores as measures of intelligence are questionable (AERA, APA, & NCME, 2014).

The impact of contrasting cultural values on intelligence behaviors has also been hypothesized as a factor in persisting group differences on cognitive test scores between African Americans and White Americans (Davies, Strickland, & Cao, 2014). Common values for African Americans include a communal focus, flexible family roles, expressive creativity, and orientation toward practical and relevant knowledge. These values stem from necessity because poor African American children must learn associated skills early in life for survival. However, this skill set is unrelated to academics and absent in academic testing (Grubb & Dozier, 1989). Thus, standardized cognitive tests may be biased against African Americans because they do not accurately assess the types of knowledge that many need to acquire to adapt to their environment (Davies et al., 2014; Grubb & Dozier, 1989). This contention is supported by studies demonstrating a positive correlation between level of acculturation to dominant Western culture for African Americans and test performance on standard neuropsychological tests (Manly et al., 1998) and a negative correlation between Black racial identity and test performance (Helms, 2002).

More directly, possessing a conception of intelligence that differs from Western notions can affect what are considered good responses on Western tests, thereby undermining the construct validity of these tests (AERA, APA, & NCME, 2014). For example, when administered an object-sorting task, the Kpelle, a farming tribe in Liberia, indicated that a wise person would sort items according to functional pairing, such as a knife and potato. By contrast, a fool would sort objects into linguistically ordered categories (M. Cole, Gay, Glick, & Sharp, 1971). Thus, Kpelle and Western criteria for wise and foolish responses on the sorting task were exact opposites. Agranovich and Puente (2007) demonstrated that cultural differences in the conception of time can have a selective impact on neuropsychological test performances. In their study, Russian and American university students were administered a battery of neuropsychological tests that included timed and untimed tasks. Given the lesser relevance that Russians place on timeliness and adherence to deadlines and the deemphasis on timed tests in the Russian educational system, the researchers predicted that Russian and American students would score similarly on untimed tests, but the Russians would score lower on timed tests. As predicted, results supported the hypothesis that cultural differences can negatively affect test performances.

Poverty and Low SES

Poverty or *low SES* is a multidimensional experience consisting of both environmental and parental/familial factors, including higher rates of perinatal complications, reduced access to medical resources, increased exposure to lead, increased exposures to acute and chronic stressors, harsh and inconsistent parenting, and less cognitive stimulation at home (for a review, see McLoyd, 1998). Low SES accounts for approximately 20% of the variance in childhood IQ (Gottfried, Gottfried, Bathurst, Guerin, & Parramore, 2003), with IQs 6 to 13 points lower than peers (Brooks-Gunn & Duncan, 1997) and lower academic achievement even when controlling for parent and family characteristics (Bornstein & Bradley, 2003). Specifically, children's exposure to books and parental reading to children are related to developing a vocabulary and listening comprehension skills that are directly related to literacy skills in Grade 3 (Sénéchal & LeFevre, 2002), parent involvement in school during childhood was associated with academic achievement in high school (Barnard, 2004), and parental aspirations/expectations are significantly predictive of academic achievement (Fan & Chen 2001).

Recent neuroimaging studies have demonstrated that negative environments can have profound effects on brain development during the highly neuroplastic period of early childhood (Sheridan, Fox, Zeanah, McLaughlin, & Nelson, 2012). For example, Luby et al. (2013) reported that stressful life events in low SES children are associated with smaller left hippocampal and amygdala volumes, whereas reduced caregiving support and hostility are associated with smaller bilateral volumes. Similarly, poor cognitive functioning and academic achievement of low SES children have been associated with smaller volumes in the hippocampus and frontal and temporal lobes, with decrements in the latter two structures accounting for 15% to 20% of the achievement deficits (Hair, Hanson, Wolfe, & Pollak, 2015).

The culture of poverty in the United States has a potentially profound impact on testing performance. A deemphasis of reading to young children would suggest that value for academics or conception of intelligent behavior may differ from persons in mainstream middle-class society. An implication is that the CDC may be uncomfortable with testing situations from a very young age. Weaker vocabularies would affect verbal skills, which are essential for responding on many Western tests. CDCs from low-resource families would also likely have reduced worldly opportunities outside the classroom, which has been an overlooked but important component of learning (AERA, APA, & NCME, 2014; Wikeley, Bullock, Muschamp, & Ridge, 2007).

Familiarity and Comfort With the Evaluation Process

According to Greenfield (1997), the experience of the testing situation, in which a client is alone in a room with a stranger who is asking questions about things that are not present for which he or she already knows the answer, is not a universal one. Thus, the perceptions and meaning of a neuropsychological test administration for a CDC can differ significantly from those of a Western examiner, thereby compromising fair treatment during the testing process (AERA, APA, & NCME, 2014). For example, Ardila (2007) identified several examples of how a Latino client's experiences with and perceptions of individual aspects of a neuropsychological evaluation may differ from the examiners:

1. *One-on-one relationship with a stranger:* The situation of being with someone you do not know and will never see again is foreign to Latinos. Questions of "Who is the tester?" and "Why does the tester have authority?" would come to mind.
2. *Isolated environment:* A private appointment with only a stranger behind a closed door may be perceived as inappropriate, particularly for a female client and male examiner. However, it is a relationship the examinee must accept.
3. *Special type of communication:* Communication in a testing situation is not normal conversation. The examiner speaks in a formal and repetitive manner. The examinee must answer questions evaluating for his or her knowledge, thus is not allowed to talk about himself or herself.
4. *Internal and subjective issues:* Intellectual testing, which includes questions such as "How is your memory?" may be perceived as humiliating and a violation of privacy.
5. *Expectations of best performance:* One puts effort into giving one's best performance only in situations perceived as extremely important, which the examinee may not ascribe to the test.
6. *Speed:* Speed, competitiveness, and high productivity are valued in many Western societies. However, for Latinos, speed and quality are contradictory. Good products result from a slow and careful process.
7. *Use of specific testing elements and testing strategies:* Manipulating materials such as blocks appear to be similar to "playing a game" with an examiner one does not know. For many Latinos, this may be perceived as a useless activity without a pertinent goal. So why perform one's best?

Another example of how testing is differentially experienced by a CDC is the phenomenon of stereotype threat (Steele, 1997). *Stereotype threat* occurs when a negative stereotype of a person's social group influences the performance of the individual (Steele, 1997). African Americans and Hispanics are particularly susceptible to this influence on intelligence tests (Gonzales, Blanton, & Williams, 2002; Steele, 1997), although not all discrepancy in test scores between Whites and these ethnic groups can be explained by this phenomenon (Sackett, Hardison, & Cullen, 2004). Schmader, Johns, and Forbes (2008) attributed negative performance with increased physiological stress, performance monitoring, and efforts to suppress negative thoughts and emotions, which reduces executive and working memory resources required for successful task performance. Studies have found that the impact of stereotype threat can be reduced by altering perceptions of the task. For example, reinforcing the idea that intelligence is malleable and can be expanded with effort versus the assumption that one's group is inherently inferior (Aronson, Fried, & Good, 2002).

Although many Asians are comfortable in testing situations, seeking assistance from a mental health professional can be highly aversive. Studies consistently report that feelings of stigma and shame instrumentally contribute to low utilization of mental health services by Asian Americans (Chu & Sue, 2011). The cultural salience of shame is embodied in terminology describing a loss of face across cultures, for example, *mianzi* among Chinese, *haji* among Japanese, *chaemyun* among Koreans, and *hiya* among Filipinos. Because seeing a mental health specialist may be perceived as a tacit admission of familial problems that would bring shame to the family if revealed to the public, many Asian Americans only seek mental health treatment if problems are too severe for family to manage (Chu & Sue, 2011). Shame may also influence a minimization of symptoms or limited self-disclosure and could conceivably affect concentration on neuropsychological tests.

Finally, perceived racism can be a significant source of stress for a CDC during a neuropsychological evaluation. A growing body of literature indicates that ethnic minorities and other disenfranchised persons such as gay men and lesbians report perceiving subtle insults or dismissive behaviors during daily interactions with persons of the majority culture (Sue et al., 2007). According to the literature, racism is communicated on an interpersonal level in the form of microaggressions, which are subtle insults, snubs, dismissive looks, gestures, or tones directed toward ethnic minorities that are frequently unconsciously or automatically delivered. Because of the subtlety and unconsciousness nature of the insults, the intent of the perpetrator may be difficult to discern; thus, the resulting confusion can be more distressing and discomforting than blatant forms of discrimination (Sue, 2010).

Sue and colleagues (2007) developed a taxonomy of microaggressions consisting of three overarching categories: (a) *Microassaults* involve hostile name-calling and racial epithets, such as calling an Asian "slant eyes." This form of aggression is most likely to be conscious and deliberate and akin to overt racism, thus unlikely to be communicated in a neuropsychological evaluation. (b) *Microinsults* are rude, insensitive, and insulting remarks that demean a person's ethnic heritage. An example is questioning African Americans on how they got their job, which could imply that the person was the recipient of affirmative action versus merit. (c) *Microinvalidations* are communications that marginalize the thoughts, values, experiences, ideas, values, or perspectives of ethnic minorities. Responses such as "you're too sensitive" when an ethnic minority complains of being given poor service at a restaurant nullifies the frustration of the experience. In addition, Sue et al. (2007) identified nine distinct themes: being an alien in one's country, ascription of intelligence, color-blindness, assumption of criminal status, denial of individual racism, myth of meritocracy, pathologizing cultural values and communication styles, second-class status, and environmental invalidation.

A significant implication of experiencing microaggressions within the context of a neuropsychological evaluation is the potential impact on test performance. Microaggressions can undermine the working alliance between clinician and client (Owen, Tao, Imel, Wampold, & Rodolfa, 2014), which is particularly salient for a CDC who may already be experiencing discomfort with the testing process. Thus, the CDC may be more reluctant to self-disclose to the clinician or engage in the testing process. The experience of micro-aggressions often results in self-doubt and frustration (Sue et al., 2007), and CDCs often spend significant mental energy discerning whether perceived slights are racially motivated (Watkins, LaBarrie, & Appio, 2010), all of which can detract from concentration required for optimal performance on neuro-psychological testing. Preliminary support for this contention comes from a study that found African American clients who perceived high levels of discrimination from a examiner of a different race scored significantly worse on memory tests compared with clients who were tested by a same-race examiner (Thames et al., 2013).

Communication

Effective communication is essential for obtaining accurate information in neuropsychological assessments and interviews. Gathering information can be challenging even when clinician and client speak the same language and share the same culture because clients may not be accurate in recall or willing to freely disclose information about themselves. Communication is more complicated with CDCs because, unbeknownst to the clinician, information can be easily misinterpreted if the clinician is not aware of the nuances of communication associated with the client's culture. Challenges in communication with CDCs can cause discomfort in the test-taking process, impede understanding of tasks and accessibility, and thereby the validity of test score interpretations (AERA, APA, & NCME, 2014).

Tannen (1984) identified eight ways that cultural differences can impair basic aspects of everyday communication and also result in negative misperceptions of the CDC:

1. *When to talk:* Cultures differ in their perception of situations when talking is appropriate. For example, Athabaskan Indians believe it is inappropriate to talk to strangers and thus speak very little when meeting a person they do not know. These situations can be awkward because the other person will essentially carry on a conversation alone. This type of cultural mismatch results in a frequently found mutual negative stereotyping in which the person who expects more talk perceives the other as uncooperative and unintelligent, whereas the person who talks less will view the other as pushy, hypocritical, and untrustworthy.

2. *What to say:* Significant differences exist as to what is considered appropriate conversation. In neuropsychological evaluations, asking questions is taken for granted as the basic method of obtaining information, yet for some cultures, such as Australian Aborigines, questions are rarely used because they are too intrusive and demand a response. Thus, in an evaluation setting, persons from these cultures would be highly uncomfortable and resentful and may passively resist by providing minimal answers to questions.

3. *Pacing and pausing:* How fast one speaks and how long one waits before concluding that the other is finished talking and one can then respond vary across cultures. Misperceptions arise when persons from cultures with different pacing and pausing expectations converse. Slower speakers perceive faster ones as not giving them a chance to speak and disinterest in what they have to say. Faster speakers often perceive slower speakers as being less engaged in conversation and not saying what is on their minds.

4. *Listenership:* This term refers to differences in how people listen. An example is eye contact norms for conversation. During counseling interviews, Erickson and Shultz (1982) found that Whites gaze when listening and break their gaze when talking, whereas African Americans do just the opposite. This discrepancy resulted in White speakers perceiving African Americans as being disinterested because of their inconsistent gaze when listening. When Whites sent a small signal for confirmation

of understanding, the African American listener often missed the cue, as she or he was looking away. This resulted in the White listener repeating what was said, which was perceived as "talking down." When the White person was the listener, the African American speaker's steady gaze appeared overbearing.

5. *Intonation:* Intonation and prosody are shifts in pitch, loudness, and rhythm that are associated with normal discourse and may also carry special meaning. Differences in intonational meaning frequently cause misunderstanding. For example, British people will raise their voices when angry, whereas Asian Indians will raise their voice to get the floor. Thus, when the Asian Indian speaker raises his voice to get the floor, the British speaker may perceive that he or she is angry and respond in turn with anger. A heated exchange may ensue in which each speaker believes that other introduced anger into the conversation.

6. *Indirectness:* Cultures differ in how much of what is communicated is stated directly or indirectly. Americans, who are highly individualistic, tend to be more direct, placing meaning primarily in the content of what is said. By contrast, in most collectivist cultures that emphasize relationships, messages are communicated indirectly to avoid conflict. Hence, the manner in which something is stated or not stated becomes more important than what is actually said. For example, Japanese who are ultrapolite may rarely disagree or decline an offer but will typically acquiesce and never say no. Thus, the listener will have to discern through nonverbals, the way a response was phrased, and what was not said whether the Japanese speaker is agreeing or disagreeing.

7. *Formulaicity:* This term refers to aphorisms or clichés that a culture will commonly use in speaking, such as "look before you leap" or "priming the pump." These statements may obfuscate understanding due to lack of familiarity, or they may be perceived as poetic or novel speech that can be associated with intelligence when in fact the meaning is trite.

8. *Cohesion and coherence:* These terms describe how information is organized within conversation. For example, British people and Asian Indians differ in how they emphasize main points. Indians will often emphasize the sentence before the main point and then lower their voice when making the main point as if for dramatic effect. By contrast, British speakers expect main points to be emphasized. Another example comes from argumentation style. Arabs highlight main points through repetition through-

out discourse, whereas Americans will build arguments up to the main point. Thus, for Americans, Arabs' arguments may appear repetitive and pointless.

Tannen (1985) identified two ramifications of communication differences across cultures. First is the attribution of negative personality traits to the culturally different person and negative stereotyping. Personality characteristics are always measured according to a cultural standard. Thus, it is difficult to accurately assess a CDC's personality characteristics if you are not aware of the standard. Second, increased exposure to another culture does not necessarily result in better understanding if behaviors are interpreted within an ethnocentric perspective (Tannen, 1985).

Given the potential differences in experience and perception that the evaluation process may hold for a CDC and potential communication pitfalls, the following are recommendations to increase comfort level with the testing situation and trust in the examiner and to maximize communication.

- Be aware of CDCs' experiences with or perceived meaning of the testing situation and address any concerns. If the culture is unfamiliar to you or discrepant from your own, it is imperative that you seek consultation from a cultural broker to gain understanding and develop a culturally informed strategy for the evaluation.
- For cultures that are uncomfortable with strangers or the testing situation, developing rapport is essential. The following are strategies to facilitate rapport:
  - To help develop a relationship, call the client before the session to introduce oneself and engaging in small talk, which may include some personal disclosure (Greenfield, 1997).
  - Schedule more frequent and shorter sessions and with additional time for rapport building.
  - Be cognizant of cultural norms for participation of family members in medical treatment and invite appropriate family members in the interview process.
  - Be sure to address clients in the manner with which they feel comfortable (e.g., with Mr. or Ms. or by first name) given the dynamics of the clinician–client relationship (e.g., age differences, differences in status).
  - Be aware of cultural norms for personal space, touch, eye contact, paralinguistic communication styles, gestures, and time conceptualization. Determine how differences could affect the evaluation process, and adapt interviewing behaviors to clients' culture.

- If a CDC's style of communication is more indirect than the clinician's, research how to phrase questions without appearing rude and learn clues to determine agreement or disagreement. Be aware of behavioral clues that would suggest the CDC is offended, uncomfortable, or disengaging from the process. Remember, in high-context cultures, miscommunication is generally attributed to the failure of the listener.
- Be aware of content areas that CDCs would consider too personal or unwilling to disclose to strangers, authority figures, elders, or someone of the same or opposite gender. Accept these limitations or strategize other methods for obtaining this information.
- Adjusting the interview process to maximize rapport with the CDC may reduce the time allowed or alter the mechanism for obtaining what the clinician may consider adequate background information. Clinicians will have to prioritize important information or accept the limitations of what the CDC is willing to provide (Hays, 2006).
- Be aware of how CDCs may perceive or react to the clinician's background. Historical or current conflicts between affiliated groups could affect rapport and dynamic of the interview. With such clients, clinicians may have to work harder to develop rapport or adjust expectations for information gathering.
- To avoid engaging in microaggressions, clinicians should be cognizant of their own biases and negative feelings toward the culture of the CDC and increase awareness of potential discriminatory communications by reviewing the taxonomy of microaggressions (for a review and listing of microaggressions, see Sue et al., 2007).
- Be aware of the potential impact of stereotype threat for client whose cultures typically perform more poorly than Whites. Attempt to diffuse the impact of this phenomenon by downplaying similarities to academic testing and emphasizing the purpose of understanding clients' profile for diagnostic purposes or addressing concerns.
- Be cognizant of the influence of shame and stigma in Asian cultures, which may affect severity of illness, when to seek help, willingness to disclose, and concentration. Attempt to diffuse shame by emphasizing medical aspects of neurological disorders, praising the client for his or her courage in seeking an assessment, and instilling hope for improved functioning with a sound diagnosis and recommendations.

- Once rapport is established, if the communication process of the evaluation (e.g., primarily questions and answers of personal or impersonal questions) is foreign to CDCs (e.g., they employ storytelling), explain this process to them, the need to gather information, and apologize for having to put them through this process.
- The informed consent process can be useful to develop rapport. It is important to have CDCs explain their understanding of the neuropsychological evaluation in their own words versus asking yes–no questions about comprehension to ensure understanding and avoid polite acquiescence. During this process, inquiring about personal goals, if appropriate for purposes of the evaluation, may also facilitate a working relationship.
- Behavioral diagnostic criteria (e.g., disinhibition, emotional lability, flat affect) are based on clinical judgment of the client's presentation compared with societal norms for behavior. Norms for behaviors such as emotional expressiveness differ across cultures. Clinicians need to be aware of the client's cultural norms for behavior, which is the standard for comparison.
- Be aware of idioms of distress for the client's culture, for example, vague somatic complaints as a sign of depression. Similarly, be aware of culture-bound psychiatric syndromes (for a list, see the DSM–5; American Psychiatric Association, 2013, pp. 833–837).
- For cultures that are reticent to freely disclose or have limited insight into symptoms or behaviors, it is imperative for the clinician to be aware of neurocognitive-behavioral syndromes associated with different neurological disorders. This knowledge base is essential for questioning to examine the impact of neurological disorder on CDCs' presentation. Clinicians may have to conceptualize how these sequelae would present within the context of the client's culture.

Language

English proficiency runs on a continuum, and different skill levels exist even for people who are "fluent." For example, Cummins (1984) highlighted a distinction between basic interpersonal fluency skills, which equate to conversational fluency, and cognitive academic language proficiency, which is needed to perform in test-taking situations. In neuropsychological assessment of CDCs, English proficiency is an integral part of the evaluation because it will determine whether translated tests and an interpreter will be needed for a valid examination. Although a final determination may not be made until the interview, basic demographics from the preassessment questions can provide clues to whether the examination should be conducted in a language other than English and guide preparation. Demographics from U.S. Census data concerning language spoken at home and ability to speak English with categories including "English only," "Language other than English," and "Speak English less than very well," can also provide information on the likelihood for need of an interpreter.

Artiola i Fortuny (2008) provided an excellent summary on language acquisition in Hispanics to guide determination for using an interpreter for neuropsychological assessment. According to the language acquisition literature, it takes about 2 years for immigrant children attending school to develop basic interpersonal communication skills (Cummins, 1984). During this early period of language acquisition, there is a normal process for losing language skills in the native tongue (Veltman, 1988), and in the first few years post-immigration, this dual process can result in difficulty in determining the child's dominant language (Veltman, 1988). After 5 to 7 years of language exposure, a more fluid decontextualized, decentered language is developed for the acquired language; however, developing cognitive academic language proficiency is related to school attendance (Cummins, 1984). Thus, for Hispanics, it should not be surprising that more than half of those immigrating before age 14 are more proficient in English than Spanish and that the younger the age at immigration, the more complete the shift to English (Artiola i Fortuny, 2008). English dominance in Hispanic children is facilitated if parents speak English in the home and hindered if the child lives in an ethnic enclave (Artiola i Fortuny, 2008). Intelligence is a moderating factor in English acquisition because native language proficiency strongly predicts acquisition of second language, and knowledge and skills acquired in one's native language transfer to the second language (Hakuta, 1991). Adults who have lived in the United States for many years and do not speak English often possess low levels of formal education and thus lack ability (Hakuta, 1991).

On the basis of the literature, Artiola i Fortuny (2008) listed the following considerations when determining the need for an interpreter:

- Interpreters are most important for first-generation immigrants and much less so for second generation. Clients who are third generation or higher are typically English dominant.
- The fewer years living in the United States, the more likely the need for an interpreter.
- For children, the need for an interpreter is more difficult to determine during the intermediary first 2 to 5 years after immigration, which is the transition period for language dominance.
- The greater exposure to English during formal schooling, the lesser the need for an interpreter.

- For an informal assessment of language dominance, have clients answer open-ended questions, describe a picture, or tell a story in both their native language and in English to compare skill levels.

For a more formal assessment of skills in both English and the client's native language, the Bilingual Verbal Abilities Test (BVAT) is recommended (Munoz-Sandoval, Cummins, Alvarado, & Ruef, 1998). The BVAT comprises three subtests from the Woodcock–Johnson Tests of Cognitive Ability and Language Proficiency Battery—Revised: Picture Vocabulary (58 items), Oral Vocabulary Synonyms (20 items) and Antonyms (20 items), and Verbal Analogies (35 items). The test requires a bilingual administrator or interpreter and takes about 30 minutes to administer. Items are initially administered in English, and missed items are then administered in the client's native language. There are translations for the following languages: Arabic, Chinese— simplified and traditional, French, German, Haitian-Creole, Hindi, Hmong, Italian, Japanese, Korean, Navajo, Polish, Portuguese, Russian, Spanish, Turkish, and Vietnamese. Norms run from ages 5 to 90.

It should be emphasized that Artiola i Fortuny's (2008) literature review and recommendations pertain primarily to a Hispanic population. Thus, clinicians should be cautious in applying concepts and recommendations for clients who emigrated from other countries and speaking other languages because exposure to English and type of exposure differs by country. For example, in the Philippines, school is taught in English from about the second grade, with stronger exposure in urban versus rural areas. By contrast, in Japan students are taught to read English with less exposure to conversational language. In addition, Spanish is a closely related to English and thus would be assumed to be easier to learn for native Spanish speakers compared with a native Japanese speaker because the language significantly differs from English in both expressive and written aspects (National Virtual Translation Center, 2007).

Similar to level and quality of education, English proficiency can have profound effects on fairness in neuropsychological testing. It is important for clinicians to determine the need for accommodations of translated tests and an interpreter to minimize biases in test administration and accessibility. Translations must be well designed to maximize equivalency at the item and test levels and to control for differential advantages or disadvantages. In certain cases, clinicians may need to modify test content or procedures that would alter the construct being measured but provide important information. An example would be providing multiple-choice cues for a verbal test in which the original instructions require open-ended responses. The clinician would then have to determine validity for test score interpretations based on the characteristics of the CDC and the accommodations or modifications made for him or her (AERA, APA, & NCME, 2014).

Assessing for Acculturation and Language

There are two steps in assessing for acculturation. First, the clinician must determine the similarities and differences between a client's culture of origin and American culture with an emphasis on the aforementioned cultural characteristics. This step is accomplished by researching the literature (for a start, see the references cited in Chapter 2). The second step is to evaluate the level of acculturation to mainstream culture for the specific client. This step is accomplished by questioning during the interview. The following are questions to guide examination of acculturation:

1. *Years in the United States:* If the CDC is native born, what generation? If foreign born, how many years has the client lived in the United States? At what age did he or she immigrate? (In general, the longer the client and family has lived in the United States and the younger the age the client immigrated, the higher level of acculturation.)
2. *Language:* What is the client's native language? What is his or her exposure to English? What percentage of English is spoken at home? Does client typically speak English to family? with friends? at work? in academic situations?
3. *Social groups:* Where does the client live? Where did the client grow up (be attentive for ethnic enclave vs. integrated neighborhood)? What percentage of socializing is spent with family? What is the ethnicity of client's closest friends?
4. *Religion:* What are the client's religious or spiritual beliefs? Does the client belong to a religious organization? How often does she or he attend services or participate in functions? Is the religion and organization associated with native or U.S. culture?
5. *Health care providers:* Does the client typically see indigenous healers/medical practitioners or Western practitioners?
6. *Foods eaten:* How frequently does the client eat native foods or shop at native grocery stores? How frequently does the person eat "American" or other nonnative foods?
7. *Activities and entertainment:* To what extent does the client prefer native entertainment (e.g., music artists, television shows) or engage in native hobbies versus those associated with mainstream culture?
8. *Reading materials:* To what extent does the client read literature in his or her native language versus English?
9. *Conceptualization of intelligence:* What is considered intelligent behavior?
10. *Heroes/idols:* Who are the client's heroes or favorite celebrities?

Answers to these questions can give clinicians an idea of assimilation to Western culture. This information will also be useful for making recommendations. A weakness of this methodology is that there is not a standardized method for measuring level of acculturation. This titrating of culture can be done by administering formal measures developed for specific cultures, such as the African American Acculturation Scale (Snowden & Hines, 1999), the Asian American Multidimensional Acculturation Scale (Gim Chung, Kim, & Abreu, 2004), and the Short Acculturation Scale for Hispanics (Marin, Sabogal, Marin, Otero-Sabogal, & Perez-Stable, 1987).

Recommendations for Using Interpreters

Once a clinician determines that an interpreter is required, the following are considerations to maximize the potential for a valid neuropsychological evaluation: (a) selecting an appropriate interpreter, (b) preparing and educating the interpreter, (c) translating tests, (d) logistics for conducting the interview, and (e) debriefing.

Selecting an Appropriate Interpreter

The interpreter is the conduit of information from the client to the clinician; thus, a successful neuropsychological evaluation hinges on selecting the right interpreter. The APA's *Ethical Principles of Psychologists and Code of Conduct* (2010) lists two considerations when choosing an interpreter for an assessment. First, the clinician is ultimately responsible for the competence of the interpreter. Hence, it is imperative that the clinician hire trained professionals or provide adequate education and training for persons who are less experienced. Second, the clinician should avoid selecting interpreters who have dual relationships with the client. Thus, clinicians are highly discouraged from using family members. Other pertinent issues include the potential negative impact on translation fidelity and the preservation of client confidentiality and autonomy (American Academy of Clinical Neuropsychology [AACN], 2007).

Given these ethical considerations, the optimal interpreter would be fluent in both English and the client's native language, familiar with the client's specific cultural group within his or her country of origin (e.g., within Iraq, there are six major ethnicities: Shiites, Sunnis, Kurds, Assyrians, Yazidis, and Turkmen), and familiar with psychological and neurological concepts. The interpreter must also understand the importance of following standardized procedures, accurately conveying the CDCs actual responses, and the role and responsibilities of an interpreter in the testing situations (AERA, APA, & NCME, 2014). In addition, for societies that make distinctions among social class or caste or have highly inequitable gender roles, considerations about social and gender matching between client and interpreter are important to avoid undesired complications (Luk, 2008).

Although less optimal, telephone interpreters, or untrained or ad hoc nonfamilial or familial persons can be used as interpreters if no other options are available. Gray, Hilder, and Stubbe (2012) identified appropriate conditions for each of these categories. Telephone interpreters would be useful when (a) no face-to-face trained interpreters are available, (b) more urgent problems would arise during an interview if no interpreter were used, (c) there is a strict deadline to complete an evaluation and no time to reschedule, and (d) communicating over the phone would not negatively impact communication. Using an ad hoc, untrained interpreter can be useful under the following conditions: (a) the interpreter has a good rapport with the client, (b) the evaluation is a relatively simple and straightforward one, (c) the clinician is familiar with the client's culture, (d) the clinician is familiar with the would-be interpreter and confident she or he can perform the role (e.g., maintain objectivity, has adequate health literacy for evaluation), and (e) the client strongly desires a supportive person who can be an advocate. Finally, a family member could be an option as a last resort if she or he (a) has a good command of English for the purpose of the evaluation, (b) is an adult, (c) is known by the clinician to be reliable and has a good relationship with the client, (d) does not have secondary gain in the outcome of the evaluation, and (e) the evaluation is relatively a straightforward and a nonsensitive one. For the latter two categories, an example of a straightforward case would be a client with severe dementia, little money, and one surviving relative who needs an evaluation for financial capacity so that a durable power of attorney can be assigned to use remaining funds for a nursing home until she or he becomes eligible for Medicaid.

Preparing and Educating the Interpreter

To ensure a competent translation, it is imperative that the clinician schedule a preassessment meeting to educate and prepare the interpreter and develop strategies for the evaluation. There are several goals to accomplish during this meeting: (a) introducing the parties, (b) providing an overview of the goals of the evaluation, (c) developing strategies for the evaluation, and (d) preparing materials and providing assignments.

The meeting should start with an introduction and brief small talk to facilitate rapport between the clinician and interpreter. Remember that most societies in the world are collectivist cultures in which relationship is important. This "getting to know you" period is also a good time to learn about the interpreter's background, training, experience, health care knowledge, and sophistication with interpreting. When this step is completed, the clinician can then introduce the agenda for the meeting.

The first agenda item is to provide the interpreter with an overview of the goals of the neuropsychological evaluation and process for accomplishing these goals. For example, the clinician could explain that she or he is evaluating a client who has demonstrated a significant decline in memory and thinking skills, which concerns the family. The specific goals of the evaluation are to determine (a) whether there is a decline in cognition, which is accomplished by comparing estimates of premorbid functioning with current functioning; (b) the severity of the decline if one exists, and if so, does it meet criteria for a dementia; (c) what is the cause of the dementia; and (d) recommendations to allow the client to continue living safely at home.

Once the interpreter understands the purpose of the evaluation, the next agenda item is to explain his or her roles and specific tasks. The first and foremost role is translating questions from the clinician and responses from the client. In this role, expectations about translation can be communicated; for example, the clinician will ask the client's understanding of the evaluation, his or her consent to undergo the evaluation, and the limits of confidentiality. Next, the clinician will ask specific questions to gather background information about the client, such as demographics, including educational, occupational, health, and immigration history; history of the illness; changes in behaviors; psychiatric symptoms; problems he or she is experiencing; and priority areas in which the client would like assistance. The clinician will then begin testing, and the interpreter will have to explain instructions, ensure the client's understanding, and may assist in translating the client's responses to test items.

For untrained interpreters, the clinician may have to go into more detail about the duties and expectations of an interpreter, such as the confidential nature of the evaluation, the importance of objectivity, and refraining from providing clues or hints during test administration. In addition, it may be useful to describe common mistakes that novice interpreters make to increase understanding of the interpretation process and reduce the likelihood of errors. Some common interpretation errors include (a) omitting information, (b) adding information that was not expressed, (c) losing information by oversimplifying long or complicated responses, (d) replacing one concept for another because of a lack of a good equivalent word, (e) taking over the interview by asking self-generated questions, and (f) biasing responses by changing open-ended to closed-ended questions (Farooq & Fear, 2003).

Clinicians should review and direct interpreters to the National Standards of Practice for Interpreters in Health Care (Ruschke et al., 2005) that define ethical and best forms of practice for interpreters. According to the standards, interpreters strive to render accurate communications by conveying both content and spirit of the message while considering the cultural context. Specifically, interpreters must communicate all verbal communication to maintain transparency in the process. Boundaries must be maintained, and interpreters must refrain from personal involvement with CDCs; they also must not allow personal or cultural values interfere with the partiality of the interpretation.

Another important role for interpreters is to function as a cultural broker or consultant. They will be asked to help the clinician develop strategies to procure accurate information and facilitate optimal motivation and effort on testing by the client. Interpreters can also be called on to assist in understanding the clients' behaviors and abilities, interpreted within the context of norms for their culture and effort on testing. Finally, interpreters may be asked to assist with translating test instructions and possibly test items.

Once the interpreter understands his or her roles in the evaluation, the clinician should discuss specifics about the case, such as the client's background and the information needed, and develop strategies for information gathering. Potential areas for consultation would include the following: (a) understanding how the client would perceive the testing situation, (b) developing strategies for gaining and maximizing rapport, (c) identifying challenges to obtaining specific types of information, (d) phrasing questions to the client's culture and level of sophistication, (e) identifying words or concepts that do not have cross-cultural equivalents, (f) developing appropriate expectations for self-disclosure, (g) identifying pertinent nonverbal signs and behaviors, (h) identifying inappropriate topics for discussion or "cultural taboos," (i) brainstorming how neurologic and psychiatric behaviors would present in the client's culture, and (j) hypothesizing the client's functioning within the context of his or her culture. From this discussion, the clinician and interpreter can map an agenda for the evaluation. Questions for the evaluation can be prepared and sent to the interpreter for translation before the interview. In addition, written materials to facilitate the interview can be procured and disseminated during the interview.

Translating Tests

Although fraught with caveats, another potential task for an interpreter is assisting in translating test instructions and materials. This is a controversial issue because of the importance of test validity in obtaining accurate information and the potential harmful ramifications of clinical decision making based on inaccurate data, particularly for ethnic minority clients. Indeed, numerous APA (2003, 2010); AERA, APA, and NCME (2014); and AACN guidelines (Heilbronner et al., 2009) underscore the ethical responsibility of the clinician for ensuring test fairness and equivalence and construct validity. Because of the complexities involved in translating tests, specifics of this task are covered in depth in a subsequent chapter detailing test selection (see Chapter 6).

Logistics for Conducting the Interview

Logistical considerations for conducting the interview with an interpreter include positioning, behaviors, general speaking rules, and troubleshooting translations. To maximize rapport and information gathering, clinicians should sit opposite the client with the interpreter on the side equidistant between them. The clinician should maintain normal eye contact or adapt eye contact to match the expectations of the client and talk directly to the client as if she were speaking the same language. Speak slowly and in short sentences. Do not interrupt or talk over others. Notes can be taken and questions written for future discussion with the interpreter; however, the focus should be on the client's nonverbal communication (Farooq & Fear, 2003; Gray et al., 2012).

Interpreting formats vary in the directness of translating the client's words and the cultural input provided by the interpreter. Each format has situational appropriateness, and formats often switch depending on the vagaries of the interview. In general, the more cultural input provided, the greater the chance for miscommunication. Hence, the knowledge and skill levels of the interpreter and the clinician's trust in him or her need to be higher for cultural interpretations (E. Lee, 1997). Interpreting formats include the following:

- *Word-for-word* interpreting entails a verbatim account of the client's responses. It is most useful when the client is expressing emotionally significant issues or disclosing delicate information.
- *Summary interpreting* highlights important points of long discourses, such as stories. It is faster but less accurate than word-for-word interpreting and requires more skill and experience.
- *Consecutive interpreting* entails providing both connotative and denotative meanings for the clinician after each statement.
- In *culture-relevant interpreting*, the interpreter translates statements in a culturally appropriate manner to minimize cultural misunderstanding.
- In *cultural-expert* interpreting, the interpreter plays an active role as a cultural consultant, providing information and explanations to both clinician and client. An example would be to explain purposes of the evaluation to motivate compliance and maximal effort in the client.

To minimize misattribution, it is recommended that clinician and interpreter discuss a process to communicate which format of interpretation the interpreter is using. For example, the interpreter may specifically state to the clinician what is a direct translation of the client, what is a summary, what is a cultural interpretation, and what explanations are provided to the client outside of the clinician's specific questions. For untrained interpreters, Gray et al. (2012) recommended that the interview be structured so that clinician and client take short turns speaking, and the interpreter employ word-for-word format. Clinicians should also seek more information from the interpreter if the client speaks for a long time but the interpreter provides a brief response.

If a cultural misunderstanding is suspected, such as when the client's statement is inconsistent with nonverbal behavior, confusion should be clarified immediately. Responses can be explored by changing wording, breaking down the question into components, or asking a related issue (Farooq & Fear, 2003). The clinician can ask the interpreter to comment on the discrepancy or provide cultural information to provide context (Gray et al., 2012). The clinician and interpreter may also discuss issues during breaks to clarify concerns or alter the agenda or strategies of the evaluation.

Postinterview Debriefing

After the evaluation is completed, a debriefing session should be scheduled. During this time, the clinician and interpreter can share observations, discuss confusing responses, process feelings, and clarify problems (Luk, 2008). In addition, the clinician should inquire about the interpreter's impressions of the normality of the conversation (Farooq & Fear, 2003); rapport and comfort with the evaluation; clinical behaviors such as premorbid functioning, decline, and psychiatric symptoms; validity of testing and effort; and culturally relevant recommendations. It is recommended that interpreters rate process dimensions or certainty of clinical opinions on a scale of 1 to 10 to determine confidence in opinions. For more information on standards of practice for medical interpreting, see International Medical Interpreters Association (2007).

5

ESTIMATING PREMORBID FUNCTIONING

A general must acquaint himself thoroughly with the terrain—its mountains and forests its halts and impasses, swamps and marshes—before he can march his army through it.

—Sun Tzu

The basic task in neuropsychological assessment is to determine the impact of a neurological disorder on cognitive and functional abilities. The basic strategy for accomplishing this goal is to compare an estimate of premorbid functioning with a measurement of current cognitive functioning (Lezak, Howieson, Bigler, & Tranel, 2012). Pattern analysis of test scores is then used to determine diagnosis or cognitive strengths and weaknesses used for recommendations. Although intelligence does not perfectly predict abilities in all cognitive domains, there are high correlations between IQ and other cognitive functions (Wechsler, 2008a; see Table 5.1). In fact, general cognitive ability or Spearman's g has been found to account for 40% of the variance in a battery of diverse cognitive tests (Jensen, 1998). IQ scores on Westerns test can also help a clinician get a sense of how acculturated a culturally different client (CDC) is to Western norms (see Chapter 8 for more details about using IQ scores when interpreting interview and test data). Thus, an accurate estimate of premorbid intelligence is crucial for performing

http://dx.doi.org/10.1037/15958-006
Conducting a Culturally Informed Neuropsychological Evaluation, by D. Fujii

TABLE 5.1
Correlations of WAIS–IV Full Scale IQ
With Various Neuropsychological Tests

Test	Full-scale IQ correlation
WAIS–IV	
Vocabulary	.78
Similarities	.77
Block Design	.73
Matrix Reasoning	.78
Symbol Search	.64
Wechsler Memory Scale—III	
Auditory Immediate Index	.63
Auditory Delayed Index	.57
Visual Immediate Index	.38
Visual Delayed Index	.34
General Memory	.59
Delis–Kaplan Executive Functioning	
Scales Number–Letter Switching	
Completion Time	.77
Letter Fluency	.54
Category Fluency	.50

Note. WAIS–IV = Wechsler Adult Intelligence Scale—IV. Data from Wechsler (2008a).

a competent neuropsychological evaluation because this is the benchmark to which all test scores are compared.

Strategies for estimating premorbid IQ are generally based on demographics that are associated with intelligence, such as education, occupation, reading levels, social economic class, or scores on select neuropsychological tests that are highly correlated with intelligence and resistant to general effects of neurological disorders (for a review, see Lezak, Howieson, Bigler, & Tranel, 2012).

For CDCs, however, standard Western strategies for estimating premorbid IQs can be problematic for several reasons. Because their culture, acculturation to Western norms, life experiences, and conception of intelligence can significantly differ from those of individuals from the dominant culture, formulas for predicting premorbid functioning in CDCs may not be valid. For similar reasons, CDCs' scores on Western tests may also not accurately reflect abilities; thus, premorbid IQ estimates should be perceived as cultural adjustments for these Western measures.

This chapter describes strategies for estimating premorbid intelligence on Western tests for different categories of CDCs. First, common Western strategies for determining premorbid intelligence for persons in the dominant culture are described, including weaknesses for each methodology. This review is followed by a discussion of problems for using these strategies with

CDCs. Next, two multistep strategies for estimating premorbid intelligence as measured by Western tests with CDCs are introduced and illustrated with a case sample. I conclude with a review of key considerations for neuropsychologists to keep in mind when framing IQ estimates within a cultural context.

Because differences in estimated country IQ score on Western tests can be a polemic issue given the perceived assumption that some ethnicities are genetically superior to others, the chapter closes with a brief literature review, which indicates that intelligence is malleable and heavily influenced by experience. Thus, intelligence, as measured by Western tests, is not static but can improve with enriching experiences and across generations.

GENERAL STRATEGIES FOR ESTIMATING PREMORBID IQ

Lezak et al. (2012) described several methods for estimating premorbid IQ: (a) historical and observational data, (b) mental ability scores, (c) word reading tests, (d) demographic variable formulas, (e) test score and demographic hybrid formulas, and (f) best performance method.

Historical and observational based estimates typically use education, occupation history, vocabulary, and expressive skills to determine premorbid intelligence. A number of studies provide support for the association between demographic variables and IQ such as occupation (full-scale IQ [FIQ], $r = .65$; verbal IQ [VIQ], $r = .65$; performance IQ [PIQ], $r = .50$), education (FIQ, $r = .58$; VIQ, $r = .59$; PIQ, $r = .43$), and race/ethnicity (White, African American, Hispanic; VIQ, $r = .35$; PIQ $r = .35$; FIQ $r = .38$; Crawford & Allan, 1997; Holdnack, 2001).

Because pertinent data for determining IQ estimates are based on self-report, it is imperative that the clinician obtain accurate data. Problems arise when a clinician fails to obtain adequate information reflecting abilities that are exceptional for a particular occupational or educational category, such as a high school dropout who is a chess master and reads *Scientific American* (Lezak et al., 2012). Inaccuracies can also result when clients overestimate premorbid abilities or minimize academic difficulties (Greiffenstein, Baker, & Johnson-Greene, 2002; Iverson, Lange, Brooks, & Rennison, 2010).

Barona, Reynolds, and Chastain (1984) attempted to standardize demographic prediction of premorbid IQ by developing a regression formula based on variables of age, gender, race, occupation, education, urban versus rural settings, and region. Predicted IQs demonstrate adequate correlations (VIQ, $r = .62$; PIQ, $r = .49$; FIQ, $r = .60$) with education, race, and occupation reported to be the strongest predictors in the equation. The Barona method has demonstrated good prediction for average range scores but tends to overestimate IQs in the lower range and underestimate higher level IQs (Lezak et al., 2012).

The mental ability score method estimates premorbid IQ by using performance on tests that are highly correlated to IQ and resistant to effects of brain damage (Lezak et al., 2012). For the Wechsler Adult Intelligence Scale—IV (WAIS–IV), the Vocabulary score is generally identified as the best estimate of premorbid IQ because it is the subtest most highly correlated with the Verbal Comprehension Index and Full Scale IQ, as well as level of education. A major weakness of this strategy is the false assumption that these subtests are resilient to most brain injuries. For example, aphasia or dementia typically compromises the expressive language skills required for the Vocabulary subtest (Lezak et al., 2012).

To control for the impact of neurological disorders on the expressive skills required for providing word definitions, word recognition reading using phonetically irregular words has been used as a proxy for vocabulary skills. Advantages of this strategy are that word recognition reading is more resistant to deterioration from brain damage and correlates highly with level of education (Lezak et al., 2012). Numerous versions of English-based word recognition tests have been developed, all reporting good correlations with WAIS IQ scores. Tests include American National Adult Reading Test (AmNART—United States; Grober, Sliwinsk, & Korey, 1991; see Lowe & Rogers, 2011; VIQ $r = .70$), Wide Range Achievement Test—4: Word Reading (Wilkinson & Robertson, 2006; see Kareken, Gur, & Saykin, 1995; VIQ, $r = .59$; PIQ, $r = .41$; FIQ, $r = .60$), and the Wechsler Test of Adult Reading (WTAR; Holdnack, 2001; VIQ, $r^2 = .66–.80$; PIQ, $r^2 = .45–.66$; FIQ, $r^2 = .63–.80$). In general, word recognition reading tests tend to perform best for estimating VIQ and FIQ and for scores in the average range. It is less accurate for estimating PIQ, IQs at the lower and superior levels, and for persons with learning disabilities and dementia (Lezak et al., 2012).

More recent strategies have used both demographic variables and test data to predict premorbid IQ via regression formula. The Oklahoma Premorbid Intelligence Estimate—3 (OPIE–3; Schoenberg, Duff, Scott, Patton, & Adams, 2006; VIQ, $r = .87$; PIQ; $r = .78$, FIQ, $r = .87$), Hopkins Adult Reading Test (HART; Schretlen et al., 2009; VIQ, $r = .81$; PIQ, $r = .60$; FIQ, $r = .78$), and WTAR (Holdnack, 2001; VIQ, $r^2 = .66$; PIQ, $r^2 = .43$; FIQ, $r^2 = .63$) are examples of this strategy.

Lezak et al. (2012) recommended the best performance method for estimating premorbid IQ. This strategy bases premorbid IQ on the strongest indicator of intelligence across different categories of behaviors. Potential sources of data include current or past test scores; behavioral observations, such as verbal language skills; or evidence of premorbid achievement, such as school grades, occupation, family reports, army rating, or other type of award that would suggest special skills or intellect. A major advantage of this method is the potential breadth of data clinicians can use on which to base their IQ estimate, as well as the flexibility it affords in making a determination. A major disadvantage is the bias toward overestimating premorbid ability. To reduce the potential for overestimation, Lezak et al. warned that clinicians should not rely on a single test score to estimate IQ. Memory scores in particular should be avoided because it is the least reliable indicator of general cognitive ability. Best performance estimates should instead be supported by corroborative evidence from history and observations. Other disadvantages of the best performance method include dependency on clinical judgment and lack of a standardized method for calculating premorbid IQ.

IMPACT OF CULTURE ON ESTIMATING IQ

Estimating premorbid intellectual functioning in CDCs can be highly challenging because language abilities and life experiences can invalidate test scores and demographic weighting in formulas used to calculate IQ estimates. For example, English proficiency and acculturation significantly affect performance on verbal tests such as vocabulary tests (Boone, Victor, Wen, Razani, & Pontón, 2007). Performances on reading levels and pronunciation of phonetically irregular words could be affected by a CDC's accent (Lezak et al., 2012). English proficiency and acculturation can also affect demographic factors used in IQ formulas, such as level of education, academic grades, and occupation. For example, there is a mismatch between jobs and educational attainment between Asian immigrants, who are often underemployed. Thus, Western demographic based formulas may underestimate their intellectual functioning (De Jong & Madamba, 2001).

The meaning of *educational level* can vary considerably for foreign-born clients when compared with those from the United States, as evidenced by the wide range of compulsory education and resources devoted to education across countries (United Nations Educational Scientific and Cultural Organization [UNESCO], 2012), as well as performances on international standardized tests such as the Programme for International Student Assessment (PISA; Organisation for Economic Co-operation and Development [OECD], 2013) and the Trends in International Mathematics and Science Study (TIMSS) and Progress in International Reading Literacy Study (PIRLS; International Association for the Evaluation of Educational Achievement [IEA], n.d.).

As of the 2012 administration, the PISA was conducted every 3 years on 15-year-olds in 65 participating countries/economies. Tests are designed to examine the application of knowledge of compulsory education in subjects such as reading, mathematics, and science to real-life situations. It is sponsored by the OECD (headquartered in Paris), the mission of which is to promote policies for improving economic and social well-being worldwide. The TIMSS and PIRLS test fourth- and eighth-grade students in math, science, and reading comprehension. These tests are administered every 4 years by the IEA with 63 countries participating in 2011. The mission of the IEA is to provide quality data to help countries develop policies to improve their educational systems. The secretariat is located in Amsterdam, the Netherlands.

Even within the United States, educational levels and academic achievement can vary among cultural groups. In a study examining reading levels of White, English-speaking Hispanic, and African American elders (Cosentino, Manly, & Mungas, 2007), researchers found that reading levels of White elders at the 10th-grade level were equivalent to Hispanic and African American elders with 15 years of education.

Race-based weighting for IQ estimates may not be applicable for cultures outside the standardization samples. In the OPIE, Barona, HART, and WTAR formulas, Blacks are associated with lower IQ weightings. This weighting may be appropriate for Black Jamaican and Haitian immigrants whose educational attainment is similar to American Blacks; however, it may not be accurate for African immigrants from countries such as Nigeria, Ethiopia, Ghana, or Liberia, where 38% hold a bachelor's degree, which is second only to Asians (Kent, 2007). Use of the "other" category for the Barona and OPIE can also be problematic because it would include East Asian ethnicities, which have reported IQs and academic achievement higher than the United States, as well as Middle Eastern ethnicities, which have lower reported achievement (E. Lynn, 2006; OECD, 2013).

The impact of region and gender may also differ by culture. For example, educational opportunities for females vary considerably across nations (UNESCO, 2012), which could have a differential impact on gender weighting when calculating premorbid IQ. For second-generation Hmong, educational attainment is relatively equal across the United States (Xiong, 2013) and thus would not correspond to regional weighting in formulas such as the Barona or OPIE.

STRATEGIES FOR ESTIMATING PREMORBID IQ FOR CDCs

Given the potential problems with current methodologies for estimating premorbid IQ on Western tests, a multifaceted strategy is proposed. The strategy applies Lezak et al.'s (2012) best performance approach within the context of the client's culture and life experiences and involves three steps: (a) obtain an initial estimate, (b) corroborate this estimate with additional data, and (c) adjust the initial score, if appropriate. Within this framework, I propose two methodologies depending on the English proficiency, ethnicity, and place of birth of the individual. The first method entails estimating premorbid IQ scores of the individual and then adjusting based on corroborative information. The second method involves obtaining an IQ estimate of the person's country of origin and then adjusting accordingly.

Strategy 1

Estimating IQ Scores for the Individual

The first strategy of estimating premorbid IQ for individuals is to use the aforementioned methods developed and validated in the United States. For word recognition reading tests, the WTAR is recommended because of its large standardization sample, which is representative of the U.S. population, and its strong correlations to the Wechsler tests, including the Wechsler Memory Scale. In addition, the WTAR is superior to the Wide Range Achievement Test 4 for more educated and higher functioning subjects (Mullen & Fouty, 2014). The WTAR would be particularly useful for African Americans and Hispanics who are proficient in English because there are demographic predictors as well as hybrid demographic and word recognition formulas. The Barona Index would provide another demographic measure with a modification that East Asians (Chinese, Japanese, and Koreans) and Singaporeans be included in the White demographic category because of the literature supporting comparable mean average level IQs (Lynn & Meisenberg, 2010).

The category of individuals for which these tests would be appropriate include the vast majority of CDCs born and raised in the United States for whom English is their primary language. Examples would be second- and later generation persons of color and those who immigrated as children and were educated primarily in the United States. American-born individuals for whom English is not a primary language, such as some older Native Americans living on reservations, would not be included.

For select countries, culture-specific word recognition reading tests would be recommended for estimating premorbid IQ. Tests have been developed in the following countries with varying levels of predictive validity: Taiwan (Y. J. Chen, Ho, Chen, Hsu, & Ryu, 2009; $r = .71–.80$ with Raven's Standard Progressive Matrices), Japan (Matsuoka, Uno, Kasai, Koyama, & Kim, 2006; $r^2 = .78$ FIQ), France (Mackinnon & Mulligan, 2005), New Zealand (Barker-Collo, Thomas, Riddick, & de Jager, 2011, $r^2 = .82$ FIQ, $r^2 = .72$ VIQ, $r^2 = .41$ PIQ; Lichtwark, Starkey, & Barker-Collo, 2013, $r = .62$ WASI), Portugal (Alves, Simões, & Martins, 2012, $r^2 = .63$ FIQ, $r^2 = .62$ VIQ, $r^2 = .47$ PIQ), Sweden (Tallberg, Wenneborg, & Almkvist, 2006, $r = .51$ FIQ), Germany (Lehrl, Triebig, & Fischer, 1995, $r = .72$), Argentina (Burin et al., 2000; $r^2 = .92$ WASI Vocabulary), and Spain (Del Ser, González-Montalvo, Martínez-Espinosa, Delgado-Villapalos, & Bermejo, 1997; $r = .837$ WAIS Vocabulary + Picture Completion, $r = .655$ RAPM). For Hispanic Americans whose primary language is Spanish, the Word Accentuation Test has been validated with a Hispanic sample representative of the U.S. population with strong correlations to the Batería Woodcock–Munoz Revisada ($r^2 = .77$), and Raven's Colored Progressive Matrices ($r^2 = .58$; Schrauf, Weintraub, & Navarro, 2006).

There are several caveats for using word recognition reading tests with CDCs. First, clinicians should be cautious when using tests validated on American samples with clients in other English-speaking countries because norms may not be equivalent. For example, Mathias, Bowden, and Barrett-Woodbridge (2007) found that, although generally comparable, the NART and WTAR produced some grossly inaccurate scores in an Australian sample that were 30 to 36 points off actual IQ scores. Second, allowances should be made for foreign accents (Lezak et al., 2012). Finally, caveats for using the WTAR with aphasics, dementia, and learning disorders would apply.

Additional Data to Corroborate and Adjust IQ Score

Once an individual premorbid IQ estimate is obtained, the next step is to corroborate estimates with other data. Sources of information include behavioral observations and hobbies, academic data, occupational data, and special awards or achievements.

Behavioral Observations and Hobbies. For behavioral observations and hobbies, clients should be evaluated for vocabulary and reading skills. How articulate is the client and vocabulary? Does the client read regularly, and if so, what type of literature (e.g., romance novels vs. Dan Brown; the local paper vs. *The New York Times*). Does the client routinely do crosswords or Sudoku, and if so, at what level?

Educational Data. Education level is one of best predictors of IQ (Crawford & Allan, 1997); thus, it is not surprising that academic data have moderate to strong correlations with IQ. Studies have reported that grade point average (GPA) demonstrates moderate to high correlations with IQ. For example, Rohde and Thompson (2007) reported a .375 correlation with Raven's Progressive Matrices, and Spinks et al. (2007) found primary school GPA correlated .64 with WAIS–III FIQ in middle adulthood. Weaknesses in using GPA to predict IQ include the strong impact of motivation and conscientiousness on GPA (Cheng & Ickes, 2009), as well as differences in curriculum rigor between academic institutions.

A more objective source for estimating premorbid IQ would be scores on standardized achievement tests. In a review of grade and middle school group administered academic tests such as the California Achievement Test or Comprehensive Test of Basic Skills. Baade and Schoenberg (2004) reported mostly moderate to high correlations with Wechsler IQ scores (range $r = -.03$ to $r = .74$). Scores on achievement tests taken by high school seniors applying to college report stronger correlations with IQ. For example, Frey and Detterman

(2004) reported a correlation of .82 between the Scholastic Achievement Test (SAT) and Armed Services Vocational Aptitude Battery (ASVAB), whereas the correlations with Raven's Advanced Progressive Matrices (RAPM) was .48. The correlation between the American College Test (ACT) and ASVAB was .77 (Koenig, Frey, & Detterman, 2008).

Given the generally high correlations between academic achievement tests and IQ, several researchers have developed formulas for estimating IQ based on achievement test scores. Baade and Schoenberg (2004) described a three-step general conversion formula that can be used to convert any standardized test to an estimated IQ. Step 1 involves calculating a z score:

z = (score – mean) SD.

Step 2 involves adjusting the predictability of the z score by multiplying it by the correlation between the achievement test and IQ test:

predicted z ability = z(correlation of achievement test with IQ test).

Step 3 involves using the adjusted z score to calculate an IQ score:

predicted IQ = predicted z ability(15) + 100

Following are examples of this calculation:

ACT composite = 30
ACT mean = 18
ACT SD = 6 (2009 data)
ACT correlation with WAIS–IV = .87 (Carvajal et al., 1989)
z = (30 – 18)/6
z = 2
Predicted Z ability = 2(.87)
Predicted Z ability = 1.74
Predicted IQ = 1.74(15) + 100
Predicted IQ = 126
SAT Verbal = 600 Quantitative = 600
SAT mean = 500
SAT SD = 100
SAT correlation with WAIS = .56 (Bailey & Federman, 1979; Verbal .73, Quantitative .39)
z = (600 + 600 / 2) / 500
z = 2
Predicted z ability = 2(.56)
Predicted z ability = 1.12
Predicted IQ = 1.12(15) + 100
Predicted IQ = 117

The authors warned that estimated IQ scores should be interpreted with caution. The sample of high school students taking the SAT or ACT is skewed with a bias toward more academic students who plan on attending colleges, which require these tests for admission. In this regard, scores may underestimate IQs.

Other IQ predictions were based on regression formulas using specific achievement tests. Frey and Detterman (2004) proposed the following formula using the Verbal and Math/Quantitative scores to predict RAPM. Correlations were reported to be .523 and .542.

IQ estimate = (0.095 * SAT Quantitative) + (0.003 * SAT Verbal) + 50.241

Following is an example of this method:

Verbal = 600
Math/Quantitative = 600
IQ estimate = (0.095 * 600) + (0.003 * 600) + 50.241
IQ estimate = 57 + 1.8 + 50.24 = 109
IQ estimate = 109

Koenig et al. (2008) developed this formula to predict the first factor of the ASVAB from ACT scores. Predictions correlated .77 with the ASVAB and .61 with RAPM:

estimated VIQ = (.685 * ACT Total) + 87.76.

An example is as follows:

ACT Total = 30
Estimated VIQ = (.685 * 30) + 87.76
Estimated VIQ = 20.55 + 87.76
Estimated VIQ = 108

As can be seen from these samples, scores vary depending on formula. Although some of the differences can be attributed to correlations with different measures of IQ (e.g., RAPM vs. WAIS), differences should underscore that calculations are indeed estimates.

Because it may be difficult to obtain accurate SAT or ACT scores due to imperfect memory combined with the fact that it is often difficult and time-consuming to obtain records, another strategy for calculating an estimate would be based on SAT or ACT data for students accepted into a particular college. This information is often available on the university's admission website, although you may have to search for this data. Another source for this information is the *U.S. News and World Report Magazine* annual college edition. The magazine also has a special college website, although SAT and

ACT data are only available for an additional fee. If race-based norms are available for a given institution, these norms may be more accurate for calculating IQ estimates. Clinicians should also inquire about participation in college athletics as this may negatively skew the estimated test score.

Occupational Data. Occupation is the other demographic that correlates highly with IQ (Crawford & Allan, 1997). Childhood IQ has been found to be predictive of occupation success in adulthood (Huang, 2001), and IQs of retired professional and managers were 16 points higher than retired operatives/laborers (Ryan, Paolo, & Dunn, 1995). Table 5.2 summarizes estimated IQs for various occupations. Column 1 reports IQ estimates

TABLE 5.2
Estimated IQ by Occupation

Occupation	NLSY79[a]	WLS[b]	GSS[c]
Physicians	124.8	118.8	117
Pharmacist		119.2	108.7
Mathematical scientists	124.8	118.7	117.1
Armed forces commissioned officers		117.9	
Attorneys	124.5	116.2	114.5
Judges			111
Architects	121.9	108.9	106.5
Management analysts	117.6		
Chemists	117.4	113.5	110.3
Authors	117.2	117.5	115.1
Technical writer/editors/reporters	117	112.1	
Optometrist			112.9
Researchers/statistician		117.1	111.4
Biological technician	113.7		
Science technician	111.7		
Computer occupations	116.6	109.8	
Systems analyst			111.3
Programmer			104.1
Engineers	116.2	110.8	
Electrical			107.9
Mechanical			106.5
Civil			104
Photographers	115.2		100.8
Clergy	114.3	110.9	108.9
Natural scientists	114.1	116.5	
Meteorologist			116.7
Geologist			116.7
Biologist			113.7
Social scientists	114.1	114.7	
Psychologist			110.3
Agronomist			107.9
Sociologist			107.4
Economist			106.6

(*continues*)

TABLE 5.2
Estimated IQ by Occupation   (Continued)

Occupation	NLSY79[a]	WLS[b]	GSS[c]
Typesetter and compositors	113.9		101.6
Librarians	113.9	113.7	114.6
College teachers	113.7	116.6	115.9
Stock and bonds salesman		113.8	107.8
Writers, artists, entertainers		112.6	
Actor			110.3
Fine artist			107.4
Museum curator			110.1
Airline pilots		112.1	105.6
Accountants	112.9	108.3	104.1
Health diagnosing practitioners	112.7		
Therapists		113.3	
Physical therapists			107.4
Office machine repairers	112.6		
Proofreaders	112.3		
Musicians and composers	112.1	114.3	
Dentists	111.9	114.9	110.3
Public relations and publicity writers		111.8	
College administrators		111.5	
Health administrators		111.1	
Social workers		110.2	105
Designers		110	
Teacher			108.1
High school		109	
Elementary school		103	
Real estate agent		109	105.7
Dental hygienist			105.5
Registered nurse		106	104.9
Stenographer			104.6
Government official		109	104.1
Insurance agent		109	104.1
Undertaker			103.6
Jeweler			103.2
Secretary		101	103.1
Engineering technician		105	102.6
Police officer		101	102.5
Industrial machine repairer		98	102.4
Photographic process worker			102.4
Debt collector			101.7
Sales representative		101	101.6
Fashion designer			101.4
Receptionist		100	100.8
Machine tool operator		93	100.6
Veterinarian			100.4
Communications equipment mechanic		98	100.2
Broadcast technician			100.2
Glazier		95	99.3
Mail carrier			99.1
Retail salesperson		101	99

TABLE 5.2
Estimated IQ by Occupation

Occupation	NLSY79[a]	WLS[b]	GSS[c]
Telephone operator		97	98.7
Dressmaker		97	98.4
Bank teller		100	97.8
Licensed practical nurse		96	97.5
Plumber		95	97.3
Maid		91	97.1
Waiter/bartender		93	96.5
Aircraft mechanic		97	96.3
Barber		93	96.2
Data entry clerk		97	96
Carpet and tile installer		95	95.8
Painter		95	95.8
Child care worker		95	95.4
Tool maker		95	95.3
Telephone installer/repairer		97	95.1
Security guard		98	95
Farmer		94	94.7
Bus driver		93	94.6
Firefighter			94.6
Insulation installer		95	93.9
Cashier		93	93.8
Furniture upholsterer		96	93.7
Electrician		96	93.6
Taxi driver		94	93.5
Bookbinder		95	93
Welder		93	92.7
Automobile mechanic		97	91.6
Dietitian			91.5
Truck driver		92	90.6
Railroad conductor		94	90.4
Sailor			90.4
Bricklayer		95	90.3
Cook		91	90.3
Construction worker		95	90
Roofer		95	89.3
Sheet metal worker		93	88.5
Carpenter		94	87.4
Janitor		91	86.9
Drill-press operator		92	86.7
Forklift operator		92	85.8
Butcher			84.3
Concrete worker		95	82.9
Surveyor		95	82.9
Shoemaker/cobbler		95	79.6
Lumberjack			75.3

Note. NLSY79 = National Longitudinal Survey of Youth; WLS = Wisconsin Longitudinal Study; GSS = General Social Survey.
[a]Data from Huang (2001). [b]Data from Hauser (2002). [c]Data from Audacious Epigone (2011).

from the National Longitudinal Survey of Youth (NLSY79), which was conducted by the U.S. Bureau of Labor Statistics (n.d.). The survey was conducted on a nationally representative sample of 12,686 male and female participants who were 14 to 22 years old in 1979. Participants were interviewed annually through 1994 and then biennially. The data set includes results from the Armed Forces Qualification Test, a battery of 10 tests administered to participants during their senior year in high school. Data for high IQ occupations reported by Huang (2001) are based on adults aged 25 to 38 from the 1983 to 1990 surveys.

Column 2 presents data from the Wisconsin Longitudinal Study (WLS), which collected Henmon–Nelson IQ scores from 10,000 seniors in 1957 and surveyed a broad sample for occupational status in 1975–1977 and 1992–1994. The data from Column 2 come from the 1992–1994 survey (Hauser, 2002). Within the reference, most data are presented in a figure, and thus IQ score for occupations below 105 are based on sight estimates. Finally, the third column reports estimated IQ scores (Audacious Epigone, 2011) calculated from Wordsum scores, a 10-item multiple-choice vocabulary test that is a short form of the original Institute of Educational Research Completion, Arithmetic, Vocabulary, Directions intelligence scale (Thorndike, 1942). The original 20-item form of the test was estimated to correlate .82 with WAIS Verbal IQ in the general population (Miner, 1961). These data were procured from the General Social Survey (GSS) cumulative database from 1972 to 2008. The GSS is a national face-to-face survey collected by the National Opinion Research Center (n.d.) at the University of Chicago of adults in randomly selected households.

Special Awards or Achievements. The next category of personal data that should be considered when estimating premorbid IQ includes awards, rankings, positions, or recognition within an occupation. Examples would include fellow status within an organization, board membership, high ranking within an occupation, prestigious awards such as a Fulbright scholarship, rankings for intellectual activities (e.g., chess, publications in poetry journals), or membership in a selective intellectual society (e.g., Mensa).

Finally, once tests are administered and it is determined that neurological conditions have not affected "hold" tests that are typically resistant to effects of brain damage (e.g., Vocabulary or Information on verbal tests) or nonverbal reasoning tests (e.g., Matrix Reasoning or Block Design), these scores can be used for estimating premorbid IQ.

Integrating Data and Making Adjustments. There is no specific formula for integrating the aforementioned data for estimating premorbid IQ, and therefore clinical judgment must be used. Table 5.3 describes three case samples of 54-year-old ethnic minority clients, born and raised in the United States, who have sustained left hemispheric cerebral vascular accidents. They illustrate how a clinician can integrate IQ estimates and demographic data to conceptualize premorbid intellectual abilities.

TABLE 5.3
Three Case Samples of 54-Year-Old Ethnic Minority, U.S.-Born Clients

	Case 1	Case 2	Case 3
Age	54	54	54
Gender	Male	Female	Male
Region	Alabama	California	Texas
Education	JD from Yale	BA California State–Bakersfield 3.0 GPA	11th grade, GED
Occupation	Attorney	Elementary school teacher	Custodian
NLSY79	124.5	—	—
WLS	114.5	108	87
Barona Index	109.27 VIQ	114.63 VIQ	87.88 VIQ
AmNART	100	100	86
Other			Emerging chess master Hardest level Sudoku

Note. AmNART = American National Adult Reading Test; NLSY79 = National Longitudinal Survey of Youth; WLS = Wisconsin Longitudinal Study.

Case 1 describes an African American attorney who graduated from Yale Law School, yet his AmNART VIQ estimate is only 100. Occupational IQ estimates for attorneys range from mid high average to superior, whereas 2013 Law School Admission Test (LSAT) statistics from Yale indicated that the lowest LSAT score was 170/180, which is at the 98th percentile. These scores would be highly suggestive of premorbid superior-level premorbid IQ. The Barona Index for Case 1 is somewhat lower at 109; however, a weakness of the Barona is that it underestimates scores for persons with high IQs (Lezak et al., 2012). This tendency is likely due to the index's low ceiling for education, which does not discriminate between persons with a bachelor's or graduate degree. An integration of existing data would suggest that Case 1 premorbidly functioned in the superior range; however, language skills have been significantly affected by his left-sided CVA, resulting in a low AmNART score.

The Native American female elementary school teacher described in Case 2 also suffered a left-sided CVA and earned a score of 100 on the AmNART. Her current word recognition–based IQ estimate, however, is more consistent with other occupational and educational scores. According to two IQ occupational scores, the IQ of teachers typically falls in the average range. California State–Bakersfield SAT statistics from 2013 reported 25th percentile/75th percentile Reading scores of 400 of 510 and Math scores of 410 of 530. Hypothetically, if the 50th percentile is considered to be a B student, using the Baade and Schoenberg (2004) formula, her WAIS IQ estimate would be 96. In this case, the Barona Index score of 112 appears to be the outlier.

For Case 3, a Hispanic male custodian from Texas who dropped out in the 11th grade but earned his GED, IQ estimates from word recognition reading

(AmNART = 86), occupation (WLS = 91, GSS = 87), and the Barona Index (88) are highly consistent, which would strongly indicate verbal IQ in the low average range. However, this person demonstrates strong special abilities, including being an emerging chess master and an ability to solve Sudoku puzzles at a high level of difficulty. Using Lezak's best performance method (Lezak et al., 2012) for estimating IQ, it would appear that Case 3 possesses highly uneven cognitive abilities with low average verbal IQ and nonverbal reasoning skills that are above average.

Strategy 2

Estimating IQ Scores for the Country of Origin

The second strategy for estimating premorbid IQ is to obtain an estimate of IQ scores on Western tests from the client's country of origin and then adjust scores based on the client's demographic information interpreted within the context of norms for that country. This strategy would be most appropriate for immigrants educated primarily in their country of origin and for whom English is not their primary language. However, it may also be useful to calculate for persons immigrating at a young age and educated in the United States whose primary language is English for contextual purposes. There are several methods for obtaining an IQ estimate of performance on Western tests: (a) data from the literature, (b) estimates based on regional IQs, (c) calculations from standardized academic tests, and (d) calculations from gross domestic product per capita (GDP).

Searching the literature for IQ scores on Western tests is the most direct method for obtaining this data. Availability and quality of data, however, vary considerably per country. Not surprisingly, more and stronger data are available for more affluent countries, whereas there is a paucity of quality data for resource poor countries. For example, the vast majority of countries do not have Wechsler-based IQ data. Instead, many use a version of Raven's Progressive Matrices (Raven, Raven, & Court, 2003), and scores for other countries may be based on something as simple as the Draw-a-Person test.

The most comprehensive source for procuring IQ scores on Western tests from different countries is Lynn and Vanhanen (2002, 2006; Lynn & Meisenberg, 2010), who obtained IQ data from 81 countries and estimated IQs for another 104 nations based on scores for neighboring or ethnically similar countries. These data were collected to support their thesis that national IQ is associated with the economic wealth of a nation, the latter determined by country GDP. Although initially criticized for weaknesses in its methodology for obtaining IQ data and rationale for estimating data for neighboring countries (Barnett & Williams, 2004), since its publication, there has been growing support for the validity of the data with correlations between IQ scores and GDP ranging from .57 to .77 (Lynn & Vanhanen, 2002). As would be expected, strong correlations have also been found between IQ and educational data, including total years of education ($r = .77–.81$; Meisenberg, 2009, 2012); adult literacy ($r = .74$; Meisenberg, 2009); percentage of students enrolled in secondary ($r = .72$) and tertiary ($r = .74$) education (Lynn & Vanhanen, 2006); quality of education ($r = .74$; Rindermann, 2008); performance on standardized achievement tests administered to different countries, such as the 1999 TIMSS math ($r = .88$) and science ($r = .87$) (Lynn & Vanhanen, 2002) and the 2003 PISA math ($r = .87$), science ($r = .85$), and reading ($r = .81$) scores (Lynn & Vanhanen, 2006). Interestingly, there is even support for their methodology of estimating IQs based on proximity. Gelade (2008) reported a correlation ($r = .87$) between IQ and geographic distance that was stronger than distance and temperature (for a review of national IQ correlates, see Lynn & Vanhanen, 2012).

A composite of Lynn and Vanhanen's original data (2002, 2006) with updated scores (Lynn & Meisenberg, 2010) is presented in columns 1 and 2 of Table 5.2. Column 1 lists data from actual studies and includes updated IQs from select African countries calculated to exclude studies with poorer methodologies or neurologically compromised samples. Updated African scores are designated with an asterisk (Wicherts, Dolan, & van der Maas, 2010). Column 2 reports estimated IQs based primarily on proximity (Lynn & Vanhanen, 2002, 2006).

Intelligence scores on Western tests can also be calculated from standardized tests of academic achievement. Table 5.2 lists estimated IQs for select countries that were administered the PISA or TIMMS (Lynn & Meisenberg, 2010). Scores are calculated with a formula similar to the one described by Baade and Schoenberg (2004) but adjusted for multiple testing and percentage of children within the country enrolled at the grade levels in which the test was administered (TIMSS Grade 8; PISA Age 15). EAact (Column 4) is the actual calculated score from achievement tests, and EAequ (Column 5) is calculated by equalizing the mean and standard deviation with the IQ score.

The last column in Table 5.4 reports GDP per capita for 2012 (World Bank, 2014; for some countries, the data are from previous years). Although there is no specific formula for using these data in calculating an IQ estimate, it is believed that GDP per capita can provide considerations for gauging cultural resources and determining a ballpark figure.[1] For example, Tuvalu,

---

[1]Lynn and Vanhanen (2002), it should be noted, warned that the relationship between GDP per capita and IQs are inaccurate for economies that are based on natural resources, such as oil-rich countries like Qatar. Also, communist countries, such as China and Vietnam, have high IQs; however, their per capita income lags because of their governments.

TABLE 5.4
Estimated IQ on Western-Based Tests by Country[a] and GDP per Capita

Country	IQ[b]	IQ est[b]	EAact[c]	EAequ[c]	GDP PC[d] ($US)
Afghanistan		84			687
Albania		90	84.7		4,000
Algeria		83	78.4	84.4	5,348
Andorra		98			
Angola		68			5,482
Antigua/Barbuda		70			12,733
Argentina	93		79.1	84.9	11,573
Armenia	92		92.7	94.1	3,351
Australia	98		101.8	100.1	67,556
Austria	100		100.8	99.5	46,642
Azerbaijan		87	82	86.8	7,164
Bahamas		84			21,908
Bahrain	81		83.8	88.1	22,467
Bangladesh		82			752
Barbados	80				14,917
Belarus		97			6,685
Belgium	99		101.2	99.8	43,372
Belize		84	67.2	76.9	4,721
Benin		70			752
Bermuda	90				84,460
Bhutan		80			2,399
Bolivia	87				2,576
Bosnia/Herzegovina	94		89.5	91.9	4,556
Botswana	71		71	79.4	7,238
Brazil	87		75.8	82.7	11,340
Brunei		91			41,127
Bulgaria	93		93.7	94.7	6,978
Burkina Faso		68			634
Burundi		69			251
Cambodia		91			944
Cameroon		64			1,167
Canada	99		102.5	100.6	52,219
Cape Verde		76			3,695
Central Africa*	71				483
Chad		68			1,035
Chile	90		82.1	86.9	15,452
China	105		102.7	100.8	6,091
Colombia	84		75.7	82.6	7,748
Comoros		77			831
Congo R.*	75.9				3,154
Congo D.R.*	77.8				262
Cook Islands	89				
Costa Rica		89	88.6		9,386
Cote d'Ivoire		69			1,244
Croatia	99		96.2	96.4	13,881
Cuba	85				6,051
Cyprus		91	89.1	91.6	26,070
Czech Republic	98		101.4	99.9	18,683

TABLE 5.4
Estimated IQ on Western-Based Tests by Country[a]
and GDP per Capita

Country	IQ[b]	IQ est[b]	EAact[c]	EAequ[c]	GDP PC[d] ($US)
Denmark	98		96.7	96.7	56,326
Djibouti		68			
Dominica		67			6,692
Dominican Republic	82				5,746
Ecuador	88				5,425
Egypt	83		78.8	84.7	3,256
El Salvador		80	69.2	78.2	3,790
England			100.5	99.3	
Equatorial Guinea	59	59			24,036
Eritrea*	85				504
Estonia	99		103	101	16,717
Ethiopia*	69.4				454
Fiji	85	85			4,467
Finland	99		105.8	102.8	45,721
France	98		99.1	98.4	39,772
Gabon		64			11,257
Gambia		66			512
Georgia		94	82.1	86.9	3,490
Germany	99		98.7	98.1	41,863
Ghana*	73.3		54.2	68.1	1,605
Greece	92		92.8	94.1	22,083
Grenada		71			7,267
Guatemala	79				3,331
Guinea	67				492
Guinea-Bissau		67			494
Guyana		87			3,584
Haiti		67			771
Honduras	81				2,323
Hong Kong	108		106.3	103.2	36,796
Hungary	97		100.5	99.3	12,531
Iceland	101		97.9	97.5	42,416
India	82		78.2	84.3	1,489
Indonesia	87		79.4	85.1	3,557
Iran	84		83.1	87.6	6,816
Iraq	87				6,455
Ireland	92		100.9	99.5	45,932
Israel	95		93.1	94.3	33,250
Italy	97		94.3	95.1	33,072
Jamaica	71				5,440
Japan	105		106.8	103.5	46,720
Jordan	85		85.8	89.4	4,909
Kazakhstan		94	102.5	100.6	12,116
Kenya*	80.4		71	79.4	943
Kiribati		85			1,736
Korea (South)	106		108	104.3	22,590
Korea North		108			

(*continues*)

TABLE 5.4
Estimated IQ on Western-Based Tests by Country[a]
and GDP per Capita   *(Continued)*

Country	IQ[b]	IQ est[b]	EAact[c]	EAequ[c]	GDP PC[d] ($US)
Kuwait	87		77.1	83.5	51,497
Kyrgyzstan		90	64.9	75.3	1,160
Laos	89				1,417
Latvia		98	95.3	95.8	14,008
Lebanon	82		82.1	86.9	9,705
Lesotho		67	51.7	66.5	1,193
Liberia		67			414
Libya		83			10,456
Liechtenstein		100	101.7	100.1	134,617
Lithuania	91		95.2	95.7	14,183
Luxembourg		100	93.7	94.7	103,828
Macao SAR, China		101	101.9	100.2	78,275
Macedonia		91	86.6	89.9	4,565
Madagascar*	82				447
Mali*	74.1				694
Malawi	60		45.5	62.3	268
Malaysia	92		95.6	96	10,432
Maldives		81			6,567
Malta	97		92.3	93.7	20,848
Marshall Islands	84				3,471
Mauritania		76			1,106
Mauritius	89		73.7	81.3	8,120
Mexico	88		82.4	87.1	9,749
Micronesia		84			3,155
Moldova		96	89	91.6	2,038
Monaco					163,026
Mongolia		101			3,673
Montenegro			82	86.8	7,041
Morocco	84		70.5	79.1	2,902
Mozambique	64		60.8	72.6	565
Myanmar		87			
Namibia*	74		51.3	66.2	5,786
Nepal	78	78			690
Netherlands	100		103	101.1	45,955
New Caledonia	85				
New Zealand	99		99.5	98.6	37,749
Nicaragua		81			1,754
Niger		69			395
Nigeria*	83.8		60.5	72.4	1,555
Northern Marianas	81				
Norway	100		96.4	96.5	99,558
Oman	85		78.9	84.8	23,133
Pakistan	84				1,257
Palau					11,006
Palestine	86		75.9	82.7	
Panama		84			9,534
Papua New Guinea	83		89.6	92	2,184

TABLE 5.4
Estimated IQ on Western-Based Tests by Country[a]
and GDP per Capita

Country	IQ[b]	IQ est[b]	EAact[c]	EAequ[c]	GDP PC[d] ($US)
Paraguay	84				3,813
Peru	85		81		6,796
Philippines	86		68.6	77.8	2,587
Poland	95		97.8	97.5	12,708
Portugal	95		92	93.6	20,165
Puerto Rico	84				27,678
Qatar	83		65.5	75.7	89,736
Romania	91		89	91.5	9,036
Rwanda		70			620
Russia	97		97.3	97.1	14,037
St. Kitts/Nevis		67			14,314
St. Lucia	62				6,848
St. Vincent Grenadines	71				6,515
Samoa	88				3,620
Sao Tome/Principe		67			1,400
Saudi Arabia	80		72.6	80.5	25,136
Scotland			96.1	96.3	
Senegal*	66.3				1,023
Serbia/Montenegro	89		88.8	91.4	5,190
Seychelles		86	75.3	82.3	12,858
Sierra Leone*	91.3				635
Singapore	108		113	107.7	51,709
Slovakia	96		99.1	98.4	16,847
Slovenia	96		100.7	99.4	22,000
Solomon Islands		84			1,835
Somalia		68			
South Africa*	77.1		54.9	68.6	7,508
South Sudan					943
Spain	98		96	96.3	28,624
Sri Lanka		79			2,923
Sudan	71				1,580
Suriname	89				9,376
Swaziland		68	65.3	75.6	3,042
Sweden	99		99.6	98.7	55,041
Switzerland	101		101	99.7	78,925
Syria	79		82.6	87.2	3,289
Taiwan	105		108.8	104.9	
Tajikistan		87			871
Tanzania	72		67.4	77	609
Thailand	91		89.4	91.8	5,480
Timor-Leste		87			1,068
Togo		70			574
Tonga	86				4,494
Trinidad/Tobago		85	87.4	90.5	17,437
Tunisia	84		80.7	85.9	4,237
Turkmenistan		87			6,798

(*continues*)

TABLE 5.4
Estimated IQ on Western-Based Tests by Country[a]
and GDP per Capita   *(Continued)*

Country	IQ[b]	IQ est[b]	EAact[c]	EAequ[c]	GDP PC[d] ($US)
Turkey	90		86	89.5	10,666
Tuvalu					4,044
Uganda*	83.9		57.3	70.2	547
UK	100		100	99	39,093
Ukraine	95		92.4	93.8	3,867
United Arab Emirates	83		92.2	93.7	39,058
Uruguay	96		85.4	89.1	14,703
USA	98		97.4	97.2	51,749
Uzbekistan		87			1,717
Vanuatu		84			3,183
Venezuela	84		74.7	81.9	12,729
Vietnam	94	94	100.9		1,755
Yemen	83		53.3	67.5	1,494
Zambia*	78.5		50.9	65.9	1,469
Zimbabwe*	81.5		61.1	72.8	714

Note. EAact = actual calculated score from achievement tests; EAequ = calculation equalizing the mean and SD with the IQ score; GDP PC = gross domestic product per capita; IQest = estimated IQ. [a]Given differences in education, experiences, and conception of intelligent behavior across cultures, these scores are best interpreted as adjustments of how culturally different clients from different regions would perform on Western-based IQ tests and do not reflect absolute measures of intelligence. [b]Data from Lynn and Vanhanen (2002, 2006) and Lynn and Meisenberg (2010). [c]Data from Lynn and Meisenberg (2010). [d]Data from World Bank (2014). *Data from Wicherts, Dolan, and van der Maas (2010).

an island nation located in the Pacific Ocean, reports a GDP per capita of $4,044. A look at economically similar nations in close proximity reveals the following IQs: Marshall Islands (GDP = $3,471, IQ = 84), Samoa (GDP = $3,670, IQ = 88), Fiji (GDP = $4,467, IQ = 85), and Tonga (GDP = $4,497, IQ = 88). On the basis of these data, a ballpark IQ estimate for natives of Tuvalu would be in the mid- to high 80s.

Finally, Table 5.5 presents regional IQ estimates calculated by Lynn and Meisenberg (2010) based on research studies and standardized test scores.

When determining IQs on Western tests, it is recommended that clinicians use all available data and strategies but weight scores based on stronger methodologies. Thus, more confidence can be placed in estimates based on standardized tests, replicated studies, and convergence of different informational sources. When searching the literature for pertinent IQ estimates, it is important to review the study's sampling because many studies in low resource countries are limited to small convenience samples or come from epidemiological studies in which the subjects suffer from a serious medical or neurological disorder. Another consideration is to be sure that the demographics of the study sample matches your client in age, education, language, and

TABLE 5.5
Estimated IQs on Western-Based Tests by National Regions

Region	IQ	EAact	EAequ
Europe	98.3 ± 2.3	98.0 ± 4.0	97.6 ± 2.7
English speaking	97.7 ± 2.9	100.3 ± 1.8	99.2 ± 1.2
Ex-communist	94.8 ± 3.1	95.8 ± 4.72	96.1 ± 3.2
Latin America	88.9 ± 4.5	79.3 ± 4.13	85.0 ± 2.8
Middle East	84.4 ± 3.8	78.9 ± 9.74	84.8 ± 6.5
Africa	69.9 ± 3.9	58.8 ± 8.14	71.3 ± 5.4
East Asia	106.2 ± 1.5	107.6 ± 3.4	104.1 ± 2.3
Rest of Asia	87.1 ± 3.8	82.1 ± 9.74	86.9 ± 6.5
All countries	89.8 ± 10.7	86.4 ± 15.93	89.8 ± 10.7

Note. EAact = actual calculated score from achievement tests; EAequ = calculation equalizing the mean and SD with the IQ score. Given differences in education, experiences, and conception of intelligent behavior across cultures, these scores are best interpreted as adjustments of how culturally different clients of various regions would perform on Western-based IQ tests and do not reflect absolute measures of intelligence. From "National IQs Calculated and Validated for 108 Nations," by R. Lynn and G. Meisenberg, 2010, *Intelligence*, *38*, p. 359. Copyright 2010 by Elsevier. Adapted with permission.

region. In many cases, studies can be decades old and may not apply to a younger client because of upgrades in the economy and educational system. When estimating IQ on older data, be sure to make adjustments for the *Flynn effect*, a phenomenon of massive IQ gains in more than 30 countries that developed over several decades (Flynn, 2007). This can be done by determining the number of years elapsed since the publication of the data, prorating gains reported in the literature, and adding this number to the original IQ score. Conversely, data from more recent studies may not apply to older clients because of changes in the country's economy and educational system.

Additional Data to Corroborate and Adjust IQ Score

Quantity of Education. Once a national IQ estimate is determined, the next step is to adjust the score for the client based on personal demographic data interpreted within the context of his or her country of origin. Sources of information include level of education, occupation, reason for and timing of immigration, educational and occupational achievement of progeny, and English skills. Table 5.6 presents educational attainment for different countries (UNESCO, n.d.-a) and expected educational attainment for current and future students (UNESCO, n.d.-b). The data for educational attainment are from 2000 unless otherwise specified; the expected years of education estimate is from 2012.

Data from this table can assist a clinician in determining how a client's level of education compares to national peers. For example, in 2000, 30.7%

TABLE 5.6
Educational Attainment by Country

Country	Percent with no schooling	Primary (percent)		Secondary (percent)		Postsecondary (percent)		Average years	Expected[b] years
		Total	Completed	Total	Completed	Total	Completed		
Afghanistan	77.5	11.5	3.7	8.4	2.0	2.6	1.7	1.74	8.1
Albania									11.4
Algeria	31.3	33.3	11.4	29.3	8.5	6.1	2.1	5.37	13.6
Andorra									11.7
Angola									10.2
Antigua/Barbuda[c]	3.3	84.6	73.6	11.6	2.5	0.4	0.2	5.02	13.3
Argentina	3.6	45.2	27.5	31.1	10.1	20.1	7.8	8.83	16.1
Armenia									12.2
Australia	1.9	18.4	10.2	47.3	17.5	32.4	15.3	10.92	19.6
Austria	2.8	25.5	14.1	57.0	21.0	14.7	5.1	8.35	15.3
Azerbaijan									11.7
Bahamas									12.6
Bahrain	25.9	25.3	8.8	38.2	12.2	10.6	3.8	6.11	13.4
Bangladesh	50.1	32.9	9.0	14.0	4.0	3.0	1.4	2.58	8.1
Barbados	2.8	41.5	11.5	43.3	9.5	12.3	6.0	8.73	16.3
Belarus									14.7
Belgium	5.5	35.7	16.8	37.7	10.5	21.0	13.1	9.34	16.4
Belize[d]	10.0	60.6	16.8	22.0	4.8	6.4	3.1	.	12.5
Benin	64.4	23.9	5.6	10.2	1.6	1.5	0.6	2.34	9.4
Bermuda									12.4
Bhutan									12.4
Bolivia	27.4	44.8	12.4	14.8	4.4	13.0	5.6	5.58	13.5
Bosnia/Herzegovina									13.4
Botswana	24.0	36.7	20.8	35.7	8.3	3.6	1.4	6.28	11.8

Highest level attained[a]

Country								
Brazil	16.0	12.6	14.4	4.6	7.5	3.7	4.88	14.2
Brunei[e]	29.2	13.5	36.1	11.4	8.0	3.9	5.99	15
Bulgaria	5.5	27.9	37.6	12.6	18.1	12.4	9.47	14
Burkina Faso								
Burundi[d]	70.6	5.6	3.3	0.7	0.4	0.2	1.38	6.9
Cambodia								11.3
Cameroon	39.3	10.1	15.4	2.9	1.9	1.3	3.54	10.5
Canada	1.4	10.8	29.8	12.5	54.3	10.0	11.62	10.9
Cape Verde								15.1
Central Africa	56.7	7.2	10.7	2.2	1.5	0.7	2.53	12.7
Chad								6.8
Chile	7.1	9.9	34.1	11.2	14.5	7.1	7.55	7.4
China	18.0	12.8	45.3	14.8	2.8	2.1	6.35	14.7
Colombia	20.3	9.5	27.2	7.9	9.8	4.4	5.27	11.7
Comoros								13.6
Congo R.	35.2	8.0	32.3	6.8	3.8	2.1	5.14	10.2
Congo D.R.								10.1
Cook Islands								8.5
Costa Rica	10.4	12.6	15.7	4.4	17.8	8.5	6.05	13.7
Cote d'Ivoire								6.5
Croatia[e]	7.0	24.3	41.5	12.6	4.5	1.7	6.92	14.1
Cuba	5.6	14.5	46.7	14.4	10.0	5.2	7.71	16.2
Cyprus	3.4	21.1	49.8	19.6	16.8	9.8	9.15	14.9
Czech Republic	2.1	10.7	59.1	20.3	10.5	6.8	9.48	15.3
Denmark	0.0	19.9	45.3	37.7	18.6	8.4	9.66	16.8
Djibouti								5.7
Dominica[e]	4.7	21.3	16.6	3.6	1.5	0.7	4.88	12.7
Dominican Republic	31.4	8.4	16.1	3.5	14.2	5.7	4.93	12.3
Ecuador	15.1	13.3	23.8	7.3	15.1	7.6	6.41	13.7
Egypt	35.9	6.9	34.2	10.5	9.3	4.3	5.51	12.1
El Salvador	27.9	10.8	13.4	1.8	9.8	3.7	5.15	12

(continues)

TABLE 5.6
Educational Attainment by Country *(Continued)*

		Highest level attained[a]							
Country	Percent with no schooling	Primary (percent)		Secondary (percent)		Postsecondary (percent)		Average years	Expected[b] years
		Total	Completed	Total	Completed	Total	Completed		
Equatorial Guinea									7.9
Eritrea									4.6
Estonia[d]	1.9	39.0	14.7	47.4	14.0	11.7	8.2	8.97	15.8
Ethiopia									8.7
Fiji	4.6	46.3	21.7	41.5	15.4	7.6	3.3	8.30	13.9
Finland	0.4	29.7	16.4	47.6	34.0	22.3	8.9	9.99	16.9
France	0.8	46.2	21.0	35.7	14.3	17.3	6.2	7.86	16.1
Gabon									13
Gambia	64.9	20.8	4.5	13.8	1.5	0.6	0.4	2.31	8.7
Georgia									13.2
Germany	3.9	18.6	9.5	61.4	23.5	16.1	8.0	10.20	16.4
Ghana	44.8	28.6	6.6	25.7	2.5	1.0	0.5	3.89	11.4
Greece	5.1	42.1	32.7	39.0	26.6	13.8	9.1	8.67	16.3
Grenada									15.8
Guatemala	39.5	42.1	9.4	13.4	2.3	5.0	2.2	3.49	10.7
Guinea									8.8
Guinea-Bissau	70.6	26.9	2.7	2.3	0.6	0.2	0.1	0.84	9.5
Guyana	6.9	48.7	13.5	40.1	8.7	4.3	1.8	6.25	10.3
Haiti	57.4	25.2	5.5	16.5	5.5	0.9	0.5	2.77	7.6
Honduras	16.6	58.9	12.8	18.8	8.1	5.7	2.3	4.80	11.4
Hong Kong	11.3	25.2	13.1	50.2	31.2	13.3	6.3	9.41	15.6
Hungary	2.4	43.9	19.2	41.7	13.1	12.1	10.0	9.12	15.5
Iceland	1.7	39.1	21.6	42.9	14.2	16.3	6.8	8.83	18.3
India	43.9	28.2	10.5	23.8	6.5	4.1	2.2	5.06	10.7

Country									
Indonesia	32.1	35.5	17.3	27.8	8.4	4.5	0.5	4.99	12.9
Iran	34.8	24.2	8.4	33.5	12.6	7.5	2.6	5.31	14.4
Iraq	41.8	34.7	11.6	16.3	4.9	7.2	3.1	3.95	10
Ireland	3.6	24.1	13.3	51.3	17.0	21.0	8.0	9.35	18.3
Israel	10.9	19.8	6.8	42.2	16.0	27.1	10.4	9.60	15.7
Italy	12.4	34.8	16.1	38.7	11.8	14.2	5.0	7.18	16.2
Jamaica	2.9	52.1	14.4	41.0	8.4	4.0	1.7	5.26	13.1
Japan	0.2	27.5	12.6	50.1	13.8	22.2	11.7	9.47	15.3
Jordan	24.6	24.4	8.4	33.1	10.0	17.9	7.3	6.91	12.7
Kazakhstan[d]	5.9	30.1	11.4	54.1	16.0	9.9	4.6	8.87	15.3
Kenya	30.7	51.8	10.8	16.4	0.9	1.1	0.5	4.20	11.1
Kiribati									12
Korea (South)	6.5	11.9	11.4	55.2	41.4	26.3	12.1	10.84	17.2
Kuwait	37.8	9.6	3.3	38.0	17.9	14.6	8.3	6.22	14.2
Kyrgyzstan									12.6
Laos	0.5								10.1
Latvia[d]	39.0	39.0	23.4	48.9	14.4	11.5	8.0	9.45	14.8
Lebanon									13.9
Lesotho	28.8	54.8	11.0	15.3	2.8	1.1	0.8	4.23	9.6
Liberia	57.6	29.3	6.2	10.7	2.1	2.4	1.2	2.45	10.5
Libya[f]	36.9	35.3	12.1	20.7	4.7	7.1	2.6	4.47	16.2
Liechtenstein									11.9
Lithuania[d]	7.4	17.3	6.5	64.7	19.1	10.6	6.4	9.42	15.7
Luxembourg									13.5
Macao SAR, China									14.2
Macedonia									13.3
Madagascar									10.4
Mali	83.9	11.7	2.4	3.8	0.7	0.6	0.3	0.88	7.5
Malawi	40.7	54.2	11.0	4.6	1.4	0.5	0.3	3.20	10.4
Malaysia	16.2	42.4	26.0	36.2	13.5	5.2	2.9	6.80	12.6
Maldives									12.5

(*continues*)

TABLE 5.6
Educational Attainment by Country (Continued)

Country	Percent with no schooling	Primary (percent)		Secondary (percent)		Postsecondary (percent)		Average years	Expected[b] years
		Total	Completed	Total	Completed	Total	Completed		
Malta									15.1
Marshall Islands									11.7
Mauritania[d]	55.8	35.7	8.3	7.2	1.4	1.2	0.5	2.42	8.1
Mauritius	13.1	44.6	5.6	39.5	30.3	2.7	0.9	6.00	13.6
Mexico	9.7	41.8	17.1	37.9	15.8	10.6	4.4	7.23	13.7
Micronesia									11.4
Moldova[d]	10.3	14.2	5.4	65.5	19.3	10.0	5.8	9.23	11.8
Mongolia									14.3
Montenegro									15
Morocco									10.4
Mozambique	63.8	33.1	7.7	2.9	0.6	0.2	0.1	1.11	9.2
Myanmar	35.7	43.5	11.9	17.8	5.5	3.1	1.3	2.77	9.4
Namibia[d]	.	.	.	44.8	9.3	3.2	1.8	.	11.3
Nauru									9.3
Nepal	57.1	20.6	5.6	20.2	5.6	2.2	1.0	2.43	8.9
Netherlands	3.7	25.5	14.1	49.1	13.1	21.7	9.3	9.35	16.9
New Zealand	0.0	28.0	15.5	30.5	11.6	41.5	14.0	11.74	19.7
Nicaragua	28.9	43.1	9.6	19.8	3.0	8.3	4.3	4.58	10.8
Niger	80.9	15.0	3.5	3.6	0.6	0.5	0.3	1.02	4.9
Nigeria									9
Norway	1.1	9.0	5.0	66.2	44.1	23.7	7.8	11.85	17.5
Oman									13.5
Pakistan	51.0	21.8	8.3	24.9	13.9	2.3	1.5	3.88	7.3
Palau									13.7

Country									
Palestine	9.1	36.2	18.8	35.8	20.2	18.8	9.9	8.55	13.5
Panama	47.9	41.6	20.4	9.0	2.0	1.5	0.5	2.88	13.2
Papua New Guinea	5.7	62.4	20.3	24.1	11.7	7.8	4.5	6.18	5.8
Paraguay	11.9	31.4	7.7	34.5	11.1	22.2	9.7	7.58	12.1
Peru	3.1	33.1	16.5	40.6	22.4	23.2	12.0	8.21	13.2
Philippines	1.9	34.1	29.7	53.7	17.8	10.2	6.2	9.84	11.7
Poland	11.5	49.6	23.0	25.1	8.4	13.8	4.1	5.87	15.2
Portugal									16
Puerto Rico									15.6
Qatar									12.2
Romania	4.3	20.5	7.5	68.0	23.9	7.3	4.8	9.51	14.5
Rwanda	47.6	47.1	9.5	4.8	0.8	0.5	0.3	2.56	10.9
Russia	1.2	32.1	21.0	50.2	17.1	16.6	11.5	10.03	14.3
St. Kitts/Nevis[e]	0.9	20.9	4.9	76.8	16.8	1.4	0.7	8.09	12.9
St. Lucia[e]	11.6	71.3	19.7	16.3	3.5	0.9	0.4	4.95	12.7
St. Vincent Grenadines[e]	1.6	80.0	22.1	17.5	3.8	0.9	0.4	5.47	13.3
Samoa									13
Samoa Western[d]	78.2	12.9	4.9	7.9	3.2	1.0	0.3	1.48	
San Marino									12.5
Sao Tome/Principe									10.8
Saudi Arabia									14.3
Senegal	53.7	35.7	8.3	8.5	1.5	2.1	1.1	2.55	8.2
Serbia/Montenegro									13.6
Seychelles[f]	7.7	31.3	6.7	55.9	9.0	3.1	1.7	6.91	14.3
Sierra Leone	66.2	22.3	4.6	10.6	1.1	1.0	0.5	2.40	7.3
Singapore	16.4	39.0	23.2	34.6	9.9	10.0	3.7	7.05	14.4
Slovakia	2.1	32.3	12.2	54.9	18.1	10.7	7.0	9.27	14.7
Slovenia	2.3	42.6	16.1	41.7	14.0	13.3	8.5	7.11	16.9
Solomon Islands[d]	12.4	29.6	16.6	43.8	18.7	14.2	5.0	7.98	9.3
Somalia									2.4
South Africa	22.1	34.5	9.9	36.1	3.5	7.3	2.5	6.14	13.1

(continues)

TABLE 5.6
Educational Attainment by Country   (Continued)

Country	Percent with no schooling	Highest level attained[a]						Average years	Expected[b] years
		Primary (percent)		Secondary (percent)		Postsecondary (percent)			
		Total	Completed	Total	Completed	Total	Completed		
South Sudan									
Spain	3.3	44.7	20.0	36.0	11.1	16.0	5.2	7.28	16.4
Sri Lanka	14.0	33.5	12.4	50.0	15.0	2.5	0.8	6.87	12.7
Sudan	60.0	27.4	5.6	10.7	2.2	1.9	0.7	2.14	4.5
Suriname									12.4
Swaziland	21.7	41.2	10.0	33.2	3.1	3.9	1.8	6.01	10.7
Sweden	2.0	14.8	6.7	61.4	44.3	21.7	10.5	11.41	16
Switzerland	4.6	21.9	12.1	57.4	28.9	16.2	7.4	10.48	15.7
Syria	20.2	45.7	15.7	22.7	6.4	11.4	5.0	5.77	11.7
Taiwan	10.0	24.2	13.6	46.2	19.7	19.6	6.9	8.76	
Tajikistan[d]	6.7	9.6	3.6	74.8	22.1	8.9	4.7	9.79	11.5
Tanzania	42.8	53.7	9.7	2.7	0.2	0.8	0.6	2.71	9.1
Thailand	12.6	61.5	27.0	15.1	4.2	10.9	7.0	6.50	12.3
Timor-Leste									11.7
Togo	43.1	39.4	8.2	15.5	1.5	1.9	1.1	3.33	10.6
Tonga									13.7
Trinidad/Tobago	5.0	43.4	12.0	47.3	10.3	4.3	2.1	7.76	11.9
Tunisia	32.9	34.0	11.4	27.1	9.9	6.1	3.3	5.02	14.5

Turkmenistan									12.6
Turkey	20.8	50.8	43.7	19.7	5.3	8.7	3.0	5.29	12.9
Tuvalu									10.8
Uganda	38.0	49.3	10.0	11.8	1.3	0.8	0.4	3.51	11.1
UK	3.3	35.4	16.3	41.7	11.0	19.6	8.8	9.42	16.4
Ukraine									14.8
United Arab Emirates[g]	70.0	7.1	2.4	18.3	7.5	4.7	3.1	2.87	12
Uruguay	5.1	44.8	10.5	35.5	8.2	14.6	7.0	7.56	15.5
USA	0.8	8.2	3.9	42.9	20.0	48.1	24.5	12.05	16.8
Uzbekistan									11.6
Vanuatu[e]	29.6	41.3	9.8	.	.	.	.	.	10.6
Venezuela	9.8	44.0	9.8	32.5	10.7	13.7	5.3	6.64	14.4
Vietnam[d]	13.2	73.4	29.4	11.1	3.5	1.9	1.4	3.84	11.9
Yemen[d]	78.2	12.9	4.9	7.9	3.2	1.0	0.3	1.48	8.7
Yugoslavia[d]	15.0	45.5	16.7	31.4	9.5	8.1	5.4	7.06	13.4
Zaire	47.7	32.0	6.5	19.0	4.0	1.3	0.6	3.03	
Zambia	17.3	55.6	11.4	25.4	12.3	1.7	0.7	5.46	8.5
Zimbabwe	12.7	45.7	9.3	37.3	1.2	4.3	1.8	5.35	10.1

Note. [a]UNESCO (n.d.-a) data from 2000 unless noted. [b]UNESCO (n.d.-b) data for 2008–2012. [c]UNESCO (n.d.-a) data from 1960. [d]UNESCO (n.d.-a) data from 1990. [e]UNESCO (n.d.-a) data from 1980. [f]UNESCO (n.d.-a) data from 1985. [g]UNESCO (n.d.-a) data from 1975.

of Kenyans aged 15 years or older had no schooling, 1.1% received some college or vocational training, and only .5% completed college. Thus, a college graduate would be in the top 1% of the population in terms of education. If the estimated IQ on Western tests for Kenyans is 80.4 (see Table 5.4), a college graduate may be expected to be 2+ standard deviations above the mean or roughly 110+. It should be emphasized that score would be a ballpark figure.

Quality of Education. Another pertinent indicator for estimating intelligence on Western tests is quality of education (Manly, Jacobs, Touradji, Small, & Stern, 2002). Rankings for international and regional universities can be found online on websites such as Academy Rank (2011), International Universities and Colleges (International Universities and Colleges, 2013), or Academic Rankings of World Universities (Center for World Class Universities, 2013). Academy Rank also has rankings of universities by country. Although most sites do not disclose specific criteria, there does appear to be significant overlap in the rankings, which would provide some face validity for the data. Websites such as Wikipedia (n.d.) also list primary and secondary schools by country and rankings for specific countries can often be found online via search engines. It should be emphasized that all rankings have inherent biases, but these websites can nonetheless provide some insight into quality of education for a given country.

Thus, for example, a person who attended the nationally prestigious Kenya High School and then the University of Nairobi (Kenya Certificate Secondary Education, 2014) would be expected to have a higher IQ on Western tests than a person who graduated from the lower achieving North Eastern Province and attended a vocational college. Although the mean level of education for all persons 15 years of age and older in 2000 was 4.2 years, the current projection for students is a mean of 11.1 years education. A comparison of these figures indicates significant development in the Kenyan educational system over the past few decades. Hence, a 60-year-old college graduate from Kenya would be much rarer than a 30-year-old with a college degree.

Occupational and Socioeconomic Status. Occupation and socioeconomic status, both in the country of origin and in the United States, would be another indicator for determining premorbid IQ. An immigrant who owned a small textile business in Pakistan but currently works as a taxi driver likely possesses a higher premorbid intellectual ability than a fellow Pakistani taxi driver who worked as a laborer in agriculture. Similarly, a Vietnamese woman who grew up in a small rural village but now owns two manicure businesses would likely have higher premorbid functioning than a neighbor in the same village peer who works as cook in a Vietnamese restaurant. When considering occupation as an indicator of functioning, clinicians should remember that occupations and statuses differ by country and their economic level. For example, a farming supervisor may have higher status in an agricultural society from an emerging economy versus a high-income industrialized nation.

Reason and Timing of Immigration. Another important consideration when estimating premorbid intellectual abilities is reason for and timing of immigration. Leaving one's home for a foreign country is a nontrivial decision and commitment; the individual must not only give up a familiar culture and language but also adjust to an unfamiliar environment where he or she will have to start all over and assimilate. Thus, emigration is typically motivated by economic opportunities, family reunification, or political reasons, which correspond to broad eligibility categories for obtaining immigration visas in the United States.

The most common form of immigration to the United States is relative- or family-sponsored immigration, which includes spouses or fiancés of U.S. citizens, intercountry adoption of orphans, and certain family members of U.S. citizens or lawful permanent residents (LPRs). This category of immigration accounts for 65% of the roughly 1 million LPRs who immigrate annually. Within this category, 43% were an immediate relative of a U.S. citizen, and 22% entered through a family-sponsored preference. Data from 2011 (Migration Policy Institute, 2013) report the following as the top 10 countries of birth for new LPRs: Mexico (14%), China (8%), India (6%), Philippines (5%), Dominican Republic (4%), Cuba (3%), Vietnam (3%), Korea (2%), Colombia (2%), and Haiti (2%).

The second largest category for immigration is asylum, as specified by international and federal law, which accounts for about 16% of LPRs (Migration Policy Institute, 2013). To seek asylum, individuals must fear persecution that is based on one of five protected grounds—race, religion, nationality, political opinion, and social group—in which the native government is either involved in the persecution or is unable to control the conduct of private actors. The United States had historically been the nation that accepted the largest number of refugees per year, with 56,384 arriving in 2011. The birth countries with the largest refugee LPRs are as follows (Russell & Batalova, 2012): Burma (30.1%), Bhutan (26.7%), Iraq (16.7%), Somalia (5.6%), Cuba (5.2%), Eritrea (3.6%), Iran (3.6%), Democratic Republic of the Congo (1.7%), Ethiopia (1%), Afghanistan (0.8%), and other (5.2%).

Refugee immigrants typically originate from countries undergoing political instability, thus large numbers of persons are simultaneously vying to leave the country. Because large numbers leaving a country simultaneously is frequently not logistically feasible, emigration often takes years and is clustered into groups known as *waves* of immigration. The wave in which a person emigrates can be an indicator of premorbid functioning. The general pattern is that the first wave of immigrants includes the educated, professional, or affluent, and then others arrive in subsequent waves, many for family reunification. For example, members of the first wave of Vietnamese immigrants were from privileged backgrounds, many with close ties to the military. In an overwhelmingly rural society, 70% came from urban areas with more than 30% head of households in medical, technical, or managerial occupations; 16.9% in transportation occupations; and 11.7% in clerical and sales. It is interesting to note that only 4.9% of first-wave immigrants were fishermen or farmers, the occupations of the majority of Vietnamese citizens (Bankston, n.d.).

Related to wave of immigration, there can be a selection bias in the location of settlement in the United States. Many of the first-wave Vietnamese immigrants settled in Los Angeles, where a study conducted 25 years later compared the cognition of elderly Vietnamese with elderly Whites, Hispanics, and African Americans (Dick, Teng, Kempler, Davis, & Taussig, 2002). Despite having a lower level of education ($x = 8.6$) compared with Whites ($x = 11.4$), the Vietnamese sample performed comparably to the White sample, with the exception of Vietnamese performance on the Trails A, which was significantly lower. Although less educated than the American Whites, the Vietnamese sample was highly educated compared with most Vietnamese adults, with a mean of 3.84 years of education (UNESCO, n.d.-b).

In employment-sponsored immigration which accounts for 13% of annual LPRs, an employer must sponsor the potential immigrant. There is a hierarchy of categories for awarding work visas with yearly quotas for each category. Priority workers are persons with outstanding abilities in the science, arts, education, business, or athletics; outstanding professors, researchers, or managers; or executives of multinational companies. Professionals holding advanced degrees or bachelor's level educated persons of exceptional ability compose the next priority group. The last three categories include skilled workers, professionals, or unskilled workers, the latter having the lowest priority, followed by certain special immigrants and finally immigrant investors (Migration Policy Institute, 2013).

Persons immigrating for economic reasons typically come from poorer nations with patterns of immigration differing for specific countries. For example, Kenya is one of the poorest countries in the world, with a GDP per capita of US $943 (World Bank, 2014). Its Human Development Index (HDI), a composite score based on GDP, life expectancy, and educational opportunities (United Nations Development Programme, n.d.), is ranked 145 of 188 in the world (0.548); thus, the occupational opportunities for college-educated citizens are limited. In comparison, U.S. GPD per capita is $51,749 and it ranks number 8 in HDI (0.915). Given the contrasting economic conditions, it would not be surprising that educated Kenyans would be motivated to immigrate to the United States, while also having qualifications for visa eligibility. The transition is also easier because educated Kenyans are multilingual, with most speaking English (of Kenyan Americans, only 16.7% speak English less than very well). An implication is that Kenyan Americans have one of the highest rates of education (48% have a bachelor's degree, and 20.3% also hold graduate degrees) among specific ethnicities within the United States and have a high median household earnings ($58,336), with 49.2% of Kenyans working in management, business, science, and arts occupations; 22.6% in service occupations; and 18.9% in sales and office occupations (U.S. Census Bureau, n.d.-b). Although impressive, this is a select sample of the total Kenyan population; the typical adult Kenyan with only 4.2 years of education would not be eligible or have the resources to immigrate to the United States.

Although economically stronger than Kenya, Mexico also ranks far behind the United States, with a GDP per capita of $9,749 and HDI ranking of 74 (0.756; United Nations Development Programme, n.d.). Because of its close proximity and unique socioeconomic conditions, characteristics of Mexican immigrants differ considerably with those from Kenya. Mexico shares the southern border with the United States, so it is not surprising that the highest numbers of immigrants to the United States come from Mexico (estimated 11,700,000 in 2011; Migration Policy Institute, 2013). Canada also borders the United States but has a higher GDP per capita ($52,219) and has a comparable HDI (0.913); thus, Canadians are less motivated to immigrate to the United States (United Nations Development Programme, n.d.).

Similar to Kenya, Mexican immigration is also driven by work (86.8% of males and 52% of females are in the labor force; 88% are of working age, 18–54); however, the occupations where most are employed are primarily unskilled. Seventy-seven percent of Mexican males work in construction, extracting, transportation (34%); service (25%); and manufacturing, installation, repair (18%); most females work in service (39%), manufacturing (14%), and administrative support (11%) occupations (Migration Policy Institute, 2013). One reason that Mexican immigrants gravitate toward low-paying jobs is that most have limited English skills; only 26% reported speaking English very well, while the rest report not speaking English very well (Migration Policy Institute, 2013). There is considerable need to fill these positions, which tend to be low paying but ranks as low priority according to criteria for employment immigration. These factors, in combination with the relative ease of coming to the United States and the long waiting period for legal immigration procedures, results in a high percentage of illegal immigration. According to figures from the Migration Policy Institute, in 2011, only 4.9 million of 11.7 million Mexican immigrants were legal; 59% were unauthorized, while only 24% were naturalized citizens. Because of their illegal status, many Mexicans are vulnerable to exploitation from unscrupulous employers. Given that most Mexican immigrants work in low-priority jobs, it is not surprising that 89% of legal immigrants are accepted under the family reunification category, whereas only 6% enter for employment purposes (Hoefer, Rytina, & Baker, 2012).

In contrast to Kenyan immigrants who are much more likely to be highly educated, Mexican immigrants are more representative of the general population. The majority of Mexican immigrants in 2011 had less than a high school education (59%); about a third completed high school (35%), and about 5% have a bachelor's degree or higher (Migration Policy Institute, 2013). Mexican immigrants come from both poorer states, such as Michoacán (16%) and Chiapas (7%), and more affluent states, including Jalisco (10%) and Guanajuato (11%; Britz & Batalova, 2013). Despite the cross-sectional representation, there is still a selection bias toward poorer rural citizens emigrating with 25% of the population living in rural areas accounting for 44% of migrants (Consejo Nacional de Población, 2006).

The last category for immigration, which accounts for about 5% of LPRs, aims to increase diversity from countries with low immigration rates by awarding a limited number of visas via lottery (U.S. Department of State, Bureau of Consular Affairs, n.d.). Before receiving permission to immigrate to the United States, lottery winners must provide proof of a high school education or its equivalent or show 2 years of work experience within the past 5 years in an occupation that requires at least 2 years of training or experience. They also must pass a medical examination and a background check (Britz, & Batalova, 2013).

Descriptions of Vietnamese, Kenyan, and Mexican immigration illustrate how the unique particulars of a country influence who actually immigrates to the United States. Selection biases exists for each country for both timing and reasons for immigration. Awareness of specific immigration patterns for a CDC's country can assist case conceptualization by providing hypotheses of the client's education level, English exposure, and general functioning in comparison to the average person from his or her country of origin. This information can then be used in preparation for the evaluation and also for estimating premorbid intellectual abilities on Western tests.

Awareness of immigration issues can also facilitate respect for the CDC or individuals from different countries. For example, due to poor English skills and other challenges, many immigrants are underemployed in comparison to their educational level and occupation in their country of origin. Thus a foreign born taxi driver may be a college educated professional who had to settle for a nonprofessional job to support his family. Additionally, it is important to be aware that less educated immigrants working in menial jobs such as agriculture are a select group from that county and not representative of all people from that country. In many cases, the more highly educated and affluent are not motivated to leave their country. Thus it would be inaccurate to make assumptions about an entire population based upon a small biased sample of who immigrates to the United States.

Academic Achievement of Children. Similar to the use of CDCs' education and occupation to adjust IQ, another consideration is their children's academic achievement or occupation. This assumption is based on the moderately high correlation between the IQ of parents and children (.48; Jencks et al., 1972). Thus, it would be assumed that a Mexican farmer with a low level of education whose daughter is a college graduate from UCLA and works as an engineer would have a higher level of intelligence than fellow immigrants whose children have high school education or less and work in the service sector.

Finally, because communication significantly affects the ability to assimilate into a new society and obtain gainful employment, immigrants to the United States should possess and inherent desire and motivation to learn English (Artiola i Fortuny, 2008). Given this assumption, English skills could be a consideration when estimating intellectual functioning because second language acquisition is highly correlated with proficiency in the original language and level of formal education (Butler & Hakuta, 2004). This association, however, should be interpreted with caution because there are many factors in learning a second language, and English skill should always be interpreted within the context of the individual's culture. Generally, the younger the age of immigration and the longer the duration spent in one's new country, the better the English skills (Veltman, 1988). Acculturation is another important factor because people living and working in an ethnic enclave would have less opportunity and need to speak English, and thus would be less proficient (Artiola i Fortuny, 2008).

Exposure to English in a person's country of origin should be considered when evaluating for English proficiency because stronger English skills would be assumed in countries such as Singapore, where English is one of the national languages, or the Philippines, where school is taught in English from a young age. Relatedness of one's native language to English is another factor. For example, according to the Foreign Service Institute's (FSI; National Virtual Translation Center, 2007) rankings of ease in learning a foreign language, Spanish is classified as a Category 1 language, which is closely related to English. The FSI estimated that gaining some proficiency in Spanish would take 23 to 24 weeks, or 575 to 600 hours. By contrast, Chinese, Korean, Japanese, and Arabic are considered Category 5 languages, which are exceptionally difficult for native English speakers to learn. The institute estimates that proficiency can be attained in 88 weeks, or 2,200 hours, which is almost four times the training. Although reciprocity of difficulty in learning English is not exact, it is assumed that native speakers of related languages should have an easier time learning English than those who speak languages that are highly unrelated.

Integrating Data and Adjusting IQ. In summary, estimating IQ on Western tests by country, and then adjusting for the individual, is a more general process than methods that provide a specific score for an individual. Thus, the goal would be to derive a ballpark range in which the individual would likely function in comparison to peers or would likely score on Western IQ tests. This estimate can guide strategies for test selection and also provide a context for interpreting test performance, which is discussed in subsequent Chapters 6 and 9, respectively. There is no specific formula for deriving this ballpark estimate. The following is a sample of how a clinician might use contextualized data for conceptualizing a client's premorbid functioning.

Dia is a 65-year-old married Hmong man who immigrated to the United States in 1976. He was referred for neuropsychological testing secondary to right hemispheric cerebral vascular accident. Dia's father was a shaman, and his mother was an herbalist. He has a sixth-grade education from the U.S. Agency for International Development school in rural Laos. Dia is multilingual, speaking Hmong, Lao, some French, and English. He is able to read Lao and English. Dia served in General Vang Pao's Secret Army and thus was among the first wave who immigrated to the United States. He settled in Minnesota, and his family arrived later for reunification. Dia worked as a social services worker in a Hmong church, where his primary duties were to assist other Hmong in the immigration process. Dia's wife, Kiab, works in a factory. They have four sons—Keej, Huaj, Zaj, and Kub—all of whom are college educated; additionally, Keej earned a doctorate in sociology and Huaj earned an MBA.

All indicators strongly suggest that Dia's intelligence is high among his peers. His parents held high positions in a predominantly agricultural society. His level of education is strong for Hmong, as most government schools were located in the cities and very limited in high land areas were Hmong lived. Dia is literate and able to read both Lao and English, whereas many Hmong-populated provinces in the 1970s reported a 99% illiteracy rate (Duffy, Harmon, Ranard, Thao, & Yang, 2004). Dia held a professional job in the United States, whereas most contemporary first-generation Hmong work in agriculture or other unskilled jobs. All of his children are educated, and two hold advanced degrees. In comparison, although 70.1% of Hmong aged 18 to 21 attend college, only 2.6% of all Hmong 25 years and older have master's degrees or higher (Xiong, 2013). Given the estimated IQ for Laotians on Western tests was 89 (Lynn & Vanhanen, 2006), it would appear that Dia would likely score at least a standard deviation higher than the average Laotian, which would conservatively place him in the high average range. Although Dia is literate in English, because it is his third or fourth language, the accuracy of word recognition reading tests to estimate specific IQ is questionable but could be attempted, keeping in mind that this would likely be a low estimate.

PUTTING IQ ESTIMATES OF CDCs INTO CONTEXT

Given that IQ estimates on Western tests for CDCs from low-resource countries are frequently lower than Western countries, this strategy can be perceived as a polemic issue. The contentiousness is fueled by Hernstein and Murray (1994), who argued that IQ is genetically determined and thus not subject to change, and that some races are inferior. However, it is argued that the conclusions of the authors are erroneous, as they are based on a narrow conception of intelligence which is assumed to be accurately measured across cultures by Western tests. In addition, subsequent research has refuted many of the author's claims.

As discussed in Chapter 4, the conceptualization of what is considered intelligent behavior differs across cultures (M. Cole, Gay, Glick, & Sharp, 1971; Grigorenko et al., 2004; Sternberg, 2004; Sternberg et al., 2001), and numerous biases can exist when administering Western tests to CDCs (Ardila, 2007; Greenfield, 1997; Ostrosky-Solís, 2007). Even within Western society, recent theorists have argued for multiple intelligences that are not measured by a traditional IQ test (Gardner, 1993) and emotional intelligences (Salovey & Mayer, 1990) that can predict success in relationships (Mayer, Salovey, & Caruso, 2008). Because of these factors, estimates of scores have been qualified by the descriptor "on Western tests," and given the multiple factors affecting CDCs' performances, an IQ score may be more accurately perceived as an adjustment measure.

Recent genetic studies indicate that intelligence is 50% heritable; thus, the environment or environment × genetic interactions also account for half of the variance (Plomin, DeFries, Knopik, & Neiderhiser, 2013). Moreover, a growing literature from different sources reports that intelligence is malleable. Recent studies have demonstrated g-fluid intelligence, as measured by tests such as Raven's Progressive Matrices, can significantly improve after short-term training in working memory (Jaeggi, Buschkuehl, Jonides, & Perrig, 2008) and executive control (Stephenson & Halpern, 2013).

Enriched environments can also significantly improve intelligence. van IJzendoorn, Juffer, and Poelhuis (2005) found that children of low socio-economic status demonstrated IQ gains of 12 to 18 points after adoption into middle-class families, and Garber (1988) reported improvements of 10 points through prekindergarten intervention programs in combination with placement in average-achieving or above-average-achieving elementary schools.

Perhaps the strongest evidence for the long-term impact of environment on intelligence are data supporting the previously mentioned Flynn Effect— that is, significantly increased IQ scores within 30 countries that have experienced rapid development in just a few decades (Flynn, 2007). Increases in IQ are typically demonstrated in fluid intelligence and associated with differential patterns of improvements depending on a country's industrialization history. For nations that modernized before the 20th century, IQ gains average about 3 points per decade, whereas countries modernizing in the mid- or late 20th century, such as Kenya (8 points), have demonstrated more significant gains. In contrast, some countries that began modernization in the 19th century, such as Norway, Britain, and Sweden, have reached an asymptote, with negative gains during the past 2 decades. An implication is that some developing nations may close the gap in academic achievement by 2050, while countries that do not modernize will continue to lag behind (Flynn, 2013).

Flynn (2013) attributed the robust rise in IQ scores over time to a multiplicity of factors associated with modernization, including increased formal educational opportunities for preschoolers, higher numbers of college-educated adults, urbanization, development of a visual culture, more creative work roles, more leisure, better nutrition, and smaller family sizes. The United States is a good example of how increases in educational level are associated with rising national intelligence. In 1917, when the median educational level in the United States was less than 6 years, U.S. IQ scores matched the lowest IQs in the developing world today. However, steady increases in median educational levels from high school by midcentury to today's median of some college mirror steady increases in IQ scores that are currently equivalent to the highest achieving industrialized nations (Flynn, 2013).

These studies from different literatures put intelligence into perspective. Intelligence is malleable; practice, enriched environments, and a confluence of societal factors, such as higher levels of formal education and urbanization, affect scores. Lower IQ scores among many CDCs are heavily influenced by a lack of exposure to enriched environments, including formal education. Thus, estimated IQ scores on Western tests for CDCs can be viewed as an adjustment for culture and educational experiences.

6

STRATEGIES FOR TEST SELECTION AND DATA COLLECTION

According to this Ichi school, you can win with a long weapon, and yet you can also win with a short weapon. In short, the Way of the Ichi school is the spirit of winning, whatever the weapon and whatever its size.
—Musashi Miyamoto

Once a clinician builds the context for understanding and approaching a culturally different client (CDC), the next preparatory task is to plan a strategy for test selection and data collection. This step is covered in the next two chapters. First, this chapter opens with a discussion of psychometric considerations for test selection, which includes test validity, reliability, measurement bias, equivalency, and accessibility. These principles are applied to test selection for CDCs in the next section on practical consideration, which also covers issues with test translation. The chapter closes with a discussion of strategies for data collection. This information will set the stage for the next chapter, which is a review of neuropsychological tests with cross-cultural validity.

http://dx.doi.org/10.1037/15958-007
Conducting a Culturally Informed Neuropsychological Evaluation, by D. Fujii
Copyright © 2017 by the American Psychological Association. All rights reserved.

PSYCHOMETRIC CONSIDERATIONS FOR TEST SELECTION

The first step in judicious test selection is evaluating the psychometric properties of the tests chosen to measure characteristics in CDCs, including validity, reliability, and fairness. *Validity* is the extent to which evidence and theory support the interpretation of test scores for specified uses of the test (American Educational Research Association, American Psychological Association, & National Council on Measurement in Education [AERA, APA, & NCME], 2014). It is developed by identifying the construct the test is designed to measure, proposing specific interpretations of test scores, and providing a rationale for the proposed interpretations. Evidence is then collected and evaluated for consistency with the proposed interpretations. Types of evidence include expert opinion when determining test items; analysis of response processes; consistency of internal structure with the test construct; correlation to other variables, which includes convergent and discriminant evidence; and prediction of criterion variables, either currently (concurrent) or at a later time (predictive). Common threats to construct measurement include *construct underrepresentation*, which occurs when a test fails to capture crucial elements of the construct, and *construct irrelevance*, which is the extent that test scores are affected by processes extraneous to the test's intended purpose (AERA, APA, & NCME, 2014).

Reliability/precision is defined as the consistency of scores across replications of a testing procedure (AERA, APA, & NCME, 2014). Score consistency can be determined by measuring performances on alternate forms of tests, test–retest scores, consistency between different raters, or the internal consistency of test items. Test scores consist of a test taker's actual score plus error, the latter captured in the test's standard error of measurement. Reliability/precision of a test can significantly affect test validity because inconsistent scoring limits the potential for accurate predictions, strength of diagnostic evidence, and evidence-based decision making (AERA, APA, & NCME, 2014).

As mentioned in the Introduction, neuropsychological testing is a Western technology, with the majority of measurements developed in the United States and other Western countries. Historically, tests were primarily standardized and normed on predominantly middle-class White samples. Thus, evaluating for potential measurement biases, test equivalency, and the interface of specific CDC characteristics with characteristics of the test are important considerations concerning fairness when applying these technologies to CDCs (AERA, APA, & NCME, 2014).

Measurement biases are test characteristics not related to the construct being measured that can place subgroups of test takers at a disadvantage.

Content bias occurs when test content favors test takers from one subgroup over others. For example, Australian subjects were found to perform worse when asked to recall a shopping list of typical American items versus typical Australian items (Y. Y. Lim et al., 2009). *Construct bias* occurs when the construct a test is measuring is not identical across cultures—for example, conceptions of intelligence in Kenyan villagers and the United States, as I discussed in Chapter 5 (Sternberg et al., 2001). Biases can occur at the item or test levels. *Differential item functioning* entails a disadvantage of correctly answering an item between members of different subgroups despite equivalency in abilities. This bias is illustrated on the Mini-Mental State Examination "no ifs, ands, or buts" item in which 67% of nondemented elderly Japanese American men failed in comparison to 24% of predominantly White elderly persons (Jones & Gallo, 2002; Valcour, Masaki, & Blanchette, 2002). *Differential test functioning* describes a similar disadvantage at the test level. This phenomenon was demonstrated between American and Russian subjects matched for age, education, and neuropsychological functioning on timed tests of Color Trails and Category Fluency. The poorer performances of Russian subjects were attributed to less experience with timed tests and not valuing Western notions that "faster is better" (Agranovich & Puente, 2007; see also Chapter 4). Finally, *predictive bias* occurs when differences exist between subgroups in the association of test scores and other variables. For example, Kaya et al. (2014) reported lower Montreal Cognitive Assessment (MoCA) cutoff scores for dementia and mild cognitive impairment in a Turkish sample compared with the North American validation studies.

An essential issue for using a test across cultures is test *equivalency*, which is the comparability of a construct across individuals or subgroups of test takers. For a test to transcend cultural groups, it is important that it measures the same or similar abilities in each group.

According to Pedraza and Mungas (2008), equivalency can be established by selecting tests that are validated and normed for each individual group using the test. However, scores should only be interpreted within the context of the group from which the norms were derived and are not necessarily comparable across groups. In this regard, for many standard neuropsychological tests, specific cultural norms or adjustments would be required to ensure equivalency when applied to CDCs.

Although the psychometric properties of a test is a basic consideration in selection, just as important is how specific CDC characteristics interface with characteristics of the test (AERA, APA, & NCME, 2014). *Accessibility* is the ability to demonstrate one's knowledge of the construct being measured. For CDCs, this issue typically involves use of interpreters (see Chapter 4) as well as test translations. Clinicians also need to consider whether the CDC has had the opportunity to learn the content and skills measured by the test. A test would not be valid for a CDC if the construct is not something that she or he had an opportunity to develop.

PRACTICAL CONSIDERATIONS FOR TEST SELECTION

When planning an assessment, clinicians should first search for validated tests with appropriate norms, and when required, test translations in the CDC's language that meet International Test Commission (ITC) standards (ITC, 2010). A Google Scholar search with *country of origin* and *neuropsychology* as search words is recommended as an initial literature search strategy. When searching, clinicians should keep in mind that many validation studies examining illnesses such as schizophrenia or dementia have normative data for controls. Contacting members of the International Neuropsychological Society (http://www.ilc-ins.org) for test recommendations is another strategy, and there are also an International Liaison Committee and Cross Cultural E-Mail Discussion Group and a referral database. It should be stressed that when asking for assistance, clinicians should adhere to copyright laws, for example, by not copying copyrighted materials. Other resources include *The Neuropsychology of Asian Americans* (Fujii, 2011) for Asian Americans and the Hispanic Neuropsychological Society website for Latinos (http://hnps.org).

When evaluating the psychometric properties of tests, the following are important considerations to determine the strength of evidence for cross-cultural validity: study design, sampling procedures, demographics, sample sizes, processes for translation and cultural adaptations of tests, selection of and adequacy of outcome measures, and adequacy of statistical analysis. To ensure fairness in testing, clinicians should keep in mind that cultural matching is only one consideration because there is considerable variability within a given ethnic group. It is actually more important to consider individual characteristics of the CDC and how his or her characteristics interact with the contextual aspects of the testing situation. Pertinent issues include quality and quantity of education, acculturation or similarity of the CDC's personal characteristics to mainstream Western culture, and English proficiency. For example, for most African Americans who were born and raised in the United States, selecting common English-based Western tests would be appropriate. However, for diagnostic purposes, scores should be interpreted using appropriate normative corrections, such as those provided in the Revised Comprehensive Norms for an Expanded Halstead–Reitan Battery: (HRB) Demographically Adjusted Neuropsychological Norms for African

American and Caucasian Adults (Heaton, Miller, Taylor, & Grant, 2004) or the Mayo Older African American Norms (MOANS) studies (Pedraza et al., 2005). Special norms however may be inappropriate for Africans from Kenya or Somalia. Somalis may also require test translations, and those with low educational level may not have experienced opportunities for the learning skills required for many common neuropsychological tests, which would be important considerations for test selection.

Hispanics are a highly heterogeneous group. The 2010 U.S. Census reported 20 separate Hispanic ethnicities in the United States, with the majority of the population of Mexican heritage (54%; Ennis, Ríos-Vargas, & Albert, 2011). Given that the majority of research studies on Hispanics are with Mexican Americans, approximately 46% of Hispanic Americans would not match this demographic (G. D. Salazar, Garcia, & Puente, 2007). Hispanics also differ considerably in literacy, education, and acculturation (Ardila & Rosselli, 2007), with 35.6% being foreign born and 73.9% speaking Spanish at home (U.S. Census Bureau, n.d.-a). On the basis of individual characteristics, when evaluating Hispanics, clinicians would have to determine whether to test a client in English, Spanish, or both languages (Ponton & Corona-LoMonaco, 2007). In addition, special test considerations would be required for clients with low educational levels or who are illiterate (Ardila & Rosselli, 2007).

Similar to Hispanics, Asian Americans are a highly heterogeneous group, and thus test selection would also be contingent on individual characteristics. The 2010 U.S. Census identified 24 separate Asian American ethnic categories (Hoeffel, Rastogi, Kim, & Hasan, 2012). With few exceptions, most Asian groups not only have different cultures but speak different languages, and thus translated tests or normative data for one Asian ethnicity would not be appropriate for any other (Fujii, 2011). Even within an ethnic group, individual characteristics would dictate appropriate test selection. For highly acculturated and educated second-generation or higher Korean Americans, common neuropsychological tests with Western norms may be the most appropriate. However, for first-generation Korean Americans who do not speak English well, translated tests would be required.

If validation studies do not exist or are not available, an alternative strategy would be to search for validated tests from countries or cultures that are similar to the CDC. For example, countries could be matched on characteristics that have been shown to correlate highly with IQ such as geographic proximity ($r = .87$, Gelade, 2008), GDP ($r = .57–.77$, R. Lynn & Vanhanen, 2002), total years of education ($r = .77–.81$, Meisenberg, 2009, 2012), or scores on standardized achievement tests ($r = .81–.88$; R. Lynn & Vanhanen, 2002, 2006). Another strategy would be to select tests that have demonstrated validity across many cultures or countries and then use estimated IQs for that country (see Table 5.2) or estimates of regional IQs (see Table 5.3) as a mean to adjustment for norms.

When using alternative strategies for test selection, it is important to consider the validity generalization of a test, which is the degree to which a test's criterion validity evidence can be generalized to new situations without further study (AERA, APA, & NCME, 2014). *Validity generalization* is a function of the accumulated research of the test. When evaluating for validity generalization, clinicians should review prior studies and evaluate for similarities in (a) measurement of predictor constructs, (b) criterion measures, (c) characteristics of the test takers, and (d) time period when the study was conducted. Carefully controlled studies with good sample size and similar situations would provide strong evidence for the validity of generalizing test usage for a given CDC. Meta-analysis with large effect sizes in similar situations would also provide evidence for generalization.

TRANSLATING TESTS

Although validated and translated tests may be available, procuring them often entails challenges. Many studies report descriptions of translation procedures and findings, and a percentage of these have norms, but few include translations in the article. It can be difficult to contact authors or procure translations. Commercial tests such as Wechsler scales are available in different languages but are costly, and clinicians may not want to purchase a test for a one-time evaluation. Thus, despite availability of validated tests with norms, there is a good chance that clinicians will have to translate tests as an accommodation to facilitate fairness in testing and increase accessibility for the CDC. This is a controversial issue because of the importance of test validity in obtaining accurate information and the potential harmful ramifications of clinical decision making based on inaccurate data, particularly for ethnic minority clients. Indeed, numerous APA (2003, 2010) guidelines, as well as the AACN guidelines (Heilbronner et al., 2009), underscore the ethical responsibility of the clinician for ensuring test fairness and equivalence and construct validity.

To ensure cross-cultural fairness in testing, the ITC (2010) established guidelines for test development and adaptation of psychological tests. Guidelines for test adaptation can be distilled into several recommendations: (a) behavioral constructs should be present in the cultures where the test was developed and for which it was adapted; (b) adaptation process addresses linguistic and culture differences in directions, rubrics, administration procedures, and test materials, including individual items; and (c) there should be evidence for equivalence including statistical analysis, and nonequivalent items should not be used.

Despite the rigor involved in adapting psychological tests, it is argued that with certain clients and tests, clinicians can engage in a process to translate tests that could meet or approach ITC standards. There are two considerations for determining which tests are appropriate for translation. First, each ITC issue can be addressed by selecting tests that have been adapted and validated in the client's culture of origin. For example, using Block Design or Matrix Reasoning with a client who emigrated from France would be appropriate because the Wechsler Adult Intelligence Scale has been validated in that country. Although less optimal, clinicians may argue for using tests that have adequate validity generalization, for example, tests validated from countries in close proximity and with similar economies, quantity and quality of education, scores on standardized academic achievement tests, and experiences.

Second, clinicians should focus on tests that require only translation for instructions, with responses consisting of performing a task or selecting from multiple choices of nonverbal material. Tests requiring translation of verbal stimuli and ratings for quality of verbal explanations, such as vocabulary, should be avoided because of the difficulty in establishing item equivalency (Casas et al., 2012). Verbal tests that require regurgitation of responses, such as list learning or tallying responses (e.g., word fluency) may be appropriate but would require more caution to ensure equivalency.

Translation of test instructions should only be attempted if original translations of existing validated tests cannot be obtained. Translations should follow established guidelines. For example, Hambleton and Patsula (1999), cited as a source by the ITC, recommended that translations involve more than one translator with knowledge of culture and construct. An initial translation can be reviewed and revised by a second translator who can provide input about accuracy of the translation, clarity and fluency of the sentences, and level of difficulty of the words. Initial translations can be obtained through colleagues or Internet translation sites, such as Google translate (http://translate.google.com). When using the latter, the clinician should use caution because the program works best for related languages with similar grammatical structures, such as English and French. Translations can be awkward when languages are highly different, such as English and Japanese. Accuracy of Google translations can be assessed by performing a forward and backward translation. Once an initial translation is obtained, the clinician can seek input from a second translator, such as the interpreter or INS colleague for review and revision. Translation should be made available to interpreters before the evaluation so she or he can become familiar with the material before the testing session. If possible, translations can be piloted.

STRATEGIES FOR DATA COLLECTION

The next step in preparing for a cross-cultural neuropsychological evaluation is to determine a preliminary strategy for collecting data to address the goals for the evaluation. The following are strategies recommended in the AACN (2007) Practice Guidelines and by Gasquoine (2009):

- direct comparison with a group of demographically similar peers,
- individual comparison method,
- criterion-referenced testing,
- relevant supplementary information about the client's adaptive functioning within his or her "real-world" community, and
- charting behavioral changes over time.

Neuropsychological Testing–Based Strategies

Direct Comparison With Demographically Similar Peers

Administering neuropsychological tests in the CDC's most proficient language in which norms of demographically similar peers are available is the most powerful type of information. This method provides quantifiable data that allow for more sensitivity for cognitive changes as well as for strengths and weaknesses in specific cognitive domains. The versatility of the data allows for pattern analysis of cognition, which can be matched with specific neurological disorders, provides more accurate measurements needed for diagnosis in which specific metrics are required (e.g., intellectual disabilities), and identifies cognitive factors associated with functional impairments that can be used for recommendations for remediation. Limitations or disadvantages of this strategy include difficulty obtaining data for equivalent comparison group and difficulty obtaining tests in different languages when available.

This strategy would be appropriate for any CDC for whom there are racial or ethnic norms for specific tests. Common examples for the U.S. population include interpreting a broad range of tests using demographically corrected African American norms when evaluating for functional decline (Heaton et al., 2004), or administering the NEUROPSI (Ostrosky-Solís, Ardila, & Rosselli, 1997) when evaluating first-generation Mexican Americans. Normative data may also be available for CDCs immigrating from many European countries or resource-rich Asian countries such as China, Japan, and South Korea. Even if norms are available for a country, clinicians need to be cautious for appropriateness of application. For example, Asian Indian norms obtained from Kannad-speaking clients from a metropolitan area such as Bangalore may not apply to Telugu-speaking Bhil in rural Madhya Pradesh. It is also important to be aware of generational effects because there can be a significant increase in IQ per decade for developing countries (Flynn, 2013); thus, norms from a 1970 study may not apply to today's young adults.

Individual Comparison Method

The individual comparison method uses an estimate of a client's pre-morbid intellectual abilities as a benchmark to compare current performances on neuropsychological tests (Gasquoine, 2009). It is similar to the strategy proposed, by Manly, Jacobs, Touradji, Small, and Stern (2002), of adjusting for quality of education when interpreting test scores of African Americans in that norms are tailored toward the individual versus a client's scores compared directly against a group sample. As noted in Chapter 5, intelligence has been shown to be highly predictive of performance on a broad range of neuropsychological tests, particularly for person scoring below average on IQ tests. For example, Diaz-Asper, Schretlen, and Pearlson (2004) compared neuropsychological tests scores of persons with above average (AA), average (A), and below average (BA) IQs. The researchers found that the AA group performed significantly better than the A group on 19 of 28 measures, whereas the A group performed significantly higher than the BA group on 25 of 28 tests. Lezak, Howieson, Bigler, and Tranel (2012) argued that this approach is the method of choice when scores are normally distributed across a population.

This method has several advantages over the previous approach of comparing test scores to demographically similar peers. It allows for more flexibility in using different tests that lack norms for equivalent groups because the individual's scores are compared with his or her own. Theoretically, it is more accurate when an individual's scores are at the high or low end of the normal distribution (Gasquoine, 2009). Hence, this method would be highly useful for CDCs. Support for this contention comes from a study with an intact Latino sample in which adjustments using this method resulted in two thirds fewer false-positives across nine neuropsychological measures (Gasquoine, Croyle, Cavazos-Gonzalez, & Sandoval, 2007).

The approach is versatile and can be used with both translated and validated tests, and Western tests. When using tests that are translated and validated within a client's country of origin, the client's premorbid functioning is estimated in comparison with peers within his or her country. This estimate is then compared with demographics of the normative sample. If higher, then the client's premorbid abilities would be set higher than the mean, and lower than the mean if the estimate is lower. For example, in the Yepthomi et al. (2006) validation study of Color Trails 1 in southern India, the control sample consisted of 30 adults with the following demographics: 87% male, 87% employed as physical laborers or drivers, mean age 34 ($SD = 10.4$), and

9.7 ($SD = 4.4$) years of education. The mean Color Trails 1 score was 59.8 seconds ($SD = 20.5$). Thus, if the client is 36 years old with a college education, his time score would be estimated to be lower than the mean of 59.8 seconds, possibly nearing a standard deviation depending on the kurtosis of the distribution. By contrast, if the client completed 2 years of education, his time score would be estimated to be much higher than the mean.

Despite its flexibility, this method has several significant weaknesses. First, there is no standard or validated method to estimate premorbid IQ, particularly with CDCs (Gasquoine, 2009). Second, the method does not control for nor take into account differential predictive ability of IQ on neuropsychological test performances (this issue is elaborated on in Chapter 9 on test interpretation). Finally, for low-resource countries in which individuals score around the borderline range on Western IQ tests, deficits would be difficult to determine because of floor effects.

This approach would be appropriate for culturally different immigrants from most countries where norms are not available if it is determined that Western tests can provide valid data for that population. It would also be useful for second-generation CDCs living in the United States, particularly if English is not the primary language spoken at home. The individual comparison approach would not be appropriate for culturally different immigrants who are illiterate, have low education, or come from low-resource countries where IQ estimates would be in the borderline or impaired ranges.

Criterion-Referenced Testing

For many CDCs, Western tests hold questionable validity. Characteristics such as English as a second language, limited education and illiteracy, low acculturation, differences in everyday experiences, or differences in conception of intelligence can significantly affect test performances on Western tests (Greenfield, 1997). In addition, because of floor effects, use of Western norms for detecting deficits may be particularly problematic for clients who originate from countries associated with very low mean scores on Western IQ tests. For these clients, Western tests can still provide valid information if interpreted within a criterion-referenced strategy (Glaser, 1963). In this interpretive strategy, test scores above a cutoff point are associated with a mastery of, or a minimum skill level for, that domain, because despite potential threats to validity, the client was still able to achieve a minimal skill level. Thus, a client scoring solidly in the low average range for memory would be assumed to rule out dementia because basic skills exceed the impaired level. The score would not, however, inform how the client's scores compares with others as a normative approach would, because less could be assumed about the absolute skill level of the client given the unknown impact of language or educational factors.

The major advantage of using a criterion-referenced strategy is the potential to rule out deficits in specific domains with tests that are not validated for the client's culture. On the flip side, the major limitation of the strategy is that it may be difficult to interpret borderline or impaired performances because all scores are subject to biases. Thus, a clinician would not know whether an impaired-level performance for a client for whom English is a second language scored poorly because of poor unfamiliarity with the test materials or because his or her memory is impaired.

Select criterion-referenced testing would be appropriate for CDCs where IQ estimates fall within the borderline level or lower, those with a low educational level, or those who are illiterate. This manner of interpretation could be useful for all CDCs for whom English is a second language, particularly those who do not have the cognitive academic language proficiency and fluency necessary to perform in test-taking situations.

Relevant Supplementary Information About a Client's Adaptive Functioning Within His or Her "Real-World" Community

The next data collection strategy entails estimating current cognitive functioning based on functional abilities. An example would be that a person who lives independently, supports herself with a competitive work position, is capable of handling her own finances, and has a good driving record would likely not meet criteria for an intellectual disability. Although lacking the precision of formal cognitive testing, per diagnostic criteria, this strategy can provide data to differentiate between levels of functional impairment associated with minor and major neurocognitive disorders. Data can be procured through interviews or through formal testing. The advantage of this approach is the ability to estimate functioning without test data. Disadvantages include the lack of precision in measuring deficits, difficulty in determining causes for deficits, need for an informant who can provide accurate data, and difficulty in determining accuracy of data.

Although this method can be used as corroborative evidence for diagnosis and hypothesis generation for all CDCs, it could be the primary strategy if there are no translated tests for a CDC who does not speak or has poor command of English, neuropsychological testing is deemed inappropriate, or the CDC is unmotivated for testing, possibly because of poor rapport or discomfort with the testing situation.

Charting of Behavioral Changes Over Time

In this strategy, cognitive decline is determined by comparing previous functioning with current abilities. Data are collected through interviews with the client or collateral resource or records documenting events that would be associated with a decline, such as early retirement or unexpected firing for a person suspected to have major neurocognitive disorder with frontotemporal etiology. Similar to the previous strategy, data are less precise than cognitive testing and can be procured through interviews or formal testing. The advantages and disadvantages of this approach, and appropriate populations, are the same as for obtaining information about the client's adaptive functioning within his or her environment. Both strategies should be used in tandem.

SELECTING A STRATEGY FOR DATA COLLECTION

Criteria for differential diagnostic categories and legal determinations, in combination with criteria for common neurological and psychological disorders for the client's cultural group, will determine the information needed to answer the referral question. The availability of normed, validated, and, when required, translated tests, together with cultural considerations such as educational opportunities will determine data collection strategies.

Fujii, Umetsu, Schwartz, and Hostetter (2002) recommended a multi-method approach when evaluating CDCs, thereby using several of the aforementioned strategies that are applicable to a case. For example, if neuropsychological testing is appropriate for a CDC, the individual comparison method, criterion-referenced testing, and direct comparison strategies for interpreting scores can all be used and compared, the latter if normative data are available. When collecting historical data, information concerning adaptive functioning and behavioral changes over time can also be used for interpretation. In addition, neuroimaging data, psychiatric symptoms, and behaviors consistent with neurobehavioral syndromes (e.g., impulsivity, social inappropriateness, and left-sided weakness for right hemisphere stroke) are also important sources of data.

The following three cases illustrate how specific data collection strategies would be appropriate for different clients of the same ethnic background.

Ahmed is a 19-year-old, second-generation Somali American attending Minnesota State University at Moorhead. He was referred for neuropsychological testing to evaluate for attention-deficit/hyperactivity disorder. Ahmed is bilingual and fluent in English. Testing with standard neuropsychological tests interpreted with both the direct comparison and individual comparison approaches would be appropriate.

Mohammed is a 51-year-old manager who is one of the first wave of immigrants from Somalia that arrived in 1992. He grew up in Mogadishu and earned an associate's degree from one of the universities. English is Mohammed's second language. Mohammed was recently diagnosed with systemic lupus erythematosus after reporting fatigue, headaches, and problems in memory and attention. He was referred for a neuropsychological evaluation administered in both Somali and English. Data were interpreted using the individual comparison approach.

Ali is a 68-year-old Somali woman who immigrated to the United States in 2009 for family reunification. Ali is illiterate with 2 years of formal education. She was taken to a clinic by family members after she left the stove on, which almost caused a kitchen fire. Ali was referred to a neuropsychologist to assess for dementia. The Consortium to Establish a Registry for Alzheimer's Disease Neuropsychological Battery (CERAD) was administered using a criterion approach for interpretation of scores. The family was also interviewed for information about adaptive functioning and behavioral changes over time.

7

A MINI-COMPENDIUM OF NEUROPSYCHOLOGICAL TESTS WITH CROSS-CULTURAL VALIDITY

But in any case, I did poorly on the tests and so, in the first three years of school, I had teachers who thought I was stupid and when people think you're stupid, they have low expectations for you.

—Robert Sternberg

This chapter offers a mini-compendium of tests that have been validated with different cultures and countries. A brief description of each test is followed by validation studies for different cultures and countries and the advantages and disadvantages of using this test. Describing specific psychometric properties for each culture is beyond the scope of this chapter, and clinicians will have to compare studies according to the specifics of the culturally different client (CDC) to make a judicious selection. Similarly, this mini-compendium does not provide a comprehensive listing of tests by ethnicity or race, for example, a Hispanic compendium (Casals-Coll et al., 2013; Guàrdia-Olmos, Peró-Cebollero, Rivera, & Arango-Lasprilla, 2015; Ostrosky-Solís, Ardila, & Rosselli, 1997; Pena-Casanova et al., 2009; Wechsler, 2004, 2002; Woodcock & Munoz-Sandoval, 2005).

Rather, the focus is on describing tests that have the most translations or validation studies across cultures to maximize clinicians' awareness of specific resources and also on exploring validity generalization of tests for

http://dx.doi.org/10.1037/15958-008
Conducting a Culturally Informed Neuropsychological Evaluation, by D. Fujii

cultures in which no tests have been validated. Test sections are organized by data-collection strategies. First, tests for performance-based data collection strategies are described, followed by tests associated with functional abilities and the client's historical progression of functional abilities. The chapter closes with illustrative examples for test selection.

INTELLIGENCE TESTS

Raven's Progressive Matrices

Although it is not widely used in the United States, the intelligence test with by far the most cross-cultural research is Raven's Progressive Matrices (RPM; Raven, Raven, & Court 2003), which has more than 1,500 published studies (McCallum, Bracken, & Wasserman, 2000), from more than 81 countries (see R. Lynn & Vanhanen, 2006, for a list of references), to support its use. The Standard Progressive Matrices contains five sets of 12 items in which the test taker must select a missing piece of a visual pattern from six choices. The puzzles start off being relatively easy, with the first set consisting of simple visual matching. The puzzles become progressively more difficult and reasoning oriented. Strengths of the test include nonverbal nature, which controls for language effects and the need for familiarity with dominant culture; untimed instructions, which do not penalize cultures in which intelligence is not equated with speed; and a reduced motor component, which controls for this potential confound (Lezak, Howieson, Bigler, & Tranel, 2012). Given nonverbal test items, translations would entail explaining test requirements and not actual content. Still, requirements could prove challenging for CDCs with more dissimilar educational and general experiences. Weaknesses of the RPM include poor discriminatory ability to localize lesions and susceptibility to visual field lesions. As with all direct comparison tests, the clinician should review normative validation studies to ensure comparability of the sample and the need to adjust scores for the Flynn effect of increases in performances across time in a given culture (Flynn, 2013; see also Chapter 5, this volume). Hiscock, Inch, and Gleason (2002) recommended adding 6 points per decade from when a normative study was conducted, whereas Flynn (2013) argued that adjustments can vary significantly depending on the industrial development of the country (Flynn, 2013).

Wechsler Intelligence Scales

The Wechsler Intelligence Scales (WIS) have long been considered the gold standard for intelligence tests in the United States and other Western countries. Originally developed in 1955, the test has evolved into several versions for children, adolescents, and adults. The test provides a general estimate of overall intelligence as well as indices for verbal comprehension, perceptual organization, working memory and processing speed. Subscales measuring multiple cognitive domains allow for pattern analysis of cognitive strengths and weaknesses.

Wechsler Intelligence Tests have been translated, adapted, and normed in many languages. For example, versions of the Wechsler Intelligence Scales for Children have been formally developed for use in India (Wechsler, 2014), Spain (Wechsler, 2004), Portuguese (Brazil; Wechsler, 2002), the Netherlands and Flemish-speaking Belgium (Schittekatte, Kort, Resing, Vermeir, & Verhaeghe, 2003), France and Belgium (Grégoire, 2003), Germany (Tewes, 2003), Austria and Switzerland (Rossman & Schallberger, 2003), Sweden (Sonnander & Ramund, 2003), Lithuania (Gintiliene & Girdzijauskiene, 2003), Slovenia (Boben & Bucik, 2003), Greece (Georgas, Paraskevopoulos, Besevegis, Giannitsas, & Mylonas, 2003), Japan (Ueno & Nakatani, 2003), South Korea (Kwak, 2003), Taiwan (H. Y. Chen et al., 2003), Canada (Saklofske, 2003), United Kingdom (McKeown, 2003), and Vietnam (Dang, Weiss, Pollack, & Nguyen, 2012), with a partial translation for Pakistan (Ambreen & Kamal, 2011). Versions of the Wechsler Adult Intelligence Scales (WAIS) have been developed for Australian and New Zealand (Wechsler, 2008b), the United Kingdom (Wechsler, 1998), Egypt (Melika, 1987), Finland (Wechsler, 2005), France (Wechsler, 2000), Spain (TEA, 1999), Italy (Orsini & Laicardi, 2003), China (Y. H. Chen & Chen, 2002), Japan (Fujita, Maekawa, Ohroku, & Yamanaka, 2006), Korea (Yum, Park, Oh, Kim, & Lee, 1992), Turkey (Savaşir & Şahin, 1995), and India (Wechsler, 2013).

Where formally developed, versions of the WIS have been based on large representative standardization samples and demonstrate strong psychometric properties. There are also many translated versions without normative data (e.g., Thailand; Ratanadilok, 2011). Despite availability, translated versions and norms may be difficult to obtain and thus not easily administered. However, the fact that the WIS has been validated in the aforementioned developed countries would indicate that many of the task-oriented subtests would possess some face validity when administered to clients from these and other similarly developed countries if administered with translations for instructions and appropriate norms for interpretation. Cross-cultural validity would be less likely for verbal comprehension subtests. Test bias, test fairness, and cultural equivalence of these subtests would be questionable for clients originating from developing countries where the WIS has not been translated, validated, and normed, particularly cultures that are highly dissimilar to the West in terms of experiences, beliefs, values, and conceptions of intelligence. Further, because WIS versions and year of translations vary per country, scores may be vulnerable to the Flynn effect.

SCREENING BATTERIES

Montreal Cognitive Assessment

The Montreal Cognitive Assessment (MoCA; Nasreddine et al., 2005) is a 30-item cognitive screen that has been found to be a useful tool in screening for dementia and mild neurocognitive impairment (Julayanont, Brousseau, Chertkow, Phillips, & Nasreddine, 2014). Although developed primarily as a dementia screen for geriatric populations, the MoCA has also been found to be useful for identifying cognitive impairment in younger adult clinical populations, including individuals with substance abuse (Copersino et al., 2009), HIV (Nabha, Duong, & Timpone, 2013), and head injury (Whitney, Mossbarger, Herman, & Ibarra, 2012). The MoCA has been translated into 44 languages; these translations are easily accessed through the MoCA website (http://www.mocatest.org). Although not all have normative data, there is a growing number of normative studies with a list of references that is frequently updated on the website. Translated languages include the following (references are for norms): Arabic (Rahman, El Gaafary, & Mohamed, 2009), Afrikaans, Chinese—Beijing (Zheng et al., 2012), Chinese—Changsha and Hong Kong (Wong et al., 2009), Chinese—Taiwan (Tsai et al., 2012), Czech (Reban, 2006), Croatian (Martinic-Popovic, Šeric, & Demarin, 2006), Danish, Dutch (Thissen, van Bergen, de Jonghe, Kessels, & Dautzenberg, 2010), English—Singapore, Estonian, Filipino (Dominguez et al., 2013), Finnish, French (Nasreddine et al., 2005), German (Costa et al., 2014), Greek, Hebrew (Lifshitz, Dwolatzky, & Press, 2012), Hindi, Hungarian, Italian (Pasi, Salvadori, Poggesi, Inzitari, & Pantoni, 2013), Japanese (Narazaki et al., 2013), Korean (J. Y. Lee et al., 2008), Malayalam, Malay—Bahasa, Malay—Singapore, Norwegian, Persian (Sikaroodi, Yadegari, & Miri, 2013), Polish (Magierska, Magierski, Fendler, Kloszewska, & Sobów, 2012), Portuguese (Freitas, Simões, Alves, & Santana, 2011), Portuguese—Brazil (Memória, Yassuda, Nakano, & Forlenza, 2013), Romanian, Russian (Makeeva et al., 2012), Serbian, Sinhalese (Karunaratne, Hanwella, & de Silva, 2011), Slovak, Slovenia, Spanish—Columbia (F. Gómez, Zunzunegui, Lord, Alvarado, & García, 2013), Swedish, Thai (Deetong-on et al., 2013), Turkish (Selekler, Cangoz, & Uluc, 2010), Ukrainian, and Uyghur. Norms are also available for African Americans (Goldstein et al., 2014) and Hispanic Americans (Strutt & Scott, 2011).

Obvious strengths of the tests include number of translated languages and accessibility of translated tests and normative references, both of which are continually growing in number. The test can provide a global measure of cognitive decline with alternate forms in select languages (Costa et al., 2014). There are some norms for young adult populations. A weakness is that, being a screening tool, there are fewer discriminatory properties for specific cognitive domains, and translations vary in quality.

Consortium to Establish a Registry for Alzheimer's Disease Neuropsychological Battery

Morris et al. (1989) developed the Consortium to Establish a Registry for Alzheimer's Disease Neuropsychological Battery (CERAD) as a means of evaluating for dementia and tracking progression. It was adapted from the Alzheimer Disease Assessment Scale Cognitive subscale (ADAS-Cog; Rosen, Mohs, & Davis, 1984) and consists of the following tests: Animal Fluency, Boston Naming Test (15-item short form), Mini-Mental Status Examination, Constructional Praxis and Recall (copying four geometric designs) and Word List Memory (10 items, three trials), Recall, and Recognition (10 words + 10 distracter words). The CERAD has been translated and researched in numerous countries including Australia (Collie, Shafiq-Antonacci, Maruff, Tyler, & Currie, 1999), Bulgaria (Raycheva, Mehrabian, & Traykov, 2005), Korea (J. H. Lee et al., 2002), China—Hong Kong (K. P. Liu et al., 2011), India (Chandra et al., 1998), Japan (Larson et al., 1998), France (Demers et al., 1994), Finland (Karrasch, Sinervä, Grönholm, Rinne, & Laine, 2005), Brazil (Bertolucci et al., 2001), Nigeria (Hendrie et al., 1995), Mexico (Juarez-Cedillo et al., 2012), Germany (Thalmann et al., 2000), Greece (Paajanen et al., 2010), Ireland (Murphy, 2012), Italy (Lucca, Tettamanti, & Quadri, 2008), Poland (Paajanen et al., 2010), Jamaica (Unverzagt et al., 1999), and Russia (Glezerman & Drexler, 2001). Normative data is also available for American minority samples including African Americans (Fillenbaum, Heyman, Huber, Ganguli, & Unverzagt, 2001; Unverzagt et al., 1996), Hispanics (Fillenbaum et al., 2007), Cree Indians (Hendrie et al., 1993), Cherokee and Choctaw Indians (Whyte et al., 2005), and Japanese Americans (Beeri et al., 2006; Fillenbaum et al., 2005; McCurry et al., 2001). Norms have been collected by the 10/66 Dementia Research Group for the animal fluency and word list subtests in the following countries: Cuba, Dominican Republic, Peru, Venezuela, Mexico, India, and China (Sosa et al., 2009). Strengths of the CERAD include interpretability of established neuropsychological measures and international validation and norms. Disadvantages are inaccessibility of test translations and that norms are primarily for geriatric populations.

Repeatable Battery for the Assessment of Neuropsychological Status

The Repeatable Battery for the Assessment of Neuropsychological Status (RBANS; Randolph, 1998) is a neuropsychological screen that can be administered in 30 minutes. It was developed to evaluate cognition in young and older adults with norms ranging from 12 to 89. The battery consists of following subtests: List Learning, Story Memory, Line Orientation, Picture Naming, Semantic Fluency, Digit Span, Coding, List Recall, List Recognition, Story Recall, and Figure Recall. These can be scored individually or combined into the following domains: Immediate Memory, Visuospatial/Constructional, Language, Attention, and Delayed Memory. In addition, studies have validated embedded symptom validity measures within the test (Crighton, Wygant, Holt, & Granacher, 2015). The publisher developed translations of the test in Spanish, Italian, Danish, Norwegian, Swedish, and U.K. English. The RBANS has also been validated in Armenia (Azizian, Yeghiyan, Ishkhanyan, Manukyan, & Khandanyan, 2011), Australia (A. Green, Garrick, Sheedy, Blake, Shores, & Harper, 2008), China (Zhang et al., 2009; Zoghbi et al., 2014), Egypt (Fawzi, Hashim, & Mahmoud, 2013), Greece (Petsanis et al., 2011), Japan (Yamashima et al., 2002), Singapore (M. L. Lim et al., 2010), Spain (De la Torre et al., 2014), Sri Lanka (Paranawithana & De Zoysa, 2012), and Turkey (Kurt, Karakaya, Safaz, & Ateş, 2015). Norms have also been developed for African Americans (Andreotti & Hawkins, 2015). Strengths of the RBANS include interpretability of established neuropsychological measures, commercially available translations and validation for select languages, international validation and norms for younger adults, and embedded symptom validity measures. Disadvantages are inaccessibility of test translations and lack of cross-cultural norms for embedded symptom validity measures.

World Health Organization Cognitive Batteries

The World Health Organization (WHO) developed the Neurobehavioral Core Test Battery (NCTB; Anger et al., 1993) to assist in identifying the impact of chemical exposures on cognition across different countries. The battery consists of the following tests: (a) *Simple Reaction Time*—respondents must press a response button whenever they see a stimulus light in more than 64 trials of variable time intervals; (b) *Digit Span*—instructions are similar to WAIS subtests, with forward and backward trials terminating with two missed strings of the same length; (c) *Santa Ana*—a pegboard motor task in which the subject must lift pegs out of a hole, turn it 180 degrees, and place it back as quickly as possible within a 30-second time limit; (d) *Digit Symbol*—similar to WAIS subtest with a 90-second time limit; (e) *Benton Visual Retention (Recognition Form)*—subjects are shown a card with a geometric figure for 10 seconds and then asked to recognize the same figure from four choices presented on a second card; and (f) *Pursuit Aiming II*—subjects are required to place a dot in a 2-mm diameter circle following a back-and-forth pattern for two 60-second trials. The initial validation study was conducted on a sample of more than 2,300 male and female participants between the ages of

16 and 65 residing in 10 countries: Hungary, Poland, Austria, France, Italy, China, United States, Canada, and Nicaragua (Anger et al., 1993). Results indicated that performances on the Simple Reaction Time and Benton Visual Retention were similar across countries, whereas performances on the Santa Ana, Digit Symbol, Digit Span, and Pursuit Aiming demonstrated more variability. Scores from poorly educated male participants in Nicaragua was much lower than the other higher resource countries, and thus the battery is vulnerable to education effects.

Since its development, the NCTB has been used to study the effects of chemical exposures in numerous countries worldwide, including China (Zhou, Liang, & Christiani, 2002), Costa Rica (Wesseling et al., 2002), Egypt (Farahat et al., 2003), England (Stephens et al., 1995), France (Fallas, Fallas, Maslard, & Dally, 1992), Italy (Lucchini et al., 1995), Japan (Yokoyama et al., 1998), Korea (Y. C. Shin et al., 2007), Lebanon (Saddik, Williamson, Nuwayhid, & Black, 2005), Mexican migrant workers (Rothlein et al., 2006), Netherlands (Hooisma, Hänninen, Emmen, & Kulig, 1993), Nicaragua (Miranda et al., 2002), Poland (Bazylewicz-Walczak, Majczakowa, & Szymczak, 1999), Singapore (Chia, Chia, Ong, & Jeyaratnam, 1997), South Africa (Myers, Nell, Colvin, Rees, & Thompson, 1999), Spain (Roldán-Tapia, Parrón, & Sánchez-Santed, 2005), and Venezuela (D. C. Cole et al., 1997).

Strengths of the NCTB include validation and norms on young adults from numerous countries including those with low resources and educational levels. Many subtests are readily available because they are taken from common Western neuropsychological tests. Limitations include difficulties in procuring some of the tests or test translations, limited number of tests in the battery, and vulnerability to education effects.

A second WHO international study (Maj et al., 1994) evaluated neuropsychological functioning of HIV patients in five countries, including Germany, Brazil, Zaire, Kenya, and Thailand. The battery consisted of the following tests:

1. *Auditory Verbal Learning Test*—a 15-item list learning test similar to the Rey Auditory Verbal Learning Test (RAVLT) in presentation and requirements but with words that are common across cultures
2. *Color Trails 1 & 2*—trail-making tests that use numbers in colored circles, the first trial having only one color, and the second requiring the subject to alternate numbers from yellow and pink circles
3. *Picture Memory and Interference*—a series of three trials in which subjects are presented 20 line drawings on 3 × 5 cards and then immediately presented 50 cards in which the subject

must discriminate the 20 original drawings from 30 other distracter drawings

4. *Verbal Fluency*—animals and first names
5. *Escala de Inteligencia Wechsler para Adultos (EIWA) Block Design*—Block Design task from the Spanish WAIS
6. *EIWA Digit Symbol*—Digit Symbol test from the Spanish WAIS
7. *Grooved Pegboard*
8. *Trailmaking A*

A strength of this study is the larger breadth of tests, many of which are commonly used and easily obtainable by clinicians. A disadvantage is the poor normative data because the researchers merely report percentages of subjects who are HIV negative, HIV positive but asymptomatic, and HIV positive who are symptomatic and demonstrating impairments on the battery. Results do indicate higher percentages of impaired functioning in HIV-positive symptomatic versus asymptomatic subjects across countries; however, education effects were strong in African countries for HIV-positive asymptomatic subjects (Maj et al., 1994).

APHASIA

The Bilingual Aphasia Test

The Bilingual Aphasia Test (BAT; Paradis & Libben, 1987) was designed to assess language skills of aphasics who are bilingual or multilingual. Language components evaluated include spontaneous speech, pointing, simple and semi-complex commands, verbal auditory discrimination, syntactic comprehension, synonyms, antonyms, word repetition, sentence repetition, series, naming, sentence construction, semantic opposites, and listening comprehension. For literate clients, reading of words, reading of sentences, reading of paragraphs, copying, dictation of words, dictation of sentences, reading comprehension for words, and reading comprehension for sentences are also assessed. The BAT has been translated into 67 languages, including Amharic, Arabic (Jordanian, Maghrebian), Armenian (Eastern, Western), Azari, Basque, Berber, Bosnian, Bulgarian, Catalan, Chinese (Mandarin, Cantonese), Corinthian, Croatian, Czech, Danish, Dholuo, Dutch, English, Farsi, Finnish, French, Friulian, Galician, German, Greek, Hebrew, Hindi, Hungarian, Icelandic, Inuktitut, Italian, Japanese, Kannada, Korean, Kurdish, Latvian, Lithuanian, Luganda, Malagasy, Maori, Norwegian, Oriya, Polish, Portuguese (European, Brazilian), Romanian, Russian, Sardinian, Serbian,

Slovenian, Somali, Spanish (European, Castilian, American), Swahili, Swedish, Tagalog, Tamil, Tulu, Turkish, Ukrainian, Urdu, Vietnamese, and Yiddish.

Because the test is designed to evaluate for aphasia in multilinguals, for each language there are equivalent forms for the most common secondary languages. For example, for Dutch, there are forms for German, French, English, and Hebrew. The proliferation of translations can be attributed to the authors' description of methods for constructing new language versions. Thus, different clinicians have developed the majority of translations. The strength of the test is the breadth of languages into which it is translated and the accessibility of the translations, which can be downloaded from the Internet (http://www.mcgill.ca/linguistics/research/bat/#reference). Another strength is the emphasis that both the structure and culture of the particular language be considered when adapting test materials. A limitation is the availability of normative data because authors refer to a thesis paper to review psychometric properties. Data, however, appear face valid and thus can be interpreted qualitatively.

MEMORY TESTS

International Shopping List Test

Because memory problems are a hallmark of neurological disorders, memory tests are included in several of the aforementioned batteries, including the CERAD, NCTB, and WHO HIV batteries. A standalone memory test that is gaining interest in cross-cultural neuropsychology is the International Shopping List Test (ISLT; Y. Y. Lim et al., 2009). The ISLT comprises 12 shopping items presented in three trials with measures for each trial, total words, and recency and primacy process. The test has been translated into French, Mandarin, Malay, and Korean. An interesting aspect of test development was the emphasis on familiarity of shopping items across culture versus direct translation of shopping items to ensure cross-cultural equivalency. There exists a small but growing number of validation studies demonstrating good test–retest reliability for serial testing in dementia patients (Y. Y. Lim, Pietrzak, Snyder, Darby, & Maruff, 2012) and less proactive interference than the RAVLT (Rahimi-Golkhandan, Maruff, Darby, & Wilson, 2012). Strengths of the ISLT include ecological validity, process measures, superior psychometric properties for serial testing, accessible translation in the four languages, some norms for younger adults, and process for developing form equivalency across cultures. A current weakness is the limited number of existing translations and normative studies.

Fuld Object Memory Evaluation

Unlike most memory tests using words or visual representations as stimuli, the Fuld Object Memory Evaluation (FOME; Fuld, 1981) uses tangible objects. In the test, 10 small common objects are placed in a bag and identified through touch with both hands and then with sight. The initial presentations are followed by a distracter verbal fluency trial, recall, and then four learning and recall trials using a selective reminding cuing of items missed. Verbal fluency distracter trials are interspersed between recall trials. Several studies report that the FOME is unaffected by low educational or income levels in elderly Hispanics primarily originating from Mexico (Ortiz, LaRue, Romero, Sassaman, & Lindeman, 1997), the Caribbean (Loewenstein, Duara, Argüelles, & Argüelles, 1995), and Brazil (Yassuda et al., 2009). The test has also been validated in Japan (Fuld, Muramoto, Blau, Westbrook, & Katzman, 1988) and China (Hsieh & Tori, 2007). Strengths of the test include the visual modality of presentation and use of tangible objects, which would theoretically make it more valid for CDCs from low-resource countries where "cognitive realism" is the general epistemology. Weaknesses include the limited number of translations and validation studies.

PERFORMANCE VALIDITY TESTS

Cognitive

Effort has been found to have a significant impact on neuropsychological test performance, accounting for approximately 50% of the variance in test scores (P. Green, Lees-Haley, & Allen, 2003). This impact is more pronounced than severity of brain injury in contexts where there is secondary gain, such as disability or forensic evaluations (Belanger, Curtiss, Demery, Lebowitz, & Vanderploeg, 2005). Thus, measuring effort has become an essential component of the neuropsychological evaluation (Heilbronner et al., 2009).

Effort tests are deceptively easy to perform well; thus, even persons with significant neurological disorders, children, or those with low intelligence produce perfect or near perfect scores or perform much better than one would necessarily anticipate (Heilbronner et al., 2009). Hence, failure on such tests strongly suggests that poor effort was expended to complete the task. Poor effort has been associated with both intentional exaggeration of symptoms, such as in factitious disorder and malingering, and unintentional exaggeration, such as in somatoform pain disorder, cogniform disorder (Heilbronner et al., 2009), and negative symptoms in schizophrenia (Marcopulos & Fujii, 2012). For the CDC, it is argued that poor performances on effort measures could also be secondary to poor English comprehension, significant unfamiliarity of the testing situation or test stimuli, or poor motivation to perform in the unfamiliar artificial situation.

In comparison to neuropsychological testing of cognitive functioning, the cross-cultural literature on effort testing is much sparser and varies by country. This disinterest occurs despite evidence in some countries indicating similar rates of suboptimal performance on neuropsychological tests in civil and social forensic contexts (Merten et al., 2013). Proposed reasons for the lack of research and test development or validation in this area include skepticism of the effectiveness of performance validity tests (PVTs) for determining poor effort, perception that malingering is the purview of legal versus medical professionals, a hesitation to mistrust client's self-reports, and lack of available validated measures (Merten et al., 2013).

The following are a list of PVTs and validated versions in different countries.

Free-Standing Tests

Word Memory Test (WMT; P. Green, 2005), *Medical Symptom Validity Test* (MSVT; P. Green, 2004): The software for Green's tests has translations in Spanish, French, German, Dutch, Portuguese, Turkish, Russian, Danish, and Hebrew (see http://wordmemorytest.com/languages). The WMT has been validated in the Netherlands (Rienstra, Spaan, & Schmand, 2010), Puerto Rico (P. Green, Montijo, & Brockhaus, 2011), Russia (Tydecks, Merten, & Gubbay, 2006), Germany (Stevens, Friedel, Mehren, & Merten, 2008), and Portugal (Martins & Martins, 2010). The MSVT has been validated in Switzerland (Giger & Merten, 2013), Germany (Blaskewitz, Merten, & Kathmann, 2008), Puerto Rico (P. Green et al., 2011), and Canada-Quebec (Richman et al., 2006). The nonverbal version has been validated in Germany (Henry, Merten, Wolf, & Harth, 2010).

B Test (Boone et al., 2000): The B Test has been validated with Spanish-speaking Americans (Vilar-López et al., 2008).

Dot Counting Test (Boone, Lu, & Herzberg, 2002): This test has been validated with Spanish-speaking Americans (Burton, Vilar-López, & Puente, 2012); however Punjabi-Sikhs in India with little education performed poorly on the test (Weiss & Rosenfeld, 2010).

Hiscock's Forced-Choice Digit Memory Test (Hiscock & Hiscock, 1989): This test is validated in China (R. G. Liu, Gao, Li, & Lu, 2001).

Rey 15-Item Test (Rey, 1964): Validation studies have been conducted in Germany (Blaskewitz et al., 2008), and Japan (Yamaguchi, 2005) and with the following ethnic minority samples in the United States: Pacific Islanders and Asian Indians (Webb, Batchelor, Meares, Taylor, & Marsh, 2012), Spanish

(Burton et al., 2012), African Americans, Hispanics, and Asian Americans (X. Salazar, Lu, Wen, & Boone, 2007).

Test of Memory Malingering (TOMM; Tombaugh, 1996): The TOMM has been validated in the Netherlands (Rienstra et al., 2010), China— Hong Kong (Chang, 2006), Germany (Blaskewitz et al., 2008), and Spain (Jiménez Gómez, 2012). In the United States, the test has been validated with Spanish speakers (Vilar-López et al., 2008), and Pacific Islanders and Asian Indians (Webb et al., 2012).

Victoria Symptom Validity Test (VSVT; Hopp, Strauss, & Thompson, 1997): The VSVT has been validated with Spanish Americans (Vilar-López et al., 2008).

Word Completion Memory Test (WCMT; Hilsabeck, LeCompte, Marks, & Grafman, 2001): The WCMT has been validated in the Netherlands (Rienstra et al., 2010).

Embedded Measures

Reliable Digit Span (RDS; Greiffenstein, Baker, & Gola, 1994): The RDS has been validated in China (Yang et al., 2012) and Switzerland (Giger & Merten, 2013), and with African Americans, Hispanics, Asian Americans (X. Salazar et al., 2007), Pacific Islanders, and Asian Indians living in the United States (Webb et al., 2012).

Rey Auditory Verbal Learning Test Recognition (Binder, Villanueva, Howieson, & Moore, 1993): A validation study was conducted with African Americans, Hispanics, and Asian Americans (X. Salazar et al., 2007).

Rey–Osterrieth Recognition (Lu, Boone, Cozolino, & Mitchell, 2003): The measure was validated with African Americans, Hispanics, and Asian Americans (X. Salazar et al., 2007).

Indigenous

Amsterdam Short-Term Memory Test (Rienstra et al., 2010), Swiss (Giger & Merten, 2013).

Digit Memory Test, Chinese (Chiu & Lee, 2002).

Binomial Forced-Choice Digit Recognition Test (BFCR), Chinese (Gao, Li, & Chen, 2003).

Wechsler Memory Scale—III Verbal Paired Associates Recognition, Spain (Sánchez, Jimenez, Ampudia, & Merino, 2012).

As a whole, strengths of PVT measures include availability of norms for common ethnic minority groups in the United States and for select countries. Green's tests are readily available for a fee. Weaknesses include lack of translations and normative data for most countries.

Somatic and Psychological and Psychiatric Tests

Neuropsychologists are also often asked to evaluate the veracity of physical symptoms in medicolegal contexts in which the impact of secondary gain is strong, as in personal injury or workers' compensation cases (Heilbronner et al., 2009). Somatic symptom can either be specific, such as focal pain or weaknesses, or nonspecific, such as with fatigue, general weakness, general malaise, or vague generalized pain. The American Academy of Clinical Neuropsychology recommends several strategies for evaluating the authenticity of self-reports, such as noncredible sensory and motor performances skills and validity measures on personality tests (Heilbronner et al., 2009).

Similarly, neuropsychologists may also evaluate for authenticity of psychological and psychiatric conditions in medicolegal contexts, which also includes criminal cases (e.g., fitness to stand trial, insanity defense, mitigation for death penalty; Heilbronner et al., 2009). Personality tests are also commonly used within this context, as are more specific measures of psychiatric malingering.

PERSONALITY TESTS

Minnesota Multiphasic Personality Inventory—2

The Minnesota Multiphasic Personality Inventory—2 (MMPI–2; Butcher, Dahlstrom, Graham, Tellegen, & Kaemmer, 1989) is the most widely used personality test by North American neuropsychologists (Rabin, Barr, & Burton, 2005) and also has the most validated translations into different languages (for a review, see Butcher, 2004). Translations of three versions of the MMPI are available from the publisher (https://www.upress.umn.edu/test-division/translations-permissions/permissions). The MMPI–2 is available in Bulgarian, Chinese, Croatian, Czech, Danish, Cutch/Flemish, French, French-Canadian, German, Greek, Hebrew, Hmong, Hungarian, Italian, Korean, Norwegian, Polish, Romania, Swedish, and Spanish for Hispanics living in Mexico and Central America. The MMPI Restructured Form is available in French; Italian; Korean; and Spanish for Spain, South America, and Central America. The MMPI—Adolescent is available in Bulgarian; Croatian; Dutch/Flemish; French; Hungarian; Italian; Korean; and Spanish for Mexico, Central American, Spain, South America, and the United States. The MMPI–2 has also been validated in Iceland (Konráos, 1996), Russia (Koscheyev & Leon, 1996), Turkey (Savaşir & Çulha, 1996), Cuba (Quevedo & Butcher, 2005), Puerto Rico (Cabiya, 1996), Thailand (Pongpanich, 1996), Japan (Shiota, Krauss, & Clark, 1996), and Vietnam (Tran, 1996).

The validity scales of the MMPI–2 have been researched in South Korea (F, Fb, F-K, F(p), L, K, S; Hahn, 2005; VRIN and TRIN; Ketterer, Han, Hur, & Moon, 2010), Spain (FBS; Crespo, Gomez, Barragan, & Rueda, 2007), Italy (S Scale; Sirigatti & Giannini, 2000), Mexico (L, F, K; Lucio, Duran, Graham, & Ben-Porath, 2002), and China (F; Cheung, Song, & Butcher, 1991). Many international studies on the MMPI–2 with various medical conditions such as pain have been conducted, including fibromyalgia patients in Spain (Pérez-Pareja, Abad, & Ordi, 2010), musculoskeletal pain patients in Norway (Kvåle, Ellertsen, & Skouen, 2001), temporomandibular joint pain and chronic headache patients in Italy (Meldolesi et al., 2000; Mongini, Ibertis, Barbalonga, & Raviola, 2000), pain associated with psychological factors in Britain (Monsen & Havik, 2001), chronic pain patients in Australia (Strassberg, Tilley, Bristone, & Oei, 1992) and China (Y. L. Wang, Wu, & Wu, 2000), and chronic back pain patients in the Netherlands (Vendrig, de Mey, Derksen, & van Akkerveeken, 1998). The MMPI–2 has also been validated on patients with schizophrenia in the United States, Italy, Chile, Thailand, China, and India (Butcher, 1996) and in Japan (Hayama, Oguchi, & Shinkai, 1999) and has been used in studies examining malingered psychiatric disorders in Puerto Rico (Jana, 2001) and malingered head injury in China (Gao, 2001).

Strengths of the MMPI scales include the breadth of measures, cross-cultural validation, and availability from the publisher for select languages. Weaknesses include length of testing and lack of availability for most countries.

Personality Assessment Inventory

The Personality Assessment Inventory (PAI; Morey & Boggs, 1991) is an objective personality measure of psychopathological syndromes that contains validity scales as well as measures for depression and somatic complaints. It has been validated with African American and Hispanic Americans (Alterman et al., 1995) and translated to Greek (Lyrakos, 2011), German (Groves & Engel, 2007), and Spanish (Rogers, Bagby, & Dickens, 1992). The PAI is a good alternative to the MMPI; however, it has limited translations and validation in different countries.

Beck Depression Inventory—II

The Beck Depression Inventory—II (BDI–II; Beck, Steer, & Brown, 1996) is a self-report measure of depression. It has been validated in Puerto Rico (Bonilla, Bernal, Santos, & Santos, 2004), Argentina (Bonicatto, Dew, & Soria, 1998), China (Yeung et al., 2002), Brazil (Y. P. Wang, Andrade, & Gorenstein, 2005), the Middle East (Hamdi, Abu-Hijleh, & Abu Taleb, 1988), Malaysia (Mahmud, Awang, Herman, & Mohamed, 2004), and in the United

States with African Americans (Grothe et al., 2005), Hispanics (Penley, Wiebe, & Nwosu, 2003), and Hmong (Mouanoutoua, Brown, Cappelletty, & Levine, 1991). A strength of the BDI–II is its relative ease in administration in measuring a common psychiatric disorder. However, like most personality measures, there are limited translations and validations in different countries.

FORENSIC MALINGERING

Specialized malingering tests for psychiatric symptoms are limited, with availability primarily for Hispanic clients.

Miller Forensic Assessment of Symptoms (M-FAST; Miller, 2001): The M-FAST has been validated with African Americans and Hispanics (Guy & Miller, 2004) and also translated into Spanish (Montes & Guyton, 2014).

Structured Interview of Reported Symptoms (SIRS; Rogers, Bagby, & Dickens, 1992): The SIRS has been translated to Spanish (Correa, Rogers, & Hoersting, 2010).

TESTS BASED ON FUNCTIONAL ABILITIES

The following tests estimate current cognitive functioning based on functional abilities versus performance on tests.

Clinical Dementia Rating

The Clinical Dementia Rating (CDR) was developed to determine stage of dementia and to track progression (Hughes, Berg, Danziger, Coben, & Martin, 1982). In this test, the client is rated on six functional domains (orientation, memory, judgment and problem solving, community affairs, home and hobbies, and personal care) through a semistructured interview with the subject, collateral sources, or both. Each domain is rated for impairment on a 5-point scale: 0 = *none*, 0.5 = *questionable*, 1 = *mild*, 2 = *moderate*, 3 = *severe*. Scores are tallied to formulate an overall level of dementia (no impairment, questionable, mild, moderate, and severe). Domains can also be interpreted separately. The CDR has been widely used to determine dementia diagnosis in research. It has been validated in Japan (Meguro et al., 2004), China—Hong Kong (Lam et al., 2008), Taiwan (C. K. Liu et al., 1998), Korea (Choi et al., 2001), Argentina (Zuin, Ortiz, Boromei, & Lopez, 2002), Australia (Waite et al., 1999), Brazil (Chaves et al., 2007), India (Chandra et al., 2001), Thailand (Senanarong et al., 2005), Oman (Karam & Itani, 2013), Singapore (W. S. Lim, Chin, Lam, Lim, & Sahadevan, 2005), Nigeria

(Baiyewu et al., 2003), Cuba, Dominican Republic, Peru, Venezuela, Mexico, India, and China (Rodriguez et al., 2008).

Strengths of the CDR include its strong interrater reliability, ability to discriminate between normal cognition and mild stages of cognitive decline and impairment, and international validation. Weaknesses include length of administration when using formal structured interview, lack of accessible translations, and limited applicability to neurological disorders associated with lower levels of impairment. Categories are subject to the influence of culture, so the clinician would have to adapt criteria in categories to match cultural expectations for that client. Some domains require testing to aid in determination (orientation, memory, abstractions).

Cognitive Screening Instrument for Dementia

The Cognitive Screening Instrument for Dementia (CSI–D; K. S. Hall et al., 1993) is a structured interview that was developed as a screening instrument for dementia in rural areas. It was validated with Cree Indians in Manitoba and English-speaking non-Indians in Winnipeg. The test comprises a cognitive assessment and functional interview with a close informant and takes about 15 minutes to administer. The functional assessment consists of 30 items evaluating functional abilities in the following domains: memory, activities of daily living, miscellaneous, personality, and depression. Examples of items include "Does he or she talk about long ago?" and "Is he or she more stubborn in past 6 months?" A brief 17-item version has also been developed (Prince et al., 2011). The CSI–D has been used extensively by the 10/66 Dementia Group with normative data collected for Cuba, Dominican Republic, Peru, Venezuela, Mexico, India, and China (Sosa et al., 2009). The measure has been validated in Nigeria and Jamaica (K. S. Hall et al., 2000), Tanzania (Howitt et al., 2011), Congo Central and African Republic (Guerchet et al., 2013), Brazil (Scazufca et al., 2008), and Taiwan (K. P. Liu et al., 2011). Strengths of the CSI–D include its ease of administration and validation in low-resource countries with good interrater reliability. Weaknesses include lack of accessible translations, limited use in evaluating for dementia in elderly people, and limitations in measuring stages of dementia.

Informant Questionnaire on Cognitive Decline in the Elderly

The Informant Questionnaire on Cognitive Decline in the Elderly (IQCODE; Jorm & Jacomb, 1986) is a screening tool for dementia used primarily when the client is unable to undergo neurocognitive testing, such as when translated validated measures are unavailable or he or she has a very low level of education. The original measure has 26 items asking an informant how a person's functioning in a particular domain compares with 10 years ago. Examples include recalling a conversation a few days later and handling money for shopping. Items are rated on a 5-point Likert scale with the following anchors: *much improved, a bit improved, not much change, a bit worse,* and *much worse.* Scores are then tallied and averaged. The IQCODE has been validated in the following countries: China (Fuh et al., 1995), Netherlands (de Jonghe, 1997), France (Mailles et al., 2012), Canada—French (Law & Wolfson, 1995), Germany (Wolf et al., 2009), Italy (Isella, Villa, Frattola, & Appollonio, 2002), Guam (Wiederholt, Galasko, & Salmon, 1997), Japan (Yamada, Sasaki, Kasagi, & Suzuki, 2002), Korea (D. W. Lee et al., 2005), Lithuania, Norway (Nygaard, Naik, & Geitung, 2009), Iran (Shoaee, Azkhosh, & Alizad, 2013), Poland (Klimkowicz-Mrowiec, Dziedzic, Slowik, & Szczudlik, 2006), Brazil (Perroco et al., 2009), Spain (Morales, González-Montalvo, Del Ser, & Bermejo, 1991), Thailand (Siri, Okanurak, Chansirikanjana, Kitayaporn, & Jorm, 2006), and Turkey (Ozel-Kizil, Turan, Yilmaz, Cangoz, & Uluc, 2010). Translations of the IQCODE are readily available online (http://crahw.anu.edu.au/risk-assessment-tools/informant-questionnaire-cognitive-decline-elderly). Short forms are available in the following languages: English, Chinese, Danish, Dutch, Finnish, German, Greek, Lithuanian Persian, Spanish, Swedish, Thai, and Turkish. Long forms are available in English, Dutch, French Canadian, French, German, Italian, Japanese, Korean, Lithuanian, Norwegian, Persian, Polish, Portuguese (Brazilian), and Spanish.

Strengths of the IQCODE include its international validation and accessibility of translations in many languages. Items evaluate functionality; thus, scores are not affected by education and language proficiency in country of residence. Scores are affected by anxiety and depression in informant and quality of relationship between informant and subject (Jorm, 2004). Similar to the previous behavioral-based strategy, weaknesses include limited use in evaluating for dementia in elderly people and limitations in measuring stages of dementia.

SAMPLE OF TEST SELECTION PROCESS

The following are samples of test selection processes for three clients.

Case 1

Rik is a 30-year-old married man from Flanders, Belgium, who works for an international Belgian dredging company. He sustained a mild traumatic brain injury from a blunt object while working in the United States. Rik completed vocational secondary education, which is equivalent to a high school degree, and speaks some English but is not fluent.

There are many Western tests that are validated and normed in Dutch, including the WAIS, Trails A & B, Wechsler Memory Scale—III, National Adult Reading Test—Dutch, Tower of London, Boston Naming Test, Rivermead Behavioral Memory Test, Judgment of Line Orientation, Category Fluency (animals and professions), Controlled Oral Word A Test, RAVLT, Stroop, Wisconsin Card Sorting Test (WCST), as well as PVTs such as the MMPI–2, WMT, TOMM, and ASMT (for a listing, see Muslimovic, Post, Speelman, & Schmand, 2005; Rienstra et al., 2010; Schmand, Houx, & de Koning, 2004). Together, these tests would comprise a good comprehensive battery. Optimally, the neuropsychologist could obtain copies and translations of these tests from the publisher or colleagues (16 Belgian and 82 Dutch neuropsychologists are listed in the International Neuropsychological Society [INS] membership).

If validated test material cannot be procured, a second option would be to translate tests that do not rely heavily on precise semantic equivalents for stimuli or responses, such as the WAIS Vocabulary. Although there is greater potential for error, the precision requirements for translation should be less for task-oriented tests. Assistance could be solicited from colleagues from the INS membership, Google Translate (Dutch is a Category 1 language, meaning it is relatively easy for English speakers to learn [National Virtual Translation Center, 2007]), and an interpreter (see the recommended process for working with interpreters in Chapter 5). Norms from studies using Dutch versions of the test with matching demographics could then be used. If specific norms are not available, an option, although again less precise, would be to use American norms. This strategy could be justified by similarities between the two countries in terms of estimated intelligence on Western tests (Belgian mean estimated IQ = 100, U.S. mean estimated IQ = 98; R. Lynn & Meisenberg, 2010), years of education (Belgium mean = 9.35, expected = 16.9, U.S. mean = 12.5, expected = 16.8; UNESCO, n.d.-a, n.d.-b), standardized test scores for academic achievement (Belgium Programme for International Student Assessment test math = 515, science = 505, reading = 509; U.S. math = 481, science = 498, reading = 498; Organisation for Economic Co-operation and Development, 2013), and gross domestic product (Belgium $45,955, U.S. $51,749; World Bank, 2014). Whatever method is used, the process should be documented in the neuropsychological report.

Case 2

Raghda is a 41-year-old housewife from Jordan who was recently diagnosed with multiple sclerosis (MS) after her family noticed increasing fatigue, motor weakness, and memory problems. She and her two middle-school-age children immigrated to the United States in 2009 for family reunification. Raghda has a ninth-grade education and speaks some English but is not fluent. Her family lives in a Middle Eastern enclave where many people speak Arabic.

A Google Scholar search reported no validated neuropsychological tests in Jordan with the exception of the BAT. However, a number of tests have been translated into Arabic and validated in various Arabic-speaking countries, for example, the WAIS (Melika, 1987), WMS Continuous Performance Test (CPT), WCST (Radwan et al., 2013), and the RBANS (Fawzi et al., 2013) in Egypt, the Stroop, the Test of Nonverbal Intelligence—3, WCST (Al-Ghatani, Obonsawin, Binshaig, & Al-Moutaery, 2011), verbal and design fluency (Khalil, 2010), and Trailmaking tests (Razzak, 2013) in Saudi Arabia, and the RAVLT (Poreh, Sultan, & Levin, 2012) in Oman. In addition, the Bilingual Verbal Abilities Test (BVAT) is also translated into Arabic (Munoz-Sandoval, Cummins, Alvarado, & Ruef, 1998).

Although spoken versions of Arabic can differ between countries, the written Modern Standard Arabic is shared across most Arabic-speaking countries, particularly for academic and scientific writing. Justification for using tests validated in other Arabic-speaking countries with Jordanians could be based on similarities between the countries for years of education (Jordan mean = 6.91, expected = 12.7; Egypt mean = 5.51, expected = 12.1; Saudi Arabia expected = 14.3; Oman expected = 13.5; UNESCO, n.d.-b), and estimated intelligence on Western tests (Egypt IQ = 83, Jordan IQ = 85, Saudi Arabia IQ = 80, Oman IQ = 85; R. Lynn & Meisenberg, 2010). Although significant differences in gross domestic product per capita exist between Saudi Arabia ($25,136), Oman ($23,133), Jordan ($4,909), and Egypt ($3,256; World Bank, 2014), R. Lynn and Vanhanen (2002) warned that the relationship between the two indicators are not accurate for oil-rich countries.

Given the aforementioned pool of tests validated on persons from Arabic-speaking countries with similar IQ scores on Western tests, an important consideration for test selection is the availability of appropriate norms. Ideally, norms should be based on large representative samples with comparable demographics; however, these are not always available. In general, norms should pass the "smell test." For example, Fawzi et al. (2013) reported RBANS raw index scores for a normal Egyptian sample ($n = 50$) with a mean age of 36 and education of 10.5 years. Intuitively, mean scores for this sample should be lower than the U.S. RBANS standardization sample (Randolph, 1998), of which only about 4.4% did not complete high school. In addition, the mean IQ as measured by Western tests of Egyptians is estimated to be significantly lower than for persons living in the United States (83 vs. 98; R. Lynn & Vanhanen, 2006). However, in this study the Egyptian RBANS mean raw index scores are consistently higher than the U.S. standardization sample (Immediate Recall 55.9 vs. 49.8; Visuospatial 37.7 vs. 35.9; Language 42.9 vs. 31.2; Attention/Concentration 97.4 vs. 68.8; Delayed Recall 52.1 vs. 53.5). The most likely explanation is that the Egyptian sample from a medical center at Zagazig University, one of the more prestigious universities in the country, is biased toward more intelligent participants (Michael Nestor, personal communication, August 4, 2015).

Another strategy for test selection is using validated tests and then interpreting scores with American norms using the individual comparison strategy. In this method, the estimated mean IQ for Jordanians on Western tests would be about 85, which has corroboration by 2011 Trends in International Mathematics and Science Study and Progress in International Reading Literacy Study tests scores (U.S. Department of Education, Institute of Education Sciences, National Center for Education Statistics, n.d.) for Jordanian fourth-graders (math = 386, science = 409, reading = 399), where a score of 400 would be equivalent to a standard deviation below the norm or a standard score of 85 on an IQ test. With 85 as a base, the clinician would then estimate Raghda's IQ based on her demographic comparison with other Jordanians. Thus, if 9 years is the average level of education for Jordanian women in her cohort, her estimated premorbid IQ on Western tests would be 85 and would serve as the benchmark for interpreting scores using U.S. norms.

Although there are no PVTs validated with similar cultures, given Raghda's level of education, PVTs may be applicable allowing for flexibility in interpretation of normative cutoffs. Test selection should be based on familiarity of stimuli or forced choice tests that have statistical validity.

Similar to Rik's case, procuring translated tests can pose challenges; thus, the clinician may be forced to translate tests before conducting the evaluation. In Raghda's case, meeting ITC standards for translation would be difficult because Arabic is a Category 3 language, which is among the most difficult to master for English speakers (National Virtual Translation Center, 2007). Thus, Google Translate should not be used as a first pass, and the clinician would have to find additional assistance to ensure two translations for test instructions. On the INS website, there are two neuropsychologists listed in Jordan, two from Saudi Arabia, and two from Iran, and the National Academy of Neuropsychology website lists six Arabic-speaking members.

Case 3

Asdza is a 77-year-old Navajo woman who has been referred for a dementia evaluation after family voiced concerns about wandering behaviors. Asdza has a second-grade education, is illiterate, and is poorly fluent in English.

Because of the lack of validated tests for the Navajo population (the exception is the BVAT; Munoz-Sandoval et al., 1998), numerous cultural differences can affect validity of cognitive tests for Native Americans (for a review, see Griffin-Pierce et al., 2008), and potential impact of illiteracy on the client's epistemology, cognitive testing should not be the primary evaluation strategy. Instead, collecting data on adaptive functioning in her everyday life and tracking behavioral changes over time would be more appropriate, and the CSI–D and IQCODE are recommended tests. Justification for using the CSI–D would be its validation with rural, low-educated, and low-resource populations (Sosa et al., 2009), including the Cree Indian tribe (K. S. Hall et al., 1993). Similarly, the IQCODE is relatively unaffected by premorbid abilities or education (Jorm, 2004) and has been validated with individuals who are illiterate (Fuh et al., 1995). These strategies would entail interviewing a family member, and thus translations may or may not be required depending on the informant's English proficiency. An additional advantage to these approaches is comfort for the client because of involvement of a family member in the evaluation process (Griffin-Pierce et al., 2008). The CSI–D does have a short cognitive component developed for an illiterate population; thus, some cognitive data would be available. To evaluate for depression, the Composite International Diagnostic Interview (Kessler et al., 1994) was selected because it has been validated on a large Southwestern Native American sample (Beals et al., 2005).

When using alternative strategies for test selection, it is important to consider the *validity generalization* of a test, which is the degree to which a test's criterion validity evidence can be generalized to new situations without further study (American Educational Research Association, American Psychological Association, & National Council on Measurement in Education, 2014). Validity generalization is a function of the accumulated research of the test. When evaluating for validity generalization, clinicians should review prior studies and evaluate for similarities in (a) measurement of predictor constructs, (b) criterion measures, (c) characteristics of the test takers, and (d) the time period when study conducted. Carefully controlled studies with good sample size and similar situations would provide strong evidence for the validity of generalizing test usage for a given CDC. Meta-analysis with large effect sizes in similar situations would also provide evidence for generalization.

III

EVALUATION AND REPORT WRITING

8

CONDUCTING THE EVALUATION

It's the little details that are vital. Little things make big things happen.
—John Wooden

Good preparation for conducting a neuropsychological evaluation with culturally different clients (CDCs) requires extensive research and planning. Successful implementation of the testing strategy requires an attention to detail and good clinical psychological skills. Both are essential for facilitating accurate data collection. The following example illustrates the process from receiving the referral to completion of the neuropsychological evaluation. Interpretation and report writing are covered in the following chapters.

REFERRAL AND PRELIMINARY DATA GATHERING

Mr. Jae Song Kim is a 66-year-old, Korean American man, who sustained a right-sided basal ganglia stroke with left hemiparesis a week ago. He is currently receiving treatment in a rehabilitation facility. Two days after his admission, it was discovered that Mr. Kim was refusing his medications for

http://dx.doi.org/10.1037/15958-009
Conducting a Culturally Informed Neuropsychological Evaluation, by D. Fujii

hypertension. His blood pressures have been high (approximately 170/100), and his nurse and internist tried to explain to him that his medications are important to prevent a future stroke. He still refused. Mr. Kim was referred by his internist, Dr. Johnson, to a neuropsychologist who could evaluate for cognition and how it relates to medical capacity for decision-making.

Dr. Johnson was asked to describe his reason for the referral. He stated that he was puzzled by Mr. Kim. He suddenly refused his medications. Dr. Johnson tried to explain the serious consequences of noncompliance. Mr. Kim nodded his head but still refused. He said Mr. Kim appears to understand English well enough, as he responds appropriately to staff and speaks to them in English, although he speaks to his daughter in Korean. Dr. Johnson wondered about depression because Mr. Kim has not been eating well and has lost about 4 pounds since his admission. His main goal is to prevent Mr. Kim from sustaining a second stroke.

Before accepting the referral, an attempt was made to find a neuropsychologist who was familiar with Korean culture and spoke the language; unfortunately, none could be located within the vicinity or address the urgency of the referral. Mr. Kim's chart was reviewed for preliminary background information. Mr. Kim is a widower who was born and raised in Incheon, South Korea. He has a 12th-grade education and is a small business owner who lives with his youngest daughter, Yun Ji, age 28, who is studying for the bar examination. Although Mr. Kim understands and converses with staff in English, his daughter speaks to him in Korean. Mr. Kim has a 40-year-old son, Jun Ho, who lives in South Korea, and a 38-year-old daughter, Min Ji, who lives out of state.

Mr. Kim's medical history includes hypertension, nicotine dependence (one pack per day for 40 years), and regular alcohol intake (one to three glasses of Korean rice wine two to five times a week for 40 years). There is no history of head injury or psychiatric illness. A magnetic resonance imaging scan revealed an infarct of the right putamen, right globus pallidus, and posterior limb of the internal capsule. He was treated with lisinopril 40 mg for hypertension and aspirin, which were started in the acute care hospital.

PREPARATION

Estimating Premorbid IQ

Jo and Dawson (2011) recommended estimating premorbid IQ based on a detailed history of educational attainment, academic achievement, and occupational functioning before immigration. This strategy is consistent with the one described in Chapter 5, where an IQ for an immigrant CDC is determined by procuring an estimated IQ on Western tests for the client's country of origin as a base and then adjusting for the client's estimated functioning within his or her cultural context. R. Lynn and Meisenberg (2010) estimated the average IQ for South Koreans to be 106 based on the literature and scores on international tests of academic achievement, on which South Korea has consistently scored in the top three countries. Currently, South Koreans have one of the highest levels of educational attainment, with current projections for mean years of schooling at 17.2 years (UNESCO, n.d.-b). However, the educational attainment for the country has not always been this stellar; only 10.2% of adults aged 25 years or older graduated from high school in 1970 compared with 38.3% in 2005. Consistent with these numbers are significantly large gains in intelligence averaging 7.7 points per decade from 1970 to 1990 (te Nijenhuis, Cho, Murphy, & Lee, 2012). In terms of employment, a common occupation among Korean immigrants is owning a store, thus may be considered one associated with an average level IQ. Preliminary implications would be that IQ of South Koreans would be comparable with that of Americans; however, given the format of the data (mean educational level of all adults), it is difficult to determine the mean level of education for Mr. Kim's cohort.

Language

In the Korean educational curriculum, reading and writing in English are emphasized more than speaking in English (Jo & Dawson, 2011); therefore, it is not surprising that roughly 30% of Korean American households speak a language other than English at home, and 54% of Korean Americans speak English less than well (Gambino, Acosta, & Grieco, 2014). In fact, historically many Korean immigrants open their own businesses because of limited job opportunities associated with poor English proficiency (Chung-Do, Huh, & Kang, 2011). Factors that have an impact on English proficiency include age at immigration, education, generation, acculturation, and location of residence, as people living in ethnic enclaves tend to speak predominantly Korean. Language is often a strong barrier for first-generation Koreans to integrate into mainstream society, and children often act as interpreters, when parents interface with the non-Korean community (Chung-Do et al., 2011). Although Mr. Kim may have developed English skills interacting with his customers, given that he immigrated as an adult, he would be most fluent in Korean, thus it would be prudent to perform the evaluation with an interpreter.

Cultural Values

Korean culture is heavily influenced by Confucianism, a philosophy that focuses on social ethics. The primary tenets of the philosophy are that a person is defined by his or her interpersonal relationships and thus must conduct oneself in a proper manner and fulfill his or her duties to maintain harmonious relationships (Guo & Uhm, 2014). Relationships between family members are highly formalized, with the father as head of the household and children taught to respect and obey their parents and elders. The eldest son has a special place in the family system (Chung-Do et al., 2011). This hierarchical relationship and loyalty is extended to society, where those of higher status should be highly respected and not challenged by subordinates (Jo & Dawson, 2011). In turn, persons of higher status are obligated to treat subordinates with benevolence (Guo & Uhm, 2014). Another important concept is the doctrine of the mean, which encourages people to fit in and be modest in opinions and behavior to maintain harmony (Guo & Uhm, 2014). Confucianism also value education and hard work, and parents make great sacrifices so that their children can receive the best education (Chung-Do et al., 2011).

Many Korean values derive directly from Confucian influence. Collectivism, or emphasis on the group versus the individual, reflects the foundation of interdependency. The importance of "saving face," or public self-image, can be traced to an emphasis on proper conduct and fulfilling one's role. Consistent with Confucian value of maintaining harmonious relationships, Koreans are likely to communicate indirectly to prevent hurting or embarrassing others (Guo & Uhm, 2014). Confucianism's strong formalized hierarchical relationships would make it a high power-distance culture (Hofstede, 1980).

Christianity is another strong influence, and it is estimated that 70% to 80% of Korean immigrants are Christians. The religion gained a foothold in Korean society during the Japanese occupation and after the Korean War. For many Korean Americans, Christian churches are an important source of social support (Chung-Do et al., 2011). Despite their Christian faith, many Koreans are also fatalistic and believe that events in their lives are predetermined. Thus, it is not unusual for Koreans to seek advice from a shaman or fortune-teller (Chung-Do et al., 2011).

Medical and Health Beliefs and Behaviors

Koreans believe in the Chinese conception that the foundation of illness is an imbalance of harmony between yin and yang or disturbance in life energy or *chi*. Thus, traditional Chinese medicine treatments such as herbs, acupuncture, moxibustion, and cupping are important interventions, although many Korean Americans may use both Chinese and Western medicine (K. R. Shin, Shin, & Blanchette, 2001). Because of the culture's strong filial piety, families are often involved in health care, and the oldest son and daughter-in-law are traditionally responsible for care of parents as they age

(Lau, 2014). Fatalistic beliefs can result in a passive acceptance of a severe medical diagnosis (Jo & Dawson, 2011).

As a collectivist society in which saving face is important, mental illness is highly stigmatized and reflects negatively on both self and family. Thus, emotional problems tend to be underreported (Lau, 2014), and Korean Americans tend to somaticize emotional problems, expressing them in physical symptoms, which are more acceptable (Chung-Do et al., 2011). For example, although Korean Americans have the highest rates of depression among Asians, few, particularly men, talk about symptoms but instead report physical symptoms such as digestion problems, tightness in the chest, dizziness, constipation, headaches, and back pain (for a review, see Cha, Chung, & Kim, 2014). Dementia can also be stigmatized, as traditional beliefs attribute the condition to stubborn or passive personalities or a history of hardships and stress associated with unresolved personal or family problems (Moon, 2006).

Hospitalizations, which use Western rather than Chinese medicine, can be aversive for older Korean Americans. In addition, a lack of Korean-speaking providers and Korean food is discomforting (K. R. Shin et al., 2001). Korean Americans have a high risk for developing hypertension and cardiovascular disease; stomach, liver, cervix, and breast cancers; and diabetes (K. R. Shin et al., 2001). Cigarette smoking and alcohol abuse are common (Cha et al., 2014).

Communication

As with most Asian collectivist cultures, the communication style of Korean Americans tend to be more indirect to maintain harmony and avoid offending others. What is not said is often as important as what is said, and Koreans tend to read between the lines when listening to what a person is saying (Guo & Uhm, 2014). Consistent with indirect communication, eye contact is also modulated and indirect so as not to offend (Jo & Dawson, 2011). Korean Americans are also likely to underreport previous achievements or current abilities, which is consistent with a collectivist culture's emphasis on modesty (Lau, 2014).

Other aspects of communication can be confusing to Westerners. Nodding when someone is talking typically means "I am intently listening" rather than agreement, and one must ask directly if the nod actually means "yes" (Carteret, n.d.). Korean Americans are often reluctant to express positive emotions because of Confucian values of modesty (Cha et al., 2014). They also respond to negatively stated questions oppositely to how Westerners would respond. For example, a typical response to "Doesn't that make you sad?" would be "No, it doesn't make me sad," whereas a Korean American would respond "Yes, it doesn't make me sad" (Jo & Dawson, 2011).

When interacting with health care professionals, who are perceived as authority figures, Korean American clients may present as cooperative, compliant, and submissive. Lau (2014) made several recommends to capitalize on their respect for clinicians and indirect communications style.

- Clinicians should take time to explain the neuropsychological evaluation process to facilitate understanding.
- To reduce stigma, clinicians should emphasize that the evaluation is not a psychiatric examination.
- Clients should be encouraged to volunteer pertinent information and ask questions, as both are important to facilitate the data gathering process. Throughout the evaluation, clinicians should ask whether the client has any questions.
- Given their authority, clinicians can be more directive in asking questions, which should be asked in a systematic manner.
- In a rehabilitation setting, clinicians should elicit assistance from the family.
- Recommendations can be given respectfully but in an authoritative manner. Clinicians should take time to discuss prognosis, treatment compliance, and treatment effectiveness.

To minimize feelings of shame associated with stigma, Te Pou (2010) recommended the following strategies: (a) demonstrate acceptance through warmth and support, (b) avoid intense personal questioning, (c) focus on practical goals versus emotional disclosures, (d) normalize problems by describing how others have had similar experiences, (e) reinforce the confidentiality of therapy, (f) frame participation in the evaluation as a show of strength and concern for the family, (g) reframe situations positively, (h) focus on problems versus personal weaknesses, and (i) medicalize problems by providing medical explanations.

Literature on Neurological Disorder

Clinicians must be familiar with the neuropsychological and neurological literature for pertinent disorders to guide assessment, differential diagnosis, and recommendations. For example, right basal ganglia lesions are associated with cognitive deficits in attention and concentration, visuospatial skills, memory, and executive functioning (Su, Chen, Kwan, Lin, & Guo, 2007). Neurological syndromes include aprosodia (Cohen, Riccio, & Flannery, 1994), anosognosia (Starkstein, Jorge, & Robinson, 2010), left sided-neglect (Karnath, Himmelbach, & Rorden, 2002), and disinhibition/mania (Starkstein & Robinson, 1989).

Other pertinent characteristics in Mr. Kim's case would be aging and alcohol abuse. For aging, familiarity with expectations for normal aging, mild cognitive impairment, and dementia would be required for diagnostic purposes. The impact of long-term alcohol use on the integrity of the brain and cognitive functioning is an important consideration given Mr. Kim's long history of alcohol use. In this case, his drinking habits would not meet the threshold of use (five to six drinks per day) associated with cognitive inefficiencies with chronic use (for a review, see Parsons & Nixon, 1998).

Assessing Medical Decision-Making Capacity

There are four components to the client's medical decision–making capacity: (a) an ability to express a consistent choice, (b) an understanding of information concerning diagnosis and treatment options, (c) an ability to relate medical information to one's own situation, and (d) reasoning that is rational and consistent (American Bar Association & American Psychological Association [ABA & APA], 2008). In determining capacity, clinicians must weigh how cognitive deficits or psychiatric factors impact specific decisional elements. For CDCs, clinicians must consider how values, experiences, and beliefs can affect decisions and respect culturally congruent decisions even if it runs counter to the opinions of the medical staff (ABA & APA, 2008). These guidelines would indicate that the information for determining medical decision making would be procured primarily through targeted questioning during the interview.

Tentative Hypotheses Guiding the Evaluation

Given the literature review and referral information, the following are tentative hypotheses about factors that may be affecting Mr. Kim's medical decision making and sources for gathering data to address each hypothesis: (a) He is refusing medications because of his preference for Chinese medicines (interview). (b) The language barrier may affect his ability to appreciate the importance of taking his medications (interview, behavioral observations). (c) His right-sided basal ganglia stroke is affecting his ability to make sound decisions, either through impairments in reasoning or anosognosia (neuropsychological testing, behavioral observations). (d) He is depressed and thus refusing medications and losing his appetite (interview using *International Classification of Diseases, 10th Revision* [ICD–10; World Health Organization, 2015] criteria, objective depression measure, evaluate for presence of somatic symptoms associated with depression in Koreans). (e) Alternatively, or concurrently, his poor appetite may be due to dissatisfaction with hospital food (interview).

Test Selection

Many neuropsychological tests have been translated and validated with Korean samples, including those available commercially, such as the Wechsler Intelligence Scales (Yum, Park, Oh, Kim, & Lee, 1992; for a review, see Chey & Park, 2011). Because of the rarity of testing Korean-speaking clients and the costs of and difficulty in procuring tests manufactured in Korea, the test search for Mr. Kim focused on Western tests that were validated with Korean populations reported in the neuropsychological literature. Test selection was based on several factors: (a) pertinence of cognitive function for evaluating neuropathology, (b) availability of Korean test translations or ease of translating Western tests, and (c) availability of demographic matching norms, preferably with large representative samples. If norms are not available, tests could still be selected if validated in the literature with Korean samples, but these must be interpreted with caveats. Because of the need to translate tests, which is time intensive, brevity of the battery was an additional test consideration.

The following tests were preliminary selections for a brief battery with references for Korean norms or materials:

- *Verbal:* Similarities (Wechsler, 2008a); Boston Naming Test (BNT)—Short Form (H. Kim & Na, 1999; D. Y. Lee et al., 2004)
- *Visuospatial:* Matrix Reasoning (Wechsler, 2008a); Rey–Osterrieth Complex Figure (ROCF; J. S. Kim et al., 2009)
- *Attention and concentration:* Digit Span (Chi et al., 2012)
- *Memory:* Korean CVLT (J. K. Kim & Kang, 1999); ROCF Immediate and Delayed Recall (J. S. Kim et al., 2009)
- *Executive:* Trails A & B (Chi et al., 2012), Wisconsin Card Sorting Test (Chi et al., 2012), Animal Fluency (Chi et al., 2012)
- *Performance validity:* Reliable Digit Span (X. Salazar, Lu, Wen, & Boone, 2007); Digit Span Age Corrected Scaled Score (X. Salazar et al., 2007); Dot Counting (X. Salazar et al., 2007)
- *Personality:* Korean Geriatric Depression Scale (J. Y. Kim et al., 2008)

For Similarities and Matrix Reasoning, norms could not be found; however, given the comparability of tests scores on international tests or the literature, Jo and Dawson (2011) argued that Western norms can be used with caution. Likewise, there is an absence of norms for performance validity tests with specific Korean samples. Reliable Digit Span, Digit Span Age Corrected Scaled Score, and Dot Counting were selected on the basis of ease of administration, with two indicators embedded in Digit Span subtest and the availability of some cross-cultural norms with a mixed Asian American sample (X. Salazar et al., 2007).

For the short form of the BNT, D. Y. Lee et al. (2004) selected five items from the easy, medium, and difficult items on the long form of the test. Unfortunately, the researchers did not identify specific items, and thus a version using the same selection strategy with overlapping items from the Korean (H. Kim & Na, 1999) and the original version of the BNT will be used.

As this description illustrates, the availability of adequately validated, translated, and appropriately normed tests is often not perfect even for a high-resource country like South Korea.

Preparing the Interpreter

A preevaluation meeting with interpreter Ki Dong was scheduled a few days in advance to prepare and strategize for the evaluation. The meeting began with brief introductions and small talk to develop rapport. Ki Dong disclosed that he is originally from Seoul, South Korea, and immigrated when he was 9 years old. He has formal training and 5 years of experience in medical interpreting but has never worked with a neuropsychologist. Thus, he is very familiar with Korean culture and basic skills in interpreting. He was informed that the purpose of a neuropsychological evaluation is to assess cognitive strengths and weaknesses through interviews and administration of tests to determine how it will affect current and future independent functioning and to make recommendations to maximize functionality. Examples of cognitive domains include attention and concentration, memory, language skills, spatial skills, and problem solving.

Ki Dong was given a synopsis of the specific case. The client is a 66-year-old Korean American man who sustained a stroke and is currently at a rehabilitation facility. He is refusing to take his medications to prevent a future stroke, and his physician is particularly concerned about how the stroke has affected his capacity to make sound medical decisions.

Ki Dong was also informed of his roles in the evaluation process. In addition to interpreting, he will be relied on to be a cultural broker to help strategize how to develop rapport, facilitate understanding of Mr. Kim's behaviors within the context of Korean culture to assist in diagnosis, and provide feedback on cultural congruency of recommendations. Specific tasks will include helping to determine whether Mr. Kim is depressed and if his presentation is consistent with common cognitive and behavioral impairments associated with his stroke such attentional problems, impulsivity, problem solving, spatial abilities, and prosody.

Strategies for developing rapport, facilitating communication, and sensitively evaluating for depression were discussed (described in the interview in the next section). It was agreed that Ki Dong would provide a direct translation and then comment on the possible meaning if he felt that Mr. Kim was attempting to communicate something indirectly beyond the content of the message. A tentative outline of the interview was provided to Ki Dong as well as brief demonstrations and instructions for neuropsychological tests, which he will need to translate before the second session. Contact information was exchanged so either party could ask questions or comment on strategies for the neuropsychological evaluation.

INTERVIEW

The first interview lasted for about 90 minutes. Present were Mr. Kim and his youngest daughter, Yun Ji, who was allowed to stay during the initial part of the interview so that family would be involved. The client was addressed as Mr. Kim as a sign of respect. Introductions were made in English with a handshake and a slight head bow, which is a customary Asian greeting. He was informed that his internist, Dr. Johnson, referred him for a neuropsychological evaluation, which will consist of extensive interviews and administration of several tests to determine the impact of his stroke on his functioning. Before starting, Mr. Kim was asked if he preferred that the evaluation be conducted in English or in Korean with Ki Dong as an interpreter. He chose the latter. Mr. Kim and Yun Ji were invited to ask questions if they needed clarification on anything discussed or wanted more information, which they agreed to do.

The purpose of the neuropsychological evaluation was described as testing different components of cognition to determine strengths and weaknesses that could assist in making recommendations for helping Mr. Kim maximize recovery from his stroke in the hospital and then when he returns home. The evaluation would be conducted over two 60- to 90-minute sessions. The first session would consist primarily of an interview to gather information of Mr. Kim's previous functioning and how the stroke has affected his life. Testing, which would require Mr. Kim to answer questions, manipulate objects, or do paper-and-pencil tasks, would occur during the second session.

The clinician informed Mr. Kim of the specific goals of the evaluation. First, Dr. Johnson had concerns about his ability to make good medical decisions because of his refusal to take his prescribed medications, which is important to prevent future strokes. Questions would be asked about his reasons for this decision. Second, his physician was concerned about how Mr. Kim was reacting to his stroke. It is common for stroke patients to become frustrated, angry, or sad, which can have an impact on eating or sleeping, and ultimately participation in treatment. Finally, the clinician stated that he would like to help Mr. Kim achieve his goals because he would have to adapt to the limitations in functioning secondary to his stroke. Mr. Kim reported that he wanted to walk independently, regain strength in his left arm, and return to Korea. Mr. Kim was informed that recommendations could be made to facilitate achievement of these goals, although it would not provide a cure. Mr. Kim and Yun Ji were informed that information from the report would be confidential. However, it would be part of his medical records and would be shared with Dr. Johnson and his hospital treatment team on an as-needed basis to inform his treatment. Anyone else would require permission from Mr. Kim to view the report. They were asked if they had any questions. Mr. Kim was provided with an informed consent form to sign by handing it to him with two hands, which is a gesture of politeness in the Korean culture. Mr. Kim consented. At this time, Yun Ji was asked to leave. Mr. Kim consented to allow her to be interviewed alone after his interview was completed to obtain additional information.

The interview commenced by asking Mr. Kim to describe his background and how he came to the United States, which is a good opening question for Asian immigrants. His responses were followed by intermittent nodding to demonstrate the clinician was listening to him, which is a common Asian gesture. Eye contact was also attenuated to mirror Mr. Kim's, with intermittent glances downward to avoid appearing too intrusive or rude. Mr. Kim was allowed to speak freely, although direct questions were asked to obtain specific information. He was intermittently asked if he had any questions after complicated explanations or during transitions.

Mr. Kim stated that he was working as a manager for a distributing company when he immigrated with his wife and two oldest children 36 years ago to build a better life because the economy in Korea was poor. He was invited by his sister, who had married a U.S. serviceman who had been stationed in Korea. Mr. Kim borrowed money to open a souvenir shop. He and his wife worked long hours to provide for three children and ensure they all received good educations. (At this point, Ki Dong interjected to the clinician that Mr. Kim be asked about his children's education and occupation, because this appears to be a source of pride). Upon questioning, Mr. Kim reported that his son Jun Ho married a Korean national, whom he met in college at Columbia and returned to Korea with her. He is an upper-level manager at a technology company. His oldest daughter, Min Ji, is a certified public accountant who attended the University of California—Berkeley. She is married with two children. Mr. Kim's youngest daughter just completed her law degree at UCLA and is studying for the bar examination. The accomplishments of his children were acknowledged, and he was praised for his sacrifice.

Mr. Kim lives in a Korean enclave and speaks primarily Korean, except at work, where he spoke English to customers. He reads both Korean and English newspapers daily. Mr. Kim attends a Korean Christian Church, watches Korean television, eats mostly Korean foods, and his health care is provided by a Chinese medicine doctor. Mr. Kim has a high school education, where he was ranked third in his class of 80 (Ki Dong recommended he be asked his specific class rank because many Koreans can provide this information).

The topic of refusing medications was then examined through specific questioning. Mr. Kim disclosed that his doctor told him he needs to take medications or he may have another stroke because his blood pressure is too high. He is aware of the risk but has a strong preference for Chinese medicine, which can also help him walk and regain strength on his left side. He believes that he sustained a stroke because he stopped taking his Chinese medicines after his wife died. She would arrange for him to see the doctor several times a year for herbs to "boost" his health and also to receive acupuncture to relieve stress and treat body aches. Chinese medicine kept him healthy until his stroke, which occurred only after he stopped treatment.

Mr. Kim was asked if he could describe his medical condition and its likely causes. He stated that a stroke is an illness of high pressure that affects your brain, which is caused by imbalances in his body due to factors such as low qi, poor kidney functioning, aging, poor diet, and stressors. When asked about recent events in his life that may have been stressful or contributed to imbalances, Mr. Kim disclosed that he had recently sold his business last year after his wife died of cancer 2 years earlier. Mr. Kim was asked if he still smoked cigarettes. He responded that he knew it contributed to his stroke and had therefore quit.

The clinician then gave Mr. Kim a Western medical explanation that blood is supplied to the body through arteries, which is like the pipes in a house. These pipes, however, are more like a rubber hose and can burst if they become brittle and there is too much water pressure. This is what happened to his brain. It is likely his smoking caused his rubber piping to get brittle, and his high blood pressure caused the piping to leak in his brain. The leak caused brain tissue controlling the left side of his body to die; therefore, he has some weakness and slurred speech. It can also affect his thinking, which is what the clinician will be testing for during the next session. His physician wants him to take medication that will lower his blood pressure so no other arteries will burst.

Mr. Kim was asked to explain this model in his own words, which he was able to do. He was asked if it made sense to him. He stated that he respects his doctors and their deep knowledge; however, he felt that taking Chinese medicine would reduce his risk of another stroke and improve his condition. He also decided to stop smoking cigarettes because of his stroke. His plans are to return to Korea in 2 weeks, where he can receive this type of treatment. It was reiterated that his doctors feel he is at serious risk for sustaining another stroke because his blood pressure is dangerously high. He was asked if he believed their assessment, and if not, why not. Mr. Kim nodded his head. He then became a little tearful. He stated that he just wanted to go back to Korea to live with his eldest son and daughter-in-law and receive treatment there. He apologized for tearing, noting that he is not normally emotional, and quickly recomposed himself.

To help him save face, it was explained that his emotionality is a common symptom of stroke, which may improve with time. Strokes are extremely difficult for anyone to deal with, and each patient reacts differently. It is not uncommon for people to become frustrated, sad, or worry about the future. A concern would be how these reactions might affect his recovery. He was given a written questionnaire (Geriatric Depression Scale [GDS]—Korean Version) to evaluate his reactions. His GDS score was 4 of 30, endorsing a lower level of energy, poor concentration, an unclear mind, and a preference to avoid social gatherings. Mr. Kim did not meet the *ICD–10* criteria for depressive episode, presenting only with decreased energy, a diminished ability to think, and reduction in appetite, the latter of which he attributed to a strong preference for Korean foods. Mr. Kim was then asked about common somatic symptoms associated with depression in Koreans as an alternative measure of stress. He endorsed some back pain but denied other symptoms.

When asked about the reason for wanting to return to Korea, Mr. Kim responded that his son Jun Ho and his wife offered to care for him. It would be difficult for Yun Ji to do this by herself, and Min Ji has her own family. Mr. Kim was asked if he had any more questions, and, if not, they would continue the evaluation the next day. He was thanked and offered a handshake with slightly bowed head.

Yun Ji was asked about her father's premorbid behaviors and whether she had noticed any changes since his stroke. She stated that her father was always the decision maker in the household and somewhat rigid. He had always been proud, cautious, and not very emotional. After the stroke, her father was more emotional, more irritable, more rigid, and impulsive—for example, getting out of his chair by himself. Although he is stressed, she does not feel her father is depressed, but more frustrated. Yun Ji stated that her parents have always treated illness with Chinese medicine, and she suspects that her father's distrust for Western medicine increased after her mother died from cancer. Her mother had received treatment from a well-known oncologist but did not survive. Mr. Kim had had much difficulty dealing with her death but continued the business for about a year to keep busy. Yun Ji thought he has dealt well with her mother's passing. Her father had been contemplating returning to Korea because her brother and several of her father's siblings still live there. Yun Ji said that they have tried to persuade her father to take his prescribed medicine, but he has refused. He is also upset about the lack of Korean food served in the hospital. She was willing to bring in Korean food but was told by staff that it was too salty and would not be allowed. She verified estimations of her father's drinking behavior documented in his medical records.

Yun Ji was asked whether she thought her father may compromise and take his prescribed medicines in the hospital if his physician agreed to allow some Chinese medication treatment. She stated he might, but she was not certain. Family goals were to help their father become independent enough that he could tolerate the flight to Korea. Her brother would be coming to get him in 2 weeks. She stated that Korea has an excellent rehabilitation program where he can stay in treatment for months as a dependent under her brother's plan.

After the initial interview, Ki Dong was asked about his impressions. Ki Dong stated that Mr. Kim's beliefs about health are not unusual for an older Korean man, although most would listen to their children in this matter. Going back to Korea would make sense given his situation. Rapport appears to be good. Ki Dong stated that a high school education is about average for his age group, and it was agreed that Mr. Kim appears to be above average in intelligence on the bases of his class ranking and the educational attainment of his children. His ability to understand nonverbals appeared normal. Although Mr. Kim is low in emotional expression compared with U.S. norms for behavior, Ki Dong felt that Mr. Kim's affect was generally normal for Korean Americans, with the exception of tearing when talking about his wife, which was felt to be on the higher end of emotional expression for Korean men even given the emotional content.

The second session focused on testing. Mr. Kim was asked if he had any questions about yesterday's interview or today's testing. He did not. He was reminded to try his best on each task. During testing, Mr. Kim was cooperative and appeared to put forth good effort as he became noticeably frustrated when aware that he was having difficulty on test items. He responded in both Korean and English, the latter for items with simpler verbal explanations. During the verbal fluency tests, he was allowed to name animals in both Korean and English.

After testing was completed, Mr. Kim was again asked about his understanding of the risk for sustaining another stroke if he refused his medications. He stated it was elevated but felt he should be fine until he returned to Korea. He was asked his reasoning for believing he would be fine and whether refusing

Western medicine was worth the risk of another stroke. Mr. Kim nodded his head and stated that he was tired.

In the debriefing session, Ki Dong agreed that Mr. Kim understood instructions and appeared to be motivated to perform well. Ki Dong stated that Koreans are familiar with testing situations and strive to perform their best. He assisted in scoring the verbal fluency items to avoid repetitions. Ki Dong interpreted Mr. Kim's tiredness as avoidance of an emotional question.

9

INTERPRETATION AND CASE FORMULATION

A good decision is based on knowledge and not on numbers.

—Plato

This chapter introduces a systematic process for interpreting interview and testing data within the context of the culturally different clients' (CDCs') culture and experiences to develop a coherent case formulation. Specific steps include (a) scoring tests with appropriate norms, (b) identifying potential threats to validity, (c) determining effort through performance validity tests, (d) reviewing the pertinent neuropsychological literature, and (e) interpreting the data. These steps are described, and then implementation is illustrated through a continuation of Mr. Kim's case.

SCORE TESTS WITH APPROPRIATE AVAILABLE NORMS

The first step in interpretation is to score the tests using appropriate norms. Ideally, norms are based on large sample sizes that are representative of the population. More likely, however, norms will be based on small samples,

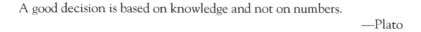

http://dx.doi.org/10.1037/15958-010
Conducting a Culturally Informed Neuropsychological Evaluation, by D. Fujii

and thus demographic matching for ethnicity, age, and education are imperative because there is much heterogeneity in demographics within a given country. Generation is another consideration as older norms may be subject to the Flynn effect (Flynn, 2007; see also Chapter 5, this volume) or may be obsolete for the level of education in the country. As mentioned previously, norms should always pass a "smell test" in which the numbers are consistent with other pertinent data of the culture before being used.

Clinicians should also be cautious when using U.S. norms as a substitute for countries similar in estimated IQ and GDP. Although norms may be generally similar, variability exists for individual tests and studies. This variability can be demonstrated by converting Dutch mean raw scores for common U.S. neuropsychological tests into scaled scores (SS; $M = 10$, $SD = 3$) using U.S. norms. Manipulating data from several Dutch studies yield the following scores: Schilt et al. (2010), $n = 20$, age $M = 46.3$, estimated IQ $M = 103$—Rey Auditory Verbal Learning Test (RAVLT; $M = 52.2$; SS = 11), Judgment of Line Orientation (JOLO; $M = 22.7$; SS = 7), Wechsler Adult Intelligence Scale—Revised (WAIS–R) Digit Span ($M = 16.8$; SS = 11), Paced Auditory Serial Addition Test 1.6 seconds ($M = 41.1$; SS = 12); van de Beek et al. (2002), $n = 25$, age $M = 43.7$; education $M = 13.4$, estimated IQ $M = 98.8$—Trails B ($M = 70.9$, SS = 9), Letter Fluency ($M = 36$, SS = 10), RAVLT immediate ($M = 45$, SS = 9), RAVLT delayed ($M = 9.6$, SS = 10), Wisconsin Card Sorting Test (WCST) perseverative errors ($M = 13.3$, SS = 9); van Hout et al. (2006), age $M = 46$, Grooved Pegboard dominant ($M = 78$, SS = 9) nondominant ($M = 84$, SS = 9), Trails A ($M = 43$, SS = 8), Trails B ($M = 94$, SS = 8), California Verbal Learning Test (CVLT) total ($M = 44$, SS = 10), CVLT long-term free recall ($M = 9$, SS = 11), CVLT recognition total hits ($M = 13.6$, SS = 13), WAIS–R Block Design ($M = 29.3$, SS = 12).

Finally, clinicians should be especially cautious about using U.S. norms on timed tests such as the Trail Making tests even for countries similar in estimated IQ and GDP because much variability exists and normal scores can be erroneously interpreted as being impaired (see Table 9.1 for a list of Trail Making norms). Possible reasons for variability include conception of intelligent behavior (Ardila, 2007) and experiences with timed-based activities (Agranovich & Puente, 2007).

IDENTIFY POTENTIAL THREATS TO TEST VALIDITY

The next step in interpretation is to identify potential threats to test validity. As described in Chapter 4, acculturation and language proficiency are moderating variables that can have an impact on the ability to obtain accurate

TABLE 9.1
Trail Making Norms for Various Countries

Country	Estimated IQ[a]	Age range (years)	Trails A Mean (SD)	Trails B Mean (SD)
United States	98	25–34	19.0 (5.9)	49.5 (17.1)
Denmark	98	20–29	26.9 (10.5)	60.9 (19.9)
Sweden	99	20–34	28.0 (10.7)	64.0 (26.0)
Argentina	93	20–29	38.9 (12.6)	72.3 (20.7)
Italy	97	20–29	33.5 (13.0)	78.1 (33.7)
China	105	20–29	24.7 (7.8)	44.7 (12.0)
Canada	99	20–29	36.1 (10.0)	85.7 (38.7)
Belgium	99	18–29	27 (6)	60 (16)

Note. Data from Fernández and Marcopulos (2008) except as noted. [a]Data from R. Lynn and Vanhanen (2002, 2006).

data. Clinicians should consider the pertinence of aspects of acculturation such as differences in (a) education quality and quantity, (b) epistemology and skills due to illiteracy, (c) cultural conceptions of intelligence, and (d) overall experiences, behaviors, and values. Clinicians should also consider how language proficiency, communication differences, and accommodation/modification efforts (e.g., quality of the interpretation service and of translated tests) affect fair treatment during the testing process. Threats to fair and valid interpretation of test scores include comfort with the testing process, differential advantages associated with test content, test context or administration biases, test response requirements or rubrics for scoring that are non–construct related, and differential opportunities to learn the content and skills measured by the test (American Educational Research Association, American Psychological Association, & National Council on Measurement in Education, 2014).

Similarly, clinicians should consider how acculturation and language proficiency/communication differences affect other aspects of data gathering, such as self-report, collateral report, and history taking, which would be particularly pertinent when evaluating the CDC's adaptive functioning within his or her "real-world" community and charting behavioral changes over time as primary data collection strategies. For example, neuropsychologists may have to titrate clinical impressions when receiving disclosures of symptoms from CDCs who come from cultures with low emotional expression and minimize problems or distress versus CDCs high in emotional expression who freely disclose problems and distress. Degree of acculturation should also be considered when formulating impressions based upon behavioral observations. Finally, clinicians should consider the context of the evaluation, particularly the potential for secondary gain.

ESTIMATE EFFORT THROUGH PERFORMANCE VALIDITY TESTS

This step has two parts. First, the clinician should check results on performance validity tests (PVTs) based on culturally appropriate normative studies (see Chapter 7). If no studies exist, allowances should be made for lower thresholds to identify response biases or insufficient effort, particularly if the CDCs' culture differs considerably from populations on which the PVTs were validated (X. Salazar, Lu, Wen, & Boone, 2007). Adjustments are important because several CDC characteristics have been associated with lower test scores on PVTs, including being foreign born (Webb, Batchelor, Meares, Taylor, & Marsh, 2012); low acculturation (Strutt, Scott, Shrestha, & York, 2011); limited education (Strutt, Scott, Lozano, Tieu, & Peery, 2012); low IQ on Western tests (Dean, Victor, Boone, & Arnold, 2008); and anxiety, depression, poor motivation for the test situation, or mistrust of the clinician (Griffin-Pierce et al., 2008). In addition, the American Academy of Clinical Neuropsychology (AACN; 2007) advises clinicians to err on side of Type I (false-negative) errors, particularly in contexts where there are high costs for response bias (e.g., diagnosis of developmental disability). Studies typically show that when scores are lower, it is only by a few points; thus, significantly low scores (e.g., at chance levels) should be interpreted as resulting from poor effort (X. Salazar et al., 2007). Other signs of poor effort include unexpected or unusually low and/or impaired levels of performance and cognitive profiles that are not consistent with patterns associated with brain disorders (AACN, 2007).

If a CDC fails PVTs, determine possible reasons for poor performance other than response bias or malingering if there is no apparent secondary gain. Consider all the aforementioned biases, as well as unfamiliarity with task or test materials. For example, select pictures on Test of Memory Malingering or pairings on the Word Memory Test may be unfamiliar to CDCs in low-resource countries. If there is secondary gain for poor performance on the evaluation, response bias or malingering are viable explanations.

REVIEW PERTINENT NEUROPSYCHOLOGICAL LITERATURE

The next step in test interpretation is to develop an awareness of the neuropsychological literature for pertinent diagnostics characteristics and factors that can have an effect on test scores. These can be both general neuropsychological factors, such as (a) cognitive profiles and associated behavioral features, prognosis, and interventions for neurological disorders and (b) general patterns and expectations for interpreting neuropsychological tests, or they can be specific cultural factors, such as (c) culturally associated factors that can affect neuropsychological test performance and (d) specific neurological and testing literature pertinent for the CDC. Knowledge of this literature is crucial for recognizing behavioral patterns and interpreting test results for accurate differential diagnosis and case conceptualization.

Cognitive Profiles and Associated Behavioral Features, Prognosis, and Interventions for Neurological Disorders

When determining a diagnosis, neuropsychologists should be familiar with the overall presentation of the neurological disorders considered for differential diagnosis and not just cognitive strengths and weaknesses. Age of onset, medical and nonmedical risk factors, and associated features including behavioral, emotional, and psychiatric symptoms are all syndrome-related characteristics that are important considerations in diagnostic pattern analysis, whereas prognosis, common challenges, and evidence-based interventions are essential for making useful recommendations.

General Patterns and Expectations for Interpreting Neuropsychological Tests

Before interpreting CDCs' neuropsychological profiles, it is important that clinicians be aware of typical test score patterns for normal Western populations (see Chapter 5, this volume). This awareness can help clinicians avoid misinterpretation due to erroneous assumptions. For example, the general assumption of a neuropsychological evaluation is that test scores gravitate around IQ scores, thus estimated premorbid IQ is the benchmark to predict and interpret test scores (Lezak, Howieson, Bigler, & Tranel, 2012). This assumption received strong support in a large, community-based study in which participants with above average IQs scored significantly better than participants with average-level IQs on a broad range of neuropsychological tests (Cohen's $d = .41$; Diaz-Asper, Schretlen, & Pearlson, 2004). Differential scoring was even stronger when comparing average versus below average IQ groups (Cohen's $d = .74$; Diaz-Asper, Schretlen, & Pearlson, 2004). However, the literature suggests that this linear relationship is too simplistic as intra-individual test scatter across a battery of neuropsychological tests is also common (Schretlen, Munro, Anthony, & Pearlson, (2003). For example, in a sample ($N = 197$) of healthy community-living adults who were administered a neuropsychologist test battery, 44% reported z scores greater than 2 SDs below their estimated IQ, while 32% of subjects' highest test score exceeded 2 SDs above their estimated IQs. In general, intraindividual variability increased with age (Schretlen, Munro, Anthony, & Pearlson, 2003).

Data from the WAIS–IV, which is standardized on a large national representative sample, also report positive correlations between IQ scores and

TABLE 9.2
Comparable Standard Scores for the WTAR, WAIS–III FSIQ,
and WMS–III Immediate Memory and General Memory Indices

WTAR	WAIS–III FSIQ	WMS–III IM	WMS–III GM
60	71	80	79
70	78	85	84
80	86	90	90
90	93	95	95
100	100	100	100
110	107	105	105
120	114	110	110
130	122	115	116

Note. FSIQ = full scale IQ; WAIS = Wechsler Adult Intelligence Scale; WMS = Wechsler Memory Scale; WTAR = Wechsler Test of Adult Reading.

cognitive domains although there is considerable variability for strengths of associations for individual tests: Wechsler Memory Scale—III (WMS–III) Auditory Delayed Index .57, WMS–III Visual Delayed Index .34, Delis–Kaplan Executive Functioning Scales Number—Letter Switching—Completion Time .77, Category Fluency .50, CVLT–II trials 1 through 5.48, CVLT–II trial B .29, and CVLT–II free recall intrusions –.10 (Wechsler, 2008a).

Various standard scores from the Wechsler Test of Adult Reading (WTAR; Wechsler, 2001) with corresponding estimated WAIS–III Full Scale IQ, WMS–III (Wechsler, 1997) Immediate Memory (IM) and General Memory (GM) indices are presented in Table 9.2. Of note is the pattern for IQs and memory indices to be higher than WTAR standard scores for below average scores, converging at the average level, and lower IQ and memory predictions for WTAR scaled scores at the higher levels. These data would indicate that there is not a perfect correspondence between IQ and various cognitive domains, although a crossover pattern of scores exists with memory and reading levels. Taken together, these findings argue for the importance of pattern analysis–based interpretation and congruence of test scores and expectations given the underlying neurological disorder.

Culturally Associated Factors That Can Affect Neuropsychological Test Performance

Acculturation

Research indicates that acculturation significantly affects test performance on standard neuropsychological tests within various cultures. In older African

Americans (Manly et al., 1998), level of acculturation, as measured by self-report and Black English use, was negatively related to WAIS–R Information, Trails B, and the Boston Naming Test (BNT). In Hispanics, formal measures of acculturation were associated with lower scores on WCST total trials and nonperseverative errors; Coffey, Marmol, Schock, & Adams, 2005) and accounted for 11% to 14% of the variance in Global Neuropsychological functioning, Verbal Fluency, and Processing Speed (Arentoft et al., 2012). A similar relationship was found between acculturation and performances on Digit Span, Digit Symbol, Trails A, and Stroop B (Razani, Burciaga, Madore, & Wong, 2007) and the Wechsler Abbreviated Scale of Intelligence (WASI) Full Scale IQ (FIQ), Verbal IQ (VIQ), Performance IQ (PIQ), Vocabulary, and Similarities (Razani, Murcia, Tabares, & Wong, 2007) in a mixed sample of Asians, Middle Easterners, and Hispanics. In an Australian study (Walker, Batchelor, Shores, & Jones, 2010), foreign-born subjects from non–English-speaking countries who were educated in English scored lower than subjects who spoke and were raised in English-speaking countries on VIQ, Vocabulary, Logical Memory, and Verbal Paired Associates.

An indicator of acculturation among immigrant samples that has demonstrated a strong relationship with scores on neuropsychological testing is years educated in the United States, which has positive associations with WASI FIQ, VIQ, Vocabulary, Similarities, and Block Design (Razani, Murcia, et al., 2007); BNT (Boone et al., 2007); Digit Symbol—Coding (Krch et al., 2015), and general WAIS–III/WMS–III performance and has been found to be a stronger predictor of performance than formal years of education (J. G. Harris, Tulsky, & Schultheis, 2003).

English as a Second Language

As would be expected, CDCs for whom English is a second language consistently score lower on verbal tests versus matched samples where English is the first language, for example, Letter and Category Fluency (Boone et al., 2007; Kisser, Wendell, Spencer, & Waldstein, 2012), VIQ, Vocabulary (Carstairs, Myors, Shores, & Fogarty, 2006; Razani, Murcia, et al., 2007; Walker et al., 2010), Similarities (Razani, Murcia, et al., 2007; Walker et al., 2010), BNT and Digit Span (Boone et al., 2007), and Logical Memory I and Verbal Paired Associates I (Walker et al., 2010). Studies also report lower scores on other timed and executive functioning tasks, such as Picture Completion and Block Design (Walker et al., 2010), PIQ (Carstairs et al., 2006; Razani, Murcia, et al., 2007; Walker et al., 2010), Trails A (Carstairs et al., 2006), Trails B and Stroop B (Razani, Burciaga, et al., 2007), Digit Symbol—Coding and WCST (Krch et al., 2015), and Cognitive Estimation (Kisser et al., 2012). Performance on verbal tests were found to be mediated by factors such as percentage of time English spoken by the CDC while growing up (Razani, Burciaga, et al., 2007), age at which conversational English was first learned (Boone et al., 2007), education in English (Walker et al., 2010) reported language preference (J. G. Harris et al., 2003), and years educated and residing in the United States (Boone et al., 2007). CDCs for whom English is a second language will often also score lower on nonverbal or performance oriented tests, which may be due to language or concomitant cultural effects.

Bilingualism

A related CDC characteristic with implications for the English as a second language (ESL) literature is bilingualism because many CDCs with ESL are bilingual. Bilingualism is a varied ability. Balanced bilinguals are equally competent in two languages, typically due to the acquisition and frequent use of both languages from an early age. Later learners start off as monolinguals and learn a second language later in life. Most clients fall somewhere in between. Research indicates that two languages are always active, thus bilinguals must inhibit activation of the nontargeted language in the conversation. It is generally easier to suppress the nondominant language because the dominant is more accessible (for a review, see Rivera Mindt et al., 2008).

There are several cognitive implications of bilingualism. Compared with monolinguals, bilinguals have smaller vocabularies within each language, which manifests in both receptive and productive speech. Bilinguals have more tip-of-the-tongue failures, are slower in confrontational picture naming, and perform worse on verbal fluency tasks, but have greater semantic fluency than letter fluency. Disadvantages are more pronounced for low-frequency words (for a review, see Rivera Mindt et al., 2008). Given the inhibitory control required to suppress the nontargeted language, it has been purported that bilinguals develop stronger executive functioning and attentional abilities than monolinguals (Bialystok, Craik, & Luk, 2012). However, support for this contention has been inconsistent (Paap & Greenberg, 2013). Studies demonstrating positive support typically use tests that are not commonly used in a neuropsychological test battery (Adesope, Lavin, Thompson, & Ungerleider, 2010).

Illiteracy

Given the profound impact of education on intelligence and cognition, it is not surprising that illiteracy and low educational levels are associated with global deficits on neuropsychological testing (Reis, Guerreiro, & Petersson, 2003). Because this finding is a given, perhaps a more important implication of the literature is providing a context for understanding behaviors and making recommendations. For example, people who are illiterate are highly influenced by direct sensory experience and perceive the world in practical functional terms versus abstract categories; memory is functional for tangible objects in the environment, but impaired for concepts or objects that are not in the immediate environment. Thus, learning is more procedural, sensory oriented, and practical, which differs significantly from people who are literate (Ardila et al., 2010). This epistemology would be essential for conceptualizing the world of those who are illiterate and making useful recommendations.

Poverty

Because many CDCs are of low socioeconomic status (SES; Macartney, Bishaw, & Fontenot, 2013), the literature on poverty and cognition may provide an important context for interpreting test data and understanding how CDCs' environment can negatively influence their cognition. For example, lower quantities and quality of linguistic exposure can retard the development of language-supporting brain regions in children and ultimately contribute to SES disparities in language skills. Similarly, exposure to stress mediates the development of the hippocampus and prefrontal cortex and limbic circuitry, which in turn can contribute to SES disparities in declarative memory and self-regulation, respectively (for a review, see Noble, 2014).

Targets for Data Interpretation

As described in Chapter 4, the evaluation should be guided by both the specific goals of the referral question and the goals of the CDC and family. Together, these make up the focus of the evaluation. Specific goals typically map onto three overlapping categories: (a) providing a diagnosis, (b) determining functionality, and (c) making recommendations.

Diagnosis is based on hypothesis testing and a "goodness of fit" between the CDC's presentation and diagnostic criteria for neurological or psychiatric disorders. Sometimes diagnostic questions involve establishing etiology, but more frequently, diagnosis entails determining the degree of cognitive impairment, as in *Dementia (ICD–10)/Major Neurocognitive Disorder (MaND) (DSM–5)* or *Mental Retardation (MR) (ICD–10) Intellectual Disability (ID) (DSM–5)*. In these cases, level of impairment is determined through a quantitative or qualitative estimate of the impact that a neurological condition has on cognition and independent functioning. Quantitative data from neuropsychological testing is needed for precision in assessing cognitive decline, useful for pattern analysis of cognitive deficits associated with etiologies, and important for determining effort and malingering when secondary gain is a salient issue. Qualitative data such as behavioral presentation, current adaptive functioning, and history of cognitive decline over time are useful as an approximate measure of cognitive impairment but lack precision to differentiate subtler levels of decline. Other potential data sources for formulating a diagnosis include medical data, such as neuroimaging, neurological examination, personal and family medical history, current cognitive, emotional, and behavioral presentation; changes in presentation over time; and performance on neuropsychological testing. An important implication of diagnosis is prognosis and specific evidence-based treatments, which can be addressed in the recommendations.

Functionality is a behavioral or real-world determination or prediction of what a CDC can or cannot do within his or her environment. Specific functions include activities of daily living (ADLs), instrumental ADLS, legal capacities, interpersonal relations, hobbies, and academic and vocational performances. Although neuropsychological test data can provide crucial information for conceptualizing functional abilities, functionality is heavily based on observations, interviews, self, family, and collateral reports of abilities, and the literature on prognosis for a given neurological disorder. The contribution of neuropsychological data can be predictive, forecasting challenges for future functioning, or explanatory, extrapolating the impact of cognitive strengths and weaknesses upon current functioning. For legal determinations, clinicians must integrate data to formulate opinions addressing legal standards.

Aside from certain legal and insurance company disability-driven assessments, the neuropsychological evaluation typically culminates in the *recommendations*, where the clinician can address the concerns of the referral sources and CDC and family. It also affords an opportunity to assist in improving other aspects of the CDC's life that are not mentioned in the goals, such as independence, functionality, and quality of life. Recommendations should be practical, strengths based, and congruent with the CDC's culture, environment, and resources.

Recommendations directed toward referral sources and clinicians should have two goals. The first is to address referral questions about diagnosis, functionality, and prognosis to assist in clinical decision making. Identifying pertinent clinical issues and efficacious treatments can contribute to this goal. A second goal is to educate clinicians about the CDC's culture to facilitate understanding about presentation and how to best work with the CDC and his or her family. Specific issues include how culture interfaces with communication, compliance, and follow-up. If there are evidence based-treatments, clinicians should explain how the intervention interfaces with cultural values, beliefs, and behaviors and what type of adaptations are needed, if any.

To maximize the usefulness of the evaluation for the CDC and family, recommendations should address their concerns and recovery goals as determined during preinterview contact or evaluation. The neuropsychologist should conceptualize how cognitive strengths and weaknesses; mood, psychiatric, or behavioral presentations; course; and prognosis interface with the CDC's functioning in everyday life and what individual, familial, or community resources are available to the CDC and family. Cultural considerations include familial and gender roles, stigma about mental health issues, saving face for families, conceptualization of health and illness, and treatment options and preferences.

A good heuristic for conceptualization of recommendations is Lewin's (1964) field theory, which argues that behavior is a function of the person and environment. Thus, to improve functioning, interventions can target improving a person's functionality or manipulating the environment. Interventions targeting the person would include medications to treat the illness, psychiatric disorder, or symptom (e.g., pain); psychotherapy to reduce distress; psychoeducation to improve understanding; rehabilitation therapies to build skills; and prosthetic devices to facilitate independence. Environmental manipulations should target both the social environment, such as teaching skills or educating caregivers and ameliorating their stress, and physical environment, which entails simplifying or modifying the environment or providing structure and routine to minimize the need for executive functioning and memory.

CONTINUATION OF CASE SAMPLE

Score Tests and Review for Appropriateness

Korean norms are available for most selected tests and should be the primary basis for interpretation, with U.S. norms being the primary basis for interpretation only when Korean norms are not available. Still, as the Dutch and Jordanian examples illustrate, unpredictable differences in norms can occur even when using norms from countries that should have comparable overall IQs with the United States. Thus, it is good practice to always score tests with both country and U.S. norms and compare scores to determine appropriateness and assist with interpretation because significant discrepancies can provide clues for cultural influences on test performances (see Table 9.3).

A review of norms indicates predominantly comparable scores typically within 1 to 2 scaled scores with the exception of Trails B (timed test) and WCST. As previously reviewed, Trails is a timed test, which can be esoteric for culture. The WCST is interesting, because the U.S. norms are significantly more stringent for categories completed, whereas the relationship is reversed for perseverative errors. One interpretation is that the two cultures may have salient differences in approaching this unstructured task. For example, on visual perception and reasoning tasks, Asians are found to emphasize relationships between objects and context, compared Westerners, who focus more on specific details of objects (for a review, see Zaroff, D'Amato, & Bender, 2014).

TABLE 9.3
Raw Test Scores Scored With Korean and American Norms

Test	Raw score	Korean scaled score	American scaled score
Similarities	15		SS = 6[d]
BNT short form	15/15	SS = 12[a]	SS = 10[e]
Matrix Reasoning	4		SS = 4[d]
ROCF	22/36	SS = ≤1[b]	SS = 2[f]
Digit Span	10	SS = 6[b]	SS = 6[d,g]
CVLT–II 1–5	44	SS = 12[c]	SS = 10[h]
CVLT–II SDFR	8		SS = 10[h]
CVLT–II LDFR	8		SS = 10[h]
ROCF immediate	10	SS = 5[b]	SS = 6[f]
ROCF delayed	8	SS = 5[b]	SS = 5[f]
Trails A	91″	SS = 4[a]	SS = 2[f]
Trails B	265″	SS = 5[a]	SS = 2[f]
WCST categories	0	SS = 7[a]	SS = 2[i]
WCST PE	23	SS = 5[a]	SS = 9[i]
Animal Fluency	12	SS = 8[a]	SS = 6[f]
Reliable Digit Span	5		cut off ≤ 6[j]
Digit Span ACSS	6		cut off ≤ 5[j]
Dot Counting E score	14		cut off ≥ 17[k]

Note. ACSS = Age-Corrected Scale Score; BNT = Boston Naming Test; CVLT = California Verbal Learning Test; ROCF = Rey–Osterrieth Complex Figure; WCST = Wisconsin Card Sorting Test. Sources for norms: [a]Chi et al. (2012); [b]Ahn et al. (2010); [c]J. K. Kim and Kang (1999); [d]Wechsler (2008a); [e]Morris et al. (1989); [f]Mitrushina, Boone, Razani, and D'Elia (2005); [g]Wechsler (1997); [h]Delis, Kramer, Kaplan, and Ober (2000); [i]Heaton, Chelune, Talley, Kay, and Curtiss (1993); [j]Babikian, Boone, Lu, and Arnold (2006); [k]Boone, Lu, and Herzberg (2002).

Given that WCST categories are based on identifying a specific characteristic of each card, it is conceivable that an examinee would complete more categories by focusing on details versus relationships between stimuli, whereas the latter process would reduce the likelihood of perseverating on a detail-oriented strategy.

Next, modified tests should be reviewed. Mr. Kim's score on the BNT would indicate item selection did not have a negative impact on performance, although it is not certain whether it was easier than the validated version. His BNT score is significantly higher than the other naming test, animal fluency; however, the latter has a timed component, and processing speed would be predicted to be affected by an acute stroke. Thus, scores on these two tests are not entirely inconsistent. His BNT score is consistent with verbal learning (CVLT), which would give credence to the validity of this score.

For interpretation strategy, both a direct comparison with a group of demographically similar peers and individual comparison methods can be employed for tests with Korean norms. Due to potential biases, an individual comparison approach would be most appropriate for tests scored with U.S. norms.

Identify Potential Threats to Test Validity

Mr. Kim strongly identifies with Korean culture and values, as evidenced by his primary spoken language, residential neighborhood, social networks, food and entertainment preferences, and preference for Chinese versus Western medicines, the latter of which is highly salient when assessing for medical decision-making capacity. Korean society highly values education, and their educational system is advanced; thus, quality of education, conception of intelligence, and familiarity and comfort with test-taking situations are likely comparable to the United States. For the same reason, threats to validity due to comfort with the testing process and differential opportunities for learning are believed to be minimal.

Mr. Kim required an interpreter for the evaluation. Ki Dong is experienced with good training and preparation for the evaluation, thus the quality of interpretation is deemed to be good, minimizing biases due to disadvantages in test response rubrics. Only tests validated in Korean culture were used in the evaluation with the CVLT and BNT using stimuli from Korean adaptations, which would control for content biases. Verbal tests, which would be highly challenging to ensure equivalent translations, were not selected. Nonetheless, translations are a weakness because it was not cross-checked by a second translator, and a back translation was not conducted. Also, the BNT was not an official version, and Trails B used English versus Korean stimuli, so validated norms may be less applicable.

Culturally Associated Factors That Can Affect Neuropsychological Test Interpretations

Although Mr. Kim immigrated to the United States 36 years ago, he was not educated in the United States. In addition, he appears marginally integrated into mainstream society; thus, acculturation could affect performances on tests scored with U.S. norms, such as Similarities, Matrix Reasoning, and individual trials of the CVLT. The literature would suggest that both acculturation and ESL can have an impact on Similarities, thus Mr. Kim's score is likely a low estimate of his abstraction abilities. ESL can also affect other nonverbal reasoning tests (e.g., Block Design, PIQ), although Matrix Reasoning was not specifically identified. For the CVLT, U.S. norms are more stringent than Korean norms on the composite score for trials I through V. Korean norms were not available for the delayed recall trials; however, scaled scores were exactly the same for all trials when scored with U.S. norms. Given that verbal learning also appears to be affected by ESL, it could be assumed that Mr. Kim's performance on the delayed recall trials of the CVLT would be at least average compared with other Korean Americans.

Estimate Effort Through Performance Validity Tests

Mr. Kim passed two of three PVTs in an evaluation that is not inherently associated with secondary gain. The test he did fail (Reliable Digit Span) is much more specific than sensitive, and he is in the acute state of recovery from stroke; thus, attentional problems are expected. Both clinician and interpreter opined that Mr. Kim put forth good effort on tests, and the test data are interpreted as being reflective of his current abilities.

Interpreting Data Within the Context of the Pertinent Neuropsychological Literature

A review of the pertinent neuropsychological literature revealed that the sequelae of Mr. Kim's cognitive and motor symptoms were typical of a right basal ganglia cerebrovascular accident (CVA), including left-sided weakness for both upper and lower extremities and deficits in visuoconstruction, nonverbal reasoning, visual memory, executive functioning, complex visual attention, and working memory, with relative sparing of confrontational naming and verbal memory. There was no evidence for aprosodia. Possible mild anosognosia and some disinhibition were observed, as was mild left-sided neglect on the Rey–Osterrieth Complex Figure (ROCF). Deficits and neurological symptoms would be expected to be most pronounced in the current acute stage of his CVA, so it is assumed that abilities should improve over time, particularly during the first 6 months postinjury.

Addressing Targets for Data Interpretation

Specific goals for this evaluation included (a) determining decision-making capacity for medical decisions (referral source); (b) assessing the client's ability to walk independently, use his left arm, and return to Korea (Mr. Kim); and (c) preventing a future stroke and gaining strength for travel (family). An additional issue is increasing Mr. Kim's food intake. These goals are addressed in accordance with general evaluation goals.

Diagnosis

Although diagnosis is not a primary goal of this evaluation, determination of a diagnosis can assist with conceptualization to address the goals of the evaluation and also to establish prognosis and identify evidence-based treatments. With the given caveats for test interpretation, Mr. Kim's pattern of test scores with weaker visual processing skills and mild left-sided neglect associated with right hemisphere lesions, executive functioning associated with connections to frontal lobes, and working memory and processing speed associated with these areas were consistent with his acute right basal ganglia stroke. His presentation and level of impairment, particularly for memory, would not meet criteria for a vascular dementia diagnosis. He only demonstrated one impaired level performance (ROCF), which is not unusual in healthy control subjects. Given his primarily borderline-level weaknesses in the acute stages of recovery, Mr. Kim's presentation would be most consistent with mild cognitive disorder. As described in Chapter 8, his disclosures and presentation would rule against a depressive disorder but are possibly consistent with an adjustment disorder unspecified (ICD–10), because his purported symptom is not overtly mood or anxiety related, but instead medication refusal.

Functionality

The referral source's functional question is capacity for medical decision making, which can be determined by addressing the following four components (American Bar Association & American Psychological Association, 2008):

1. *Does Mr. Kim have an ability to express a consistent choice?* Yes, he consistently expressed to his internist and neuropsychologist that he prefers Chinese to Western medicine.
2. *Does Mr. Kim understand the information concerning diagnosis and treatment options?* Yes, he understood he had suffered a stroke and was at risk for sustaining a second event. He was able to describe both Chinese and Western causal explanations for a stroke and knew Chinese and Western medicine treatment options.
3. *Can he relate the medical information to his own situation?* Although Mr. Kim was aware that he had sustained a stroke and was at risk for a second, he may have been underestimating the risk or downplaying or denying the potential impact of a second stroke on his health and independence. He only had about 2 weeks before he would return to Korea and receive his preferred treatment (i.e., Chinese medicine), which likely factored into his decision to stop taking Western medicines.
4. *Is his reasoning rational and consistent?* Mr. Kim's preference is consistent with cultural beliefs for illness and treatment, as well as his long-term personal preferences because he identifies strongly with Korean culture and is minimally assimilated into Western culture. He had enjoyed good health while taking Chinese medicines, and his stroke occurred after he stopped taking them. His wife's death also appears to have had a strong impact on his distrust of Western medicine, which is understandable. However, it is possible that

his stroke has had some impact on his thinking (e.g., increased rigidity in a person who the family has described as premorbidly stubborn; more concrete thinking). Because older Koreans will often listen to their children for advice on health care, his behavior may be perceived as unusual or extreme.

In weighing Mr. Kim's decision making and the factors affecting that process, there does not appear to be overwhelming evidence that he lacks capacity because his decision is highly consistent with his belief system. Although cognitive factors could have some impact on his ability to reason, it was deemed that he had capacity.

Recommendations

The primary aim of making recommendations is to address goals of the referral source, client, and family. The underlying motivation for Dr. Johnson's referral was to prevent a second stroke by treating Mr. Kim's high blood pressure. He was first educated on cultural factors related to Mr. Kim's behaviors and miscommunication between Dr. Johnson and his client, such as Mr. Kim's rationale for refusing medications; overestimation of his English skills; misinterpretation of his nodding, which was not intended to indicate agreement; and his dissatisfaction with institutional food. It was then suggested to Dr. Johnson that a compromise be made. Dr. Johnson could allow Mr. Kim to undergo acupuncture treatments, which has some empirical evidence for reducing spasticity in stroke patients (S. M. Lim et al., 2015) and work with the dietician to liberalize his diet and allow him to eat some Korean foods if he agrees to take his hypertension medications until he is discharged. Although initially reluctant, he was agreeable to offer this proposal to Mr. Kim and his family.

Mr. Kim and his family's goals were also functional and not inconsistent with Dr. Johnson's goal. For Mr. Kim, acupuncture treatments would facilitate his goal of regaining use of his arm and walking and increasing his comfort level by receiving a treatment modality in which he has confidence. Allowing Korean food in his diet would reduce dissatisfaction and increase strength, the latter of which would be important for participation in rehabilitation. The proposed compromise would also facilitate family goals of preventing a future stroke and gaining the strength needed for the flight back to Korea.

A second aim was to infuse cultural considerations into standard recommendations for clients sustaining a right hemisphere stroke. Thus, for Mr. Kim, addressing stigma associated with mental illness or dementia, saving face, maintaining behavioral controls within a collectivist culture and relinquishing his role as head of the household are pertinent cultural considerations for maximizing the usefulness of standard recommendations. For depression or poorly controlled emotional responses, efforts to medicalize and normalize symptoms can reduce the perceived stigma associated with mental health issues. Providing strategies to cope with "normal" reactions may help to prevent depressive symptoms. Strategies to facilitate cognitive functioning allow Mr. Kim some control, reducing stigma associated with dementia. Educating Mr. Kim and his family about common behaviors associated with a right hemisphere stroke, including potential impulsivity, emotionality, or poor social awareness, and strategies to control or prevent the display of these behaviors in public would help maintain behavioral decorum in a collectivist society. Facilitating maintenance of traditional family hierarchy may assuage Mr. Kim's adjustment difficulties in becoming more dependent on his children.

10

WRITING THE REPORT
AND PROVIDING FEEDBACK

Everything should be as simple as possible, but not simpler.
—Albert Einstein

REPORT WRITING

Report writing is highly individualized, and each neuropsychologist has his or her own style and templates. In addition, the content, length, and details can vary with the purpose and setting of an evaluation. For example, forensic reports or those prepared for insurance company workers' compensation cases are typically longer and more detailed than routine screens for rehabilitation inpatients. Thus, the purpose of this section is not to dictate how to write a culturally informed report but instead to describe elements that should be included in a comprehensive evaluation.

Report writing for a culturally different client (CDC) is similar to writing a routine report. It should tell a story with a beginning (reason for referral, background), a middle (data collection), and end (formulation, recommendations). The primary difference is that all the potential limitations to data validity should be documented in the CDC's report. Recommended elements

http://dx.doi.org/10.1037/15958-011
Conducting a Culturally Informed Neuropsychological Evaluation, by D. Fujii

include descriptions of (a) the clinician's fluency in the CDC's language; (b) quality of communication with the CDC; (c) uncertainties about the fidelity of translations, such as literal content, culturally mediated meanings, affective tone, and nonverbal body language; (d) impact of using an interpreter on the validity of the test results and interview data; and (e) modifications of test administration and scoring and their potential effect on the validity of the assessment results. Other recommended elements include (f) rapport and the CDC's comfort with the evaluation process; (g) rationale for test selection (American Academy of Clinical Neuropsychology, 2007; American Psychological Association, 2003, 2010); (h) formulations to be made, with caveats; and (i) specific conclusions, qualified by a confidence level. A general heuristic for these elements is to "make the implicit explicit."

Another way to conceptualize the specific goals for writing a culturally informed neuropsychological report is that the writer should inform the reader of his or her (a) awareness of cultural factors that can affect or limit the validity of data collection and interpretation; (b) efforts to address these issues; and (c) confidence in the test results, diagnoses, or clinical opinions. Because cultural factors will vary depending on the CDC's ethnic background, acculturation, and English skills, cultural details will also differ by report.

The following is a sample report for Jae Song Kim. Recommended cultural elements are italicized and identified throughout the report.

JAE SONG KIM REPORT

Reason for Referral

Jae Song Kim is a 66-year-old, Korean American man who sustained a right-sided basal ganglia stroke with left hemiparesis. A magnetic resonance imaging scan revealed an infarct of the right putamen, right globus pallidus, and posterior limb of the internal capsule. After transfer to a rehabilitation facility, he started to refuse his hypertension medications and would not comply even after informed of the risk for sustaining a second stroke. Mr. Kim was referred by his internist, Dr. Johnson, to evaluate for cognition and how it relates to medical capacity for decision making, with the underlying goal of medication adherence to prevent a future stroke. Mr. Kim has also lost weight, and thus depression is another concern.

Before his stroke, Mr. Kim enjoyed good health. His medical history includes hypertension (diagnosed at the time of his stroke), nicotine dependence (one pack per day for 40 years), and social drinking (one to two glasses of Korean rice wine two to five times a week for 40 years). There is no history of head injury or psychiatric illness.

Brief Background History

Mr. Kim is a widower who was born and raised in Incheon, South Korea. He graduated from high school and was ranked third in his class of 80. He initially worked as a manager in a distributing company before immigrating to the United States 36 years ago. Mr. Kim opened up a souvenir shop with his wife, which he sold a year ago, a year after his wife died. Mr. Kim has three children and was able to finance their education from universities with highly competitive and selective admissions. They have professional occupations, including certified public accountant, attorney, and upper-level management in a large Korean company. Mr. Kim lives in a Korean enclave, eats primarily Korean food, and socializes almost exclusively with other Korean speakers. He speaks English primarily to customers. He reads both Korean and English papers.

The clinician is not familiar with Korean language (clinician's fluency), thus the evaluation was conducted through a *formally trained interpreter with several years of medical interpreting experience. He was also born in South Korea and thus is very familiar with Korean culture. He was prepped on the purpose of the evaluation, his role, and expectations* (quality of communication).

Behavioral Observations and Interview

Mr. Kim was a neatly groomed 66-year-old Korean American with a left-sided hemiplegia who appeared about his chronological age. His speech was fluent, and thought processes were linear. He spoke primarily in Korean but also responded in English. He appeared to understand the purpose of the evaluation and limits to confidentiality and agreed to the evaluation and use of an interpreter. *The fidelity of interpreter-mediated translation, including literal content, culturally mediated meanings, and nonverbals, was believed to be good* (fidelity, nonverbal), as was the *writer's rapport with Mr. Kim* (rapport). *He appeared open in answering questions. Thus, information collected is believed to be valid* (impact of using interpreter on validity of data collection). The evaluation was conducted in two sessions held on consecutive days. On questioning, Mr. Kim stated that his goal was to walk independently, regain use of his left arm, and return to Korea to live with his son and continue his rehabilitation. Family goals were preventing a future stroke and gaining strength for travel back to Korea.

Mr. Kim was interviewed about his reason for refusing medications to prevent a future stroke. He explained that he preferred and believed in Chinese versus Western medicines. He had been healthy all his life until he stopped taking Chinese medicines. His wife recently died of cancer even with expensive Western treatments, which exacerbated his distrust of Western medicine. His goal is to return to Korea with his son in 2 weeks to continue his rehabilitation, which will include Chinese medicine. Mr. Kim was able to describe both Chinese and Western causal explanations for a stroke and knew both Chinese and Western treatment options. He understood he had suffered a stroke and is at risk for sustaining a second event; however, he appeared avoidant when asked for the cost–benefit of taking Western medicines versus sustaining a second stroke.

Mr. Kim denied feeling depressed despite a moment of tearing. On the Korean version of the Geriatric Depression Scale, his score of 4 out of 30 was significantly below criteria for depression, only endorsing items for a lower level of energy, poor concentration, an unclear mind, and a preference to avoid social gatherings. His poor appetite was attributed to a strong preference for Korean foods, which were unavailable at the rehabilitation facility. Mr. Kim only endorsed one somatic symptom (back pain; somatic symptoms are commonly associated with depression in Koreans). His daughter did not feel he was depressed.

Tests Administered and Results

Selected neuropsychological tests have all been validated in Korea; however, these materials could not be procured, and thus instructions to tests were translated by the interpreter before the evaluation. To maximize test equivalency, only tests requiring minimal responses for verbal stimuli were administered (rationale for test selection). *Exceptions included the California Verbal Language, for which words from the Korean version* (J. K. Kim & Kang, 1999) *were back-translated to Korean, and the short form of the Boston Naming Test, for which item selection was based on strategy for test development from the Korean version or the test* (H. Kim & Na, 1999; modifications in test administration). *Although the translation was not back-translated nor reviewed by an independent translator, it is believed to be adequate for purposes of testing, as demonstrated by client's apparent ability to understand and follow instructions well* (uncertainties about fidelity). *Tests were administered in a standardized manner and deviated only to the extent that translations differed from validated versions* (modifications in test administration).

Test results were interpreted both with Korean and American norms, the latter primarily when Korean norms were not available. Although cultural biases may exist, the applicability of American norms are based on comparability in education, IQ, and scores on tests of academic achievement between Korea and the United States. Because of potential biases, test scored with American norms were be interpreted broadly (modifications in scoring). (For list of tests and test results refer to Table 9.3.)

Formulation

Mr. Kim passed two of three performance validity tests, including the Digit Span Age-Corrected Scale Score and Dot Counting Test. He failed the Reliable Digit Span; however, he is in the acute-stage poststroke recovery in which attentional deficits are expected, and the test is much more specific than it is sensitive. In addition, there is no apparent secondary gain for poor performances, and he appeared to put good effort on tests, thus *results are believed to be a fairly accurate estimate of his abilities at the time of testing, given the limitations of the U.S. norms for test interpretation* (conclusions qualified by confidence level).

Mr. Kim's premorbid intellectual functioning is estimated to be above average for Korean American peers based on his academic class ranking, successful business, and children's education and occupational levels. Relative strengths were demonstrated on verbal tasks, including confrontational naming, verbal fluency, and verbal learning, which generally fell within the average range. By contrast, consistent weaknesses were demonstrated on tests of visual construction that fell within the impaired range and nonverbal reasoning and visual memory that fell within the borderline range. A mild left-sided neglect was also demonstrated. Borderline-level functioning was also returned on tests associated with executive functioning and complex attention, whereas Mr. Kim demonstrated low-average-level performance on tests of working memory and abstract reasoning, which are sensitive to acute stages of brain injuries.

Mr. Kim's pattern of test scores, with weaker visual processing and memory skills, executive functioning, attention/processing speed, and his mild left-sided neglect are highly consistent with his acute right basal ganglia stroke. His primarily borderline-level weaknesses in the acute stages of recovery would be most consistent with mild cognitive disorder. Mr. Kim does not appear to be depressed, but his presentation would be consistent with an adjustment disorder with other specified predominant symptoms because his primary symptoms include refusing medications and food. *These clinical opinions are made with a high degree of confidence* (conclusions qualified by confidence level).

In terms of medical decision-making capacity, Mr. Kim is aware of his medical condition, possible treatments, and risk of sustaining a second stroke when refusing Western medications. His preference for Chinese medicine treatments is consistent with his strongly held traditional Korean beliefs and values, and he is consistent in voicing his preferences. He does, however, appear to minimize the possibility of a second stroke, and his reasoning may be more rigid and concrete secondary to his cerebrovascular accident (CVA). Still, there does not appear to be overwhelming evidence that he lacks capacity.

Thus, it is opined with a reasonable degree of confidence that Mr. Kim has medical decision-making capacity for refusing his hypertension medications (conclusion qualified by confidence level).

Recommendations

1. Given the converging goals of internist, Mr. Kim, and his family of preventing a future stroke and preparing him for a return to Korea, it is recommended that the rehabilitation team meet with him and his family for a compromise solution. For example, Mr. Kim could be allowed acupuncture treatments for spasticity in his hemiplegia and a more liberal diet, allowing for certain Korean foods brought in by his daughter to facilitate his rehabilitation and strength, if Mr. Kim would agree to take his prescribed medications while at the facility to prevent a future stroke. Reframing the issue as working together to help him reach his goals and motivational interviewing techniques could be used. If scheduled, it is recommended that an interpreter be present because staff may overestimate Mr. Kim's English comprehension and expressive language.

2. Once he returns to Korea, it is recommended that Mr. Kim immediately see a Chinese medicine doctor to treat hypertension, if he refuses Western medicines from a Korean physician. Lifestyle changes such as smoking cessation, a healthy diet, routine exercise, stress management, and judicious alcohol intake should also be implemented.

3. In addition to cognitive deficits, Mr. Kim and his family should be informed of common emotional and behavioral sequelae of a right CVA, such as increased impulsivity and emotionality, poor social awareness, increased rigidity, and poor safety awareness, as well as typical course so that they can adequately prepare for his return to the community. If stroke-related symptoms associated with culturally inappropriate behaviors persist, interventions may include educating others about the behavioral sequelae of right hemispheric stroke or minimizing interaction in situations in which Mr. Kim or the family may "lose face"; the latter may include chaperoning in public, minimizing alcohol intake, or avoiding situations that may be upsetting to Mr. Kim.

4. Mr. Kim and the family should be informed of the potential for depressive reactions when reaching a plateau in recovery as a normal part of the adjustment process, and possible cognitive behavioral interventions should be discussed.

5. Mr. Kim and the family should be aware of additional adjustment challenges, such as moving back to Korea, as well as increased dependency on his children for instrumental activities of daily living.
6. Mr. Kim should follow recommendations by physical, occupational, and speech therapists, including stimulating cognitive activities to facilitate his recovery.
7. Mr. Kim should be retested in 6 months to a year to allow for recovery and determine the long-term effects of his CVA.

PROVIDING FEEDBACK

The feedback session is the payoff for both the clinician and the CDC because it is here where the hard work that both parties put into the assessment comes to fruition. During the session, it is essential that CDCs and families fully comprehend and appreciate the feedback, or else they may not follow recommendations. This goal can be highly challenging when working with individuals who come from different cultures and do not speak the same language. It is argued that the clinician bears the responsibility for communicating feedback in a manner that the CDC hears. Similar to preparing for the assessment, clinicians should consult with a cultural broker to identify likely emotional reactions to feedback, challenging family dynamics, and challenges to communication given the type and severity of medical condition, as well as to assist in developing strategies to communicate effectively. The following are general recommendations for providing feedback from the neuropsychological evaluation to maximize engagement and optimize communication:

- Use motivation as an ally by addressing the CDC's and family's concerns and goals, identified during preinterview or assessment.
- If family or another support network accompanies a CDC, determine who the spokesperson is and speak directly to this person when giving feedback.
- To diffuse defensiveness or anxieties associated with concerns about stigma or loss of face, diagnoses or challenging behaviors should be normalized or medicalized.
- Feedback presentation should consider roles of family members and how deficits associated with the disorder can undermine those roles.
- For severe conditions, reframe client perception by emphasizing positives or something to be grateful for, instilling hope, and emphasizing cultural strengths for coping (e.g., family, community, church).

- Words should be carefully selected to address the unique communication style of the CDC's culture. For example, for CDCs with indirect communication styles, feedback may need to be less direct or more vague to avoid being perceived as rude or upsetting family, thereby reducing the likelihood of accepting feedback and following recommendations. Be aware of nonverbal reactions and particularly what is not said. Potential reactions and presentation can be discussed with a cultural broker beforehand.
- For CDCs who have passive response styles, such as nodding simply to indicate listening rather than agreement, clinicians should ask open questions about understanding.
- Avoid jargon or complicated explanations unless the CDC or family member has medical sophistication and is requesting technical feedback.
- Metaphors can be an effective aid for communicating the impact of neurological disorders on everyday functioning (see Postal & Armstrong, 2013); however, the content of metaphors should be familiar to the CDC and family.
- Acculturation will typically determine acceptance of Western concepts of medical disorders. To the extent that it aids in understanding, for less acculturated CDCs, conditions can be framed within their worldview.
- If the CDC and family are willing, facilitate problem solving for pertinent issues identified by them.

In preparing for Mr. Kim's feedback session, strategies for presenting key issues of accepting the revised treatment plan, reducing stigma associated with mental illness or cognitive deficits, maintaining behavior controls within a collectivist society, accepting increased dependency on his children, and relinquishing his role as head of the household were discussed with Ki Dong beforehand. A particularly salient issue was developing the wording to minimize defensiveness and maximize acceptance of feedback and recommendations. Although interpreters will typically translate messages independently on their own, open discussion of specific messages can aid clinicians in understanding the nuances of communication.

Feedback Session

The feedback session was conducted with Mr. Kim, son Jun Ho and daughter Min Ji via conference call, daughter Yun Ji, and Ki Dong the interpreter. Feedback was primarily directed to Mr. Kim, and secondarily to Jun Ho, because of his position as oldest son and future caregiver. Mr. Kim was thanked for participating in the evaluation, which can be highly challenging so early in his recovery, and it was noted that it demonstrated his concern for his family because the information would assist them in providing care for him. Mr. Kim's children were also thanked for attending because family support is essential for successful rehabilitation planning when recovering from a stroke. Family was informed of the session agenda, explaining the context and reason for the evaluation, describing test results and recommendations, and then addressing family concerns. The cooperative nature of treatment was emphasized, and family was strongly encouraged to ask questions at any time.

The family was first informed that Dr. Johnson initiated neuropsychological testing because he was concerned that Mr. Kim's refusal to take his medications may make him vulnerable to sustaining a second stroke. He wanted to determine whether his stroke was affecting his thinking and decision making. However, Dr. Johnson is most concerned about Mr. Kim's health and recovery. His concerns are consistent with Mr. Kim's goal of walking and using his arm again and the family's goal of preparing their father for his return trip to Korea.

Results of neuropsychological testing were then presented. Testing and history indicated that Mr. Kim is an intelligent person, as evidenced by his successful business and accomplished children. However, as would be expected, he is currently experiencing cognitive problems because of his recent stroke, which affected half of his brain. His ability to speak and understand spoken and written language and to reason with words is generally intact. However, at this time, Mr. Kim may have some problems focusing his attention on a task and processing information quickly. Most problems will occur with processing visual information, and he may misperceive things in his environment and have problems remembering things he experiences or sees. He can be easily overloaded with information and mentally tire when thinking. New and complex tasks will be particularly difficult. Fortunately, Mr. Kim is early in recovery, and his thinking should improve with time, although it is difficult to predict how much improvement he will experience. Most recovery will occur in the first 6 months.

As mentioned, the original reason for referral was evaluating his ability to make rational medical decisions. Test results and the interview indicate that Mr. Kim maintains this ability because his refusal to take Western medication is consistent with his values and experiences and not due to deficits secondary to stroke. However, despite his preference for Chinese medical treatment, Mr. Kim and his family were asked whether they agreed that preventing a future stroke is still a very real and important health issue. If this happened, it would certainly undermine Mr. Kim's goal of walking again and returning to Korea in the next 2 weeks. Jun Ho verbalized agreement with this statement. It is therefore recommended that Mr. Kim's care plan be expanded to include acupuncture to assist in rehabilitation of his left arm and leg and allow for some Korean foods so Mr. Kim can eat better and get stronger, which would facilitate rehabilitation and his goal of walking again. Although not his treatment of choice, it is also strongly recommended that Mr. Kim temporarily take prescribed Western medications at the facility until he returns to Korea, to make sure he does not sustain a second stroke. If Mr. Kim agrees, Dr. Johnson and the rehabilitation team will incorporate recommendations into his care plan. Family allowed time to discuss recommendations with each other for a few minutes, and Jun Ho informed the clinician of his father's approval.

It was then explained that a stroke affects not only thinking but also behaviors. Mr. Kim's increased emotionality and doing or saying things he would not normally do is likely due to his stroke. These behaviors should improve with time, particularly within the first 6 months after the stroke. However, if these behaviors persist, to avoid future stress, Mr. Kim may wish to avoid situations associated with strong emotions, refrain from alcohol in public gatherings, require a family escort, or educate others about sequelae associated with stroke.

Mr. Kim and family were next informed of the potential for becoming frustrated with the recovery process. The process is generally slow, and it is easy for a person to get upset and down on himself if improvement is not being made. If Mr. Kim experiences these feelings, he should keep in mind that this is a normal reaction and part of the adjustment process, which can occur early or later in recovery. Some strategies to deal with frustrations include staying positive and patient, focusing on the many things he can still do, perceiving his condition as a challenge, accepting that he will have some residual limitations, and maintaining a sense of control through an exercise regimen, lifestyle changes, and engaging in cognitive activities to continue his recovery.

Mr. Kim was also informed that a significant challenge for most men sustaining a stroke is trying to do too much. This is a normal reaction. However, Mr. Kim will also have to adjust back to life in Korea, which can be stressful for anyone, particularly if recovering from a stroke. Although Korea is his native country, it will not be the same because there have been many changes since he lived there. Taking care of home and bills will also be complicated because he will be living in a different country. Thus, at this time, it would be best for him to focus on his recovery and allow Jun Ho to fulfill his duty as eldest son in caring for him and assist with managing affairs, at least until he is able to resume this role. In addition, he is lucky to have daughters who are an accountant and attorney and can assist with managing his affairs here in the United States. He can still be involved in decision making. Jun Ho had a brief discussion with Mr. Kim and stated that his father agreed.

Finally, other lifestyle changes important for preventing future strokes, such as smoking cessation, a healthy diet, routine exercise, stress management, and alcohol use in moderation, were also discussed. Mr. Kim and family were asked if they had any questions or concerns.

Jun Ho thanked the clinician for the feedback, which would assist in their preparation, and stated that family will discuss it with their father. He then inquired about the availability of a Korean-speaking companion for Mr. Kim to provide support while at the rehabilitation hospital because this is a common intervention in Korea. The clinician responded that a companion may be helpful, but that this type of intervention is not standard in the United States and can be quite expensive and that the family would typically have to pay for this out of pocket. Visitors would certainly be welcome. Yun Ji interjected that church friends have stopped by in large groups. However, she can try to coordinate more frequent visits from individual church members. She then asked her father in Korean if this is something he would like. He agreed. Family also had questions about travel logistics, and these were directed to the rehabilitation team.

Understanding and respecting cultural values transformed Mr. Kim from a challenging to a motivated client, with better-than-expected outcome. He took all his medications, which reduced his blood pressure to normal levels. Yun Ji brought in Korean food approved by the dietician, and arrangements were made for church visitors and acupuncture treatment. Thus, he demonstrated more strength and energy for rehabilitation. Mr. Kim returned to Korea with Jun Ho without incident.

APPENDIX: CULTURAL RESOURCES

The following are resources for researching cultural information. These websites provide a good overview of history and facts for understanding a culture or a client's country of origin:

- Countries and Their Cultures: http://www.everyculture.com/
- Dimensions of Culture: Cross Cultural Communication for the Healthcare Professional: http://www.dimensionsofculture.com
- Library of Congress Country Studies: http://www.photius.com/countries
- BBC: http://news.bbc.co.uk/2/hi/country_profiles
- Wikipedia (specific cultures, educational systems, languages spoken)

Data clearinghouse websites are a good source of statistics, facts, and history about a culture:

- Nationmaster.com: http://www.nationmaster.com/index.php
- The World Bank: http://data.worldbank.org
- CIA World Fact Book: https://www.cia.gov/index.html

Search engines for finding references and norms for neuropsychological tests within a specific country:

- Google Scholar: Google Scholar is the preferred search engine for retrieving research articles with neuropsychological norms for culturally different clients as specific ethnicities can be used as key words to focus the search. Links to the full text PDFs or html are provided for select articles. Other useful click features for an article includes access to abstracts of articles that cite it, related articles, and citations in several publication formats, the latter useful for referencing. A major disadvantage of this engine is that the most recent articles are placed in later screens, thus not easily accessible.
- Google: Google searches are similarly guided by specific key words and is most useful for finding webpage resources such as government data, information from non-scientific periodicals such as technical reports, newspaper or magazine articles, or other online data sources such as Wikipedia. It is the search engine of choice for finding cultural resources for building a context.
- Pubmed: Pubmed is most useful for finding the latest scientific journal articles as listings are organized temporally starting with

the most recent articles. Similar to Google Scholar, there are links to similar articles and access to full texts, although links to the latter are primarily to publishers who charge fees. The major disadvantage of this engine is the limited number of set key words used for searches. Thus searches tend to be general versus focused on specific topics.

U.S. Government websites are good sources of census data on ethnic minorities, information on immigration, and information on mental health and health disparities:

- U.S. Department of Commerce United States Census Bureau Race Publications: http://www.census.gov/topics/population/race/publications.html
- Centers for Disease Control (CDC) Office of Minority Health and Health Equity (OMHHE): http://www.cdc.gov/minorityhealth/index.html
- U.S. Department of Health and Human Services (DHHS), Office of Minority Health (OMH): http://minorityhealth.hhs.gov/
- U.S. National Library of Medicine/National Institute of Health Medline Plus: https://www.nlm.nih.gov/medlineplus/
- Substance Abuse Mental Health Services Administration (SAMHSA): http://store.samhsa.gov/facet/Professional-Research-Topics/term/Cultural-Competence
- Migration Policy Institute: http://www.migrationpolicy.org/

Seek out books that provide general information on cultural beliefs, values, behaviors, family structures, and cultural considerations when working with CDCs. When searching for relevant books, neuropsychologists should not limit their searches to neuropsychology or psychology because resources in cultural anthropology, sociology, epidemiology, and counseling psychology can provide useful information. Here is one such book:

McGoldrick, M., Giordano, J., & Garcia-Preto, N. (Eds.). (2005). *Ethnicity and family therapy* (3rd ed.). New York, NY: Guilford Press.

Neuropsychological association websites provide links specific to culture and neuropsychology. They are also a good resources for finding neuropsychologists from different countries or those who speak different languages. These colleagues could be asked for cultural consultation. Here is a list of these websites:

- National Academy of Neuropsychology (NAN): https://www.nanonline.org/Default.aspx
  The membership directory can identify colleagues who speak specific languages.

- International Neuropsychological Society (INS): http://www.
  the-ins.org/member-directory
  The membership directory can be sorted by country to find international consultants.
- INS International Liaison Committee Cross-Cultural Referrals:
  http://www.ilc-ins.org/language.cfm
  Provides a list of clinicians who perform bilingual/cultural
  assessments.

Finally, seeking assistance from cultural brokers is essential for a nuanced
understanding of a culturally different client. Local cultural resources should
be sought out and utilized. Partnerships are best (seek to provide what they
need as they are providing for you). Similar to searching for book references,
neuropsychologists should not overlook professors in other social scientific
disciplines as resources for cultural expertise.

REFERENCES

Abe-Kim, J., Takeuchi, D. T., Hong, S., Zane, N., Sue, S., Spencer, M. S., . . . Alegría, M. (2007). Use of mental health-related services among immigrant and US-born Asian Americans: Results from the National Latino and Asian American Study. *American Journal of Public Health, 97,* 91–98. http://dx.doi.org/ 10.2105/AJPH.2006.098541

Academy Rank. (2011). *World academies rank.* Retrieved from http://academyrank. com/rank.php

Adeponle, A. B., Thombs, B. D., Groleau, D., Jarvis, E., & Kirmayer, L. J. (2012). Using the cultural formulation to resolve uncertainty in diagnoses of psychosis among ethnoculturally diverse patients. *Psychiatric Services, 63,* 147–153. http:// dx.doi.org/10.1176/appi.ps.201100280

Adesope, O., Lavin, T., Thompson, T., & Ungerleider, C. (2010). A systematic review and meta-analysis of the cognitive correlates of bilingualism. *Review of Educational Research, 80,* 207–245. http://dx.doi.org/10.3102/0034654310368803

Agranovich, A. V., & Puente, A. E. (2007). Do Russian and American normal adults perform similarly on neuropsychological tests? Preliminary findings on the relationship between culture and test performance. *Archives of Clinical Neuropsychology, 22,* 273–282. http://dx.doi.org/10.1016/j.acn.2007.01.003

Ahn, H. J., Chin, J., Park, A., Lee, B. H., Suh, M. K., Seo, S. W., & Na, D. L. (2010). Seoul Neuropsychological Screening Battery-Dementia Version (SNSB-D): A useful tool for assessing and monitoring cognitive impairments in dementia patients. *Journal of Korean Medical Science, 25,* 1071–1076.

Al-Ghatani, A. M., Obonsawin, M. C., Binshaig, B. A., & Al-Moutaery, K. R. (2011). Saudi normative data for the Wisconsin Card Sorting test, Stroop test, Test of Non-verbal Intelligence—3, Picture Completion and Vocabulary (subtest of the Wechsler Adult Intelligence Scale—Revised). *Neurosciences (Riyadh), 16,* 29–41.

Alterman, A., Zaballero, A., Lin, M., Siddiqui, N., Brown, L., Rutherford, M., & McDermott, P. (1995). Personality Assessment Inventory (PAI) scores of lower-socioeconomic African American and Latino methadone maintenance patients. *Assessment, 2,* 91–100. http://dx.doi.org/10.1177/1073191195002001009

Alves, L., Simões, M. R., & Martins, C. (2012). The estimation of premorbid intelligence levels among Portuguese speakers: The Irregular Word Reading Test (TeLPI). *Archives of Clinical Neuropsychology, 27,* 58–68. http://dx.doi.org/ 10.1093/arclin/acr103

Ambreen, S., & Kamal, A. (2011). Adaptation and validation of the Verbal Comprehension Index (VCI) Subtests of WISC–IV UK in Pakistan. *Journal of Behavioural Science, 21,* 18–34.

American Academy of Clinical Neuropsychology Board of Directors. (2007). American Academy of Clinical Neuropsychology (AACN) practice guidelines for neuropsychological assessment and consultation. *The Clinical Neuropsychologist, 21*, 209–231. http://dx.doi.org/10.1080/13825580601025932

American Bar Association & American Psychological Association. (2008). *Assessment of older adults with diminished capacity: A handbook for psychologists.* Washington, DC: American Bar Association Commission on Law and Aging and American Psychological Association.

American Educational Research Association, American Psychological Association, & National Council on Measurement in Education. (2014). *Standards for educational and psychological testing* (2nd ed.). Washington, DC: American Education Research Association.

American Psychiatric Association. (2013). *The diagnostic and statistical manual of mental disorders* (5th ed.). Arlington, VA: Author.

American Psychological Association. (2003). APA guidelines on multicultural education, training, research, practice, and organizational change for psychologists. *American Psychologist, 58*, 377–402. Retrieved from http://www.apa.org/pi/oema/resources/policy/multicultural-guidelines.aspx

American Psychological Association. (2010). *Ethical principles of psychologists and code of conduct (2002, Amended June 1, 2010).* Retrieved from http://www.apa.org/ethics/code/index.aspx

American Psychological Association. (2011). *Revised competency benchmarks for professional psychology.* Retrieved from http://www.apa.org/ed/graduate/competency.aspx

Andreotti, C., & Hawkins, K. A. (2015). RBANS norms based on the relationship of age, gender, education, and WRAT-3 reading to performance within an older African American sample. *The Clinical Neuropsychologist, 29*, 442–465. http://dx.doi.org/10.1080/13854046.2015.1039589

Anger, W. K., Cassitto, M. G., Liang, Y. X., Amador, R., Hooisma, J., Chrislip, D. W., . . . Fournier, L. (1993). Comparison of performance from three continents on the WHO-recommended Neurobehavioral Core Test Battery. *Environmental Research, 62*, 125–147. http://dx.doi.org/10.1006/enrs.1993.1097

Ardila, A. (2007). The impact of culture on neuropsychological test performance. In B. Uzzell, M. Ponton, & A. Ardila (Eds.), *International handbook of cross-cultural neuropsychology* (pp. 23–44). Mahwah, NJ: Erlbaum.

Ardila, A., Bertolucci, P. H., Braga, L. W., Castro-Caldas, A., Judd, T., Kosmidis, M. H., . . . Rosselli, M. (2010). Illiteracy: The neuropsychology of cognition without reading. *Archives of Clinical Neuropsychology, 25*, 689–712. http://dx.doi.org/10.1093/arclin/acq079

Ardila, A., & Rosselli, M. (2007). Illiterates and cognition: The impact of education. In B. Uzzell, M. Ponton, & A. Ardila (Eds.), *International handbook of cross-cultural neuropsychology* (pp. 181–198). Mahwah, NJ: Erlbaum.

Arentoft, A., Byrd, D., Robbins, R. N., Monzones, J., Miranda, C., Rosario, A., . . . Rivera Mindt, M. (2012). Multidimensional effects of acculturation on English-language neuropsychological test performance among HIV+ Caribbean Latinas/os. *Journal of Clinical and Experimental Neuropsychology, 34,* 814–825. http://dx.doi.org/10.1080/13803395.2012.683856

Aronson, J., Fried, C., & Good, C. (2002). Reducing the effects of stereotype threat on African American college students by shaping theories of intelligence. *Journal of Experimental Social Psychology, 38,* 113–125. http://dx.doi.org/10.1006/jesp.2001.1491

Artiola i Fortuny, L. (2008). Research and practice: Ethical issues with immigrant adults and children. In J. Morgan & J. Ricker (Eds.), *Textbook of clinical neuropsychology* (pp. 960–982). New York, NY: Psychology Press.

Aud, S., Fox, M., & KewalRamani, A. (2010). *Status and trends in the education of racial and ethnic groups* (NCES 2010-015). U.S. Department of Education, National Center for Education Statistics. Washington, DC: U.S. Government Printing Office.

Audacious Epigone. (2011, January 22). *Average IQ by occupation (estimated from wordsum scores).* Retrieved from http://anepigone.blogspot.com/2011/01/average-iq-by-occupation.html

Azizian, A., Yeghiyan, M., Ishkhanyan, B., Manukyan, Y., & Khandanyan, L. (2011). Clinical validity of the Repeatable Battery for the Assessment of Neuropsychological Status among patients with schizophrenia in the Republic of Armenia. *Archives of Clinical Neuropsychology, 26,* 89–97. http://dx.doi.org/10.1093/arclin/acq100

Baade, L. E., & Schoenberg, M. R. (2004). A proposed method to estimate premorbid intelligence utilizing group achievement measures from school records. *Archives of Clinical Neuropsychology, 19,* 227–243. http://dx.doi.org/10.1016/S0887-6177(03)00092-1

Babikian, T., Boone, K. B., Lu, P., & Arnold, G. (2006). Sensitivity and specificity of various digit span scores in the detection of suspect effort. *The Clinical Neuropsychologist, 20,* 145–159. http://dx.doi.org/10.1080/13854040590947362

Bailey, K. G., & Federman, E. J. (1979). Factor analysis of breadth and depth dimensions on Wechsler's Similarities and Vocabulary Subscales. *Journal of Clinical Psychology, 35,* 341–345. http://dx.doi.org/10.1002/1097-4679(197904)35:2<341::AID-JCLP2270350224>3.0.CO;2-C

Baiyewu, O., Smith-Gamble, V., Akinbiyi, A., Lane, K. A., Hall, K. S., Ogunniyi, A., . . . Hendrie, H. C. (2003). Behavioral and caregiver reaction of dementia as measured by the neuropsychiatric inventory in Nigerian community residents. *International Psychogeriatrics, 15,* 399–409. http://dx.doi.org/10.1017/S1041610203009645

Bankston, C. (n.d.). *Vietnamese Americans.* Retrieved from http://www.everyculture.com/multi/Sr-Z/Vietnamese-Americans.html

Barker-Collo, S., Thomas, K., Riddick, E., & de Jager, A. (2011). A New Zealand regression formula for premorbid estimation using the National Adult Reading Test. *New Zealand Journal of Psychology, 40*(2), 47–55.

Barnard, W. (2004). Parent involvement in elementary school and educational attainment. *Children and Youth Services Review, 26*, 39–62. http://dx.doi.org/ 10.1016/j.childyouth.2003.11.002

Barnes, A. (2004). Race, schizophrenia, and admission to state psychiatric hospitals. *Administration and Policy in Mental Health, 31*, 241–252. http://dx.doi.org/10.1023/ B:APIH.0000018832.73673.54

Barnett, S., & Williams, W. (2004). National intelligence and the emperor's new clothes. *Contemporary Psychology: APA Review of Books, 49*, 389–396.

Barona, A., Reynolds, C., & Chastain, R. (1984). A demographically based index of premorbid intelligence for the WAIS–R. *Journal of Consulting and Clinical Psychology, 52*, 885–887. http://dx.doi.org/10.1037/0022-006X.52.5.885

Bazylewicz-Walczak, B., Majczakowa, W., & Szymczak, M. (1999). Behavioral effects of occupational exposure to organophosphorous pesticides in female greenhouse planting workers. *Neurotoxicology, 20*, 819–826.

Beals, J., Manson, S. M., Shore, J. H., Friedman, M., Ashcraft, M., Fairbank, J. A., & Schlenger, W. E. (2002). The prevalence of posttraumatic stress disorder among American Indian Vietnam veterans: Disparities and context. *Journal of Traumatic Stress, 15*, 89–97. http://dx.doi.org/10.1023/A:1014894506325

Beals, J., Novins, D. K., Whitesell, N. R., Spicer, P., Mitchell, C. M., & Manson, S. M., & the American Indian Service Utilization, Psychiatric Epidemiology, Risk and Protective Factors Project Team. (2005). Prevalence of mental disorders and utilization of mental health services in two American Indian reservation populations: Mental health disparities in a national context. *The American Journal of Psychiatry, 162*, 1723–1732. http://dx.doi.org/10.1176/ appi.ajp.162.9.1723

Beck, A. (1979). *Cognitive therapy and the emotional disorders.* New York, NY: Plume.

Beck, A., Steer, R., & Brown, G. (1996). *The Beck Depression Inventory—II.* San Antonio, TX: The Psychological Corporation.

Beeri, M. S., Schmeidler, J., Sano, M., Wang, J., Lally, R., Grossman, H., & Silverman, J. M. (2006). Age, gender, and education norms on the CERAD neuropsychological battery in the oldest old. *Neurology, 67*, 1006–1010. http://dx.doi.org/10.1212/01.wnl.0000237548.15734.cd

Belanger, H. G., Curtiss, G., Demery, J. A., Lebowitz, B. K., & Vanderploeg, R. D. (2005). Factors moderating neuropsychological outcomes following mild traumatic brain injury: A meta-analysis. *Journal of the International Neuropsychological Society, 11*, 215–227. http://dx.doi.org/10.1017/S1355617705050277

Bennett, M. (1993). Towards ethnorelativism: A developmental model of intercultural sensitivity. In R. M. Paige (Ed.), *Education for the intercultural experience* (pp. 21–71). Yarmouth, ME: Intercultural Press.

Bertolucci, P. H., Okamoto, I. H., Brucki, S. M., Siviero, M. O., Toniolo Neto, J., & Ramos, L. R. (2001). Applicability of the CERAD neuropsychological battery to Brazilian elderly. *Arquivos de Neuro-Psiquiatria, 59*, 532–536. http://dx.doi.org/10.1590/S0004-282X2001000400009

Bialystok, E., Craik, F. I., & Luk, G. (2012). Bilingualism: Consequences for mind and brain. *Trends in Cognitive Sciences, 16*, 240–250. http://dx.doi.org/10.1016/j.tics.2012.03.001

Binder, L. M., Villanueva, M. R., Howieson, D., & Moore, R. T. (1993). The Rey AVLT recognition memory task measures motivational impairment after mild head trauma. *Archives of Clinical Neuropsychology, 8*, 137–147. http://dx.doi.org/10.1016/0887-6177(93)90031-U

Blaskewitz, N., Merten, T., & Kathmann, N. (2008). Performance of children on symptom validity tests: TOMM, MSVT, and FIT. *Archives of Clinical Neuropsychology, 23*, 379–391.

Boben, D., & Bucik, V. (2003). Slovenia. In J. Georgas, L. G. Weiss, F. J. van de Vijver, & D. H. Saklofske (Eds.), *Culture and children's intelligence: Cross-cultural analysis of the WISC–III* (pp. 182–199). San Diego, CA: Academic Press.

Boivin, M., & Giordani, B. (Eds.). (2013). *Neuropsychology of children in Africa: Perspectives on risk and resilience.* New York, NY: Springer. http://dx.doi.org/10.1007/978-1-4614-6834-9

Bonicatto, S., Dew, A. M., & Soria, J. J. (1998). Analysis of the psychometric properties of the Spanish version of the Beck Depression Inventory in Argentina. *Psychiatry Research, 79*, 277–285. http://dx.doi.org/10.1016/S0165-1781(98)00047-X

Bonilla, J., Bernal, G., Santos, A., & Santos, D. (2004). A revised Spanish version of the Beck Depression Inventory: Psychometric properties with a Puerto Rican sample of college students. *Journal of Clinical Psychology, 60*, 119–130. http://dx.doi.org/10.1002/jclp.10195

Boone, K., Lu, P., & Herzberg, D. (2002). *The dot counting test.* Los Angeles, CA: Western Psychological Services.

Boone, K. B., Lu, P., Sherman, D., Palmer, B., Back, C., Shamieh, E., . . . Berman, N. G. (2000). Validation of a new technique to detect malingering of cognitive symptoms: The b Test. *Archives of Clinical Neuropsychology, 15*, 227–241.

Boone, K. B., Victor, T. L., Wen, J., Razani, J., & Pontón, M. (2007). The association between neuropsychological scores and ethnicity, language, and acculturation variables in a large patient population. *Archives of Clinical Neuropsychology, 22*, 355–365. http://dx.doi.org/10.1016/j.acn.2007.01.010

Bornstein, M., & Bradley, R. (2003). *Socioeconomic status, parenting, and child development.* Mahwah, NJ: Erlbaum.

Britz, E., & Batalova, J. (2013). *Frequently requested statistics on immigrants and immigration in the United States.* Retrieved from Migration Policy Institute website: http://www.migrationpolicy.org/article/frequently-requested-statistics-immigrants-and-immigration-united-states

Brooks-Gunn, J., & Duncan, G. J. (1997). The effects of poverty on children. *The Future of Children, 7*, 55–71. http://dx.doi.org/10.2307/1602387

Burin, D. I., Jorge, R. E., Arizaga, R. A., & Paulsen, J. S. (2000). Estimation of premorbid intelligence: The word accentuation test—Buenos Aires version. *Journal of Clinical and Experimental Neuropsychology, 22*, 677–685. http://dx.doi.org/10.1076/1380-3395(200010)22:5;1-9;FT677

Burton, V., Vilar-López, R., & Puente, A. E. (2012). Measuring effort in neuropsychological evaluations of forensic cases of Spanish speakers. *Archives of Clinical Neuropsychology, 27*, 262–267. http://dx.doi.org/10.1093/arclin/acs026

Butcher, J. (Ed.). (1996). *International adaptations of the MMPI–2: Research and clinical applications*. Minneapolis: University of Minnesota Press.

Butcher, J. N. (2004). Personality assessment without borders: Adaptation of the MMPI–2 across cultures. *Journal of Personality Assessment, 83*, 90–104. http://dx.doi.org/10.1207/s15327752jpa8302_02

Butcher, J. N., Dahlstrom, W., Graham, J., Tellegen, A., & Kaemmer, B. (1989). *MMPI–2: Manual for administration and scoring*. Minneapolis: University of Minnesota Press.

Butler, Y., & Hakuta, K. (2004). Bilingualism and second language acquisition. In W. Ritchie & T. Bhatia (Eds.), *The handbook of bilingualism* (pp. 114–144). Malden, MA: Blackwell.

Cabiya, J. J. (1996). Use of the MMPI and the MMPI–2 in Puerto Rico. In J. N. Butcher (Ed.), *International Adaptation of the MMPI–2* (pp. 284–304). Minneapolis: University of Minnesota Press.

Carstairs, J., Myors, B., Shores, E., & Fogarty, G. (2006). Influence of language background on tests of cognitive abilities: Australian data. *Australian Psychologist, 41*, 48–54. http://dx.doi.org/10.1080/00050060500391878

Carteret, M. (n.d.). *Non-verbal behavior in cross-cultural interactions*. Retrieved from http://www.dimensionsofculture.com/2010/11/non-verbal-behavior-in-cross-cultural-interactions

Carvajal, H., McKnab, P., Gerber, J., Hewes, P., & Smith, P. (1989). Counseling college-bound students: Can ACT scores be predicted? *School Counselor, 36*, 186–191.

Casals-Coll, M., Sánchez-Benavides, G., Quintana, M., Manero, R. M., Rognoni, T., Calvo, L., . . . Peña-Casanova, J. (2013). Spanish normative studies in young adults (NEURONORMA young adults project): Norms for verbal fluency tests. *Neurología (English Edition), 28*, 33–40.

Casas, R., Guzmán-Vélez, E., Cardona-Rodriguez, J., Rodriguez, N., Quiñones, G., Izaguirre, B., & Tranel, D. (2012). Interpreter-mediated neuropsychological testing of monolingual Spanish speakers. *The Clinical Neuropsychologist, 26*, 88–101. http://dx.doi.org/10.1080/13854046.2011.640641

Centers for Disease Control and Prevention. (2002). Fetal alcohol syndrome—Alaska, Arizona, Colorado, and New York, 1995–1997. *MMWR Weekly, 51*, 433–435.

Centers for Disease Control and Prevention. (2011). CDC Health Disparities and Inequalities Report—United States, 2011. *MMWR Weekly, 60.*

Center for World Class Universities. (2013). *Academic rankings of world universities.* Shanghai Jiao Tong University. Retrieved from http://www.shanghairanking.com/ARWU2013.html

Cha, N., Chung, M., & Kim, S. C. (2014). Cross-cultural considerations in Korean American clients: A perspective on psychological assessment. In L. Benuto, N. Thaler, & B. Leany (Eds.), *Guide to psychological assessment with Asians* (pp. 43–60). New York, NY: Springer.

Chandra, V., Ganguli, M., Pandav, R., Johnston, J., Belle, S., & DeKosky, S. T. (1998). Prevalence of Alzheimer's disease and other dementias in rural India: The Indo–US study. *Neurology, 51,* 1000–1008. http://dx.doi.org/10.1212/WNL.51.4.1000

Chandra, V., Pandav, R., Dodge, H. H., Johnston, J. M., Belle, S. H., DeKosky, S. T., & Ganguli, M. (2001). Incidence of Alzheimer's disease in a rural community in India: The Indo–US study. *Neurology, 57,* 985–989. http://dx.doi.org/10.1212/WNL.57.6.985

Chang, S. (2006). Development of a test battery for assessing memory malingering in Hong Kong and its application on depressed patients (China). *Dissertation Abstracts International Section B: The Sciences and Engineering, 68.*

Chaves, M. L., Camozzato, A. L., Godinho, C., Kochhann, R., Schuh, A., De Almeida, V. L., & Kaye, J. (2007). Validity of the clinical dementia rating scale for the detection and staging of dementia in Brazilian patients. *Alzheimer Disease & Associated Disorders, 21,* 210–217. http://dx.doi.org/10.1097/WAD.0b013e31811ff2b4

Chen, H. Y., Chen, Y. H., & Zhu, J. J. (2003). Taiwan. In J. Georgas, L. G. Weiss, F. J. van de Vijver, & D. H. Saklofske (Eds.), *Culture and children's intelligence: Cross-cultural analysis of the WISC–III* (pp. 241–254). San Diego, CA: Academic Press.

Chen, Y. H., & Chen, X. Y. (2002). *Wechsler Adult Intelligence Scale—III (Chinese)* [in Chinese]. Taipei, Taiwan: Chinese Behavioral Science Corporation.

Chen, Y. J., Ho, M. Y., Chen, K. J., Hsu, C. F., & Ryu, S. J. (2009). Estimation of premorbid general fluid intelligence using traditional Chinese reading performance in Taiwanese samples. *Psychiatry and Clinical Neurosciences, 63,* 500–507. http://dx.doi.org/10.1111/j.1440-1819.2009.01970.x

Cheng, W., & Ickes, W. (2009). Conscientiousness and self-motivation as mutually compensatory predictors of university-level GPA. *Personality and Individual Differences, 47,* 817–822. http://dx.doi.org/10.1016/j.paid.2009.06.029

Cheung, F. M., Song, W. Z., & Butcher, J. (1991). An infrequency scale for the Chinese MMPI. *Psychological Assessment: A Journal of Consulting and Clinical Psychology, 3,* 648–653.

Chey, J., & Park, H. (2011). Neuropsychology in Korea. In D. E. M. Fujii (Ed.), *The neuropsychology of Asian Americans* (pp. 247–267). New York, NY: Taylor & Francis.

Chi, Y. K., Kim, T. H., Han, J. W., Lee, S. B., Park, J. H., Lee, J. J., . . . Kim, K. W. (2012). Impaired design fluency is a marker of pathological cognitive aging; results from the Korean longitudinal study on health and aging. *Psychiatry Investigation, 9*, 59–64. http://dx.doi.org/10.4306/pi.2012.9.1.59

Chia, S. E., Chia, H. P., Ong, C. N., & Jeyaratnam, J. (1997). Cumulative blood lead levels and neurobehavioral test performance. *Neurotoxicology, 18*, 793–803.

Chiu, V., & Lee, T. (2002). Detection of malingering behavior at different levels of task difficulty in Hong Kong Chinese. *Rehabilitation Psychology, 47*, 194–203. http://dx.doi.org/10.1037/0090-5550.47.2.194

Choi, S., Na, D., Lee, B., Hahn, D., Jeong, J., Yoon, S., . . . Dementia Research Group. (2001). Estimating the validity of the Korean version of expanded clinical dementia rating (CDR) scale. *Journal of the Korean Neurological Association, 19*, 585–591.

Chu, J., & Sue, S. (2011). Asian American mental health: What we know and what we don't know. *Online Readings in Psychology and Culture, 3*(1), 4.

Chung-Do, J., Huh, J., & Kang, M. (2011). The Koreans. In J. McDermott & N. Andrade (Eds.), *People and cultures of Hawai'i: The evolution of culture and ethnicity* (pp. 176–200). Honolulu: University of Hawaii Press.

Coffey, D. M., Marmol, L., Schock, L., & Adams, W. (2005). The influence of acculturation on the Wisconsin Card Sorting test by Mexican Americans. *Archives of Clinical Neuropsychology, 20*, 795–803. http://dx.doi.org/10.1016/j.acn.2005.04.009

Cohen, M., Riccio, C., & Flannery, A. (1994). Expressive aprosodia following stroke to the right basal ganglia: A case report. *Neuropsychology, 8*, 242–245. http://dx.doi.org/10.1037/0894-4105.8.2.242

Colby, J., & Ortman, J. (2015). *Projections of the size and composition of the U.S. population: 2014–2060.* Retrieved from https://www.census.gov/content/dam/Census/library/publications/2015/demo/p25-1143.pdf

Cole, D. C., Carpio, F., Julian, J., Leon, N., Carbotte, R., & De Almeida, H. (1997). Neurobehavioral outcomes among farm and nonfarm rural Ecuadorians. *Neurotoxicology and Teratology, 19*, 277–286. http://dx.doi.org/10.1016/S0892-0362(97)00019-6

Cole, M., Gay, J., Glick, J., & Sharp, D. (1971). *The cultural context of learning and thinking.* New York, NY: Basic Books.

Collie, A., Shafiq-Antonacci, R., Maruff, P., Tyler, P., & Currie, J. (1999). Norms and the effects of demographic variables on a neuropsychological battery for use in healthy ageing Australian populations. *Australian and New Zealand Journal of Psychiatry, 33*, 568–575. http://dx.doi.org/10.1080/j.1440-1614.1999.00570.x

Consejo Nacional de Población. (2006). *Mexico–United States migration: Regional and state overview.* Mexico City: Author.

Copersino, M. L., Fals-Stewart, W., Fitzmaurice, G., Schretlen, D. J., Sokoloff, J., & Weiss, R. D. (2009). Rapid cognitive screening of patients with substance use disorders. *Experimental and Clinical Psychopharmacology, 17*, 337–344. http://dx.doi.org/10.1037/a0017260

Cornelius, S. W., & Caspi, A. (1987). Everyday problem solving in adulthood and old age. *Psychology and Aging, 2*, 144–153. http://dx.doi.org/10.1037/0882-7974.2.2.144

Correa, A. A., Rogers, R., & Hoersting, R. (2010). Validation of the Spanish SIRS with monolingual Hispanic outpatients. *Journal of Personality Assessment, 92*, 458–464. http://dx.doi.org/10.1080/00223891.2010.497430

Cosentino, S., Manly, J., & Mungas, D. (2007). Do reading tests measure the same construct in multiethnic and multilingual older persons? *Journal of the International Neuropsychological Society, 13*, 228–236. http://dx.doi.org/10.1017/S1355617707070257

Costa, A. S., Reich, A., Fimm, B., Ketteler, S. T., Schulz, J. B., & Reetz, K. (2014). Evidence of the sensitivity of the MoCA alternate forms in monitoring cognitive change in early Alzheimer's disease. *Dementia and Geriatric Cognitive Disorders, 37*, 95–103. http://dx.doi.org/10.1159/000351864

Costa, P., & McCrae, R. (1992). *Revised NEO Personality Inventory (NEO PI–R) and NEO Five-Factor Inventory (NEO–FFI) professional manual.* Odessa, FL: Psychological Assessment Resources.

Crawford, J., & Allan, K. (1997). Estimating premorbid WAIS–R IQ with demographic variables: Regression equations derived from a UK sample. *Clinical Neuropsychologist, 11*, 192–197. http://dx.doi.org/10.1080/13854049708407050

Crespo, G. S., Gomez, F. J., Barragan, V. M., & Rueda, A. A. (2007). Una pobre contribucion de la Escala Fingirse enfermo (FBS) a la adaptacion Espanola del MMPI–2. [The contribution of the Fake Bad Scale (FBS) to the Spanish adaptation of the MMPI–2]. *Revista de Psicología General y Aplicada, 60*, 299–313.

Crighton, A. H., Wygant, D. B., Holt, K. R., & Granacher, R. P. (2015). Embedded effort scales in the repeatable battery for the assessment of neuropsychological status: Do they detect neurocognitive malingering? *Archives of Clinical Neuropsychology, 30*, 181–185. http://dx.doi.org/10.1093/arclin/acv002

Cross, T. L. (2003). Culture as a resource for mental health. *Cultural Diversity and Ethnic Minority Psychology, 9*, 354–359. http://dx.doi.org/10.1037/1099-9809.9.4.354

Cummings, J. L., & Mega, M. (2003). *Neuropsychiatry and behavioral neuroscience.* New York, NY: Oxford University Press.

Cummins, J. (1984). *Bilingualism and special education: Issues in assessment and pedagogy.* Clevedon, England: Multilingual Matters.

da Silva, C. G., Petersson, K. M., Faísca, L., Ingvar, M., & Reis, A. (2004). The effects of literacy and education on the quantitative and qualitative aspects of semantic verbal fluency. *Journal of Clinical and Experimental Neuropsychology, 26*, 266–277. http://dx.doi.org/10.1076/jcen.26.2.266.28089

Dang, H. M., Weiss, B., Pollack, A., & Nguyen, M. C. (2012). Adaptation of the Wechsler Intelligence Scale for Children—IV (WISC–IV) for Vietnam. *Psychological Studies, 56*(4), 387–392. http://dx.doi.org/10.1007/s12646-011-0099-5

Davies, M. S., Strickland, T. L., & Cao, M. (2014). Neuropsychological evaluation of culturally diverse populations. In F. Leong (Ed.), *APA handbook of multicultural psychology: Vol. 2. Applications and testing* (pp. 231–251). Washington, DC: American Psychological Association. http://dx.doi.org/10.1037/14187-014

Dean, A. C., Victor, T. L., Boone, K. B., & Arnold, G. (2008). The relationship of IQ to effort test performance. *The Clinical Neuropsychologist, 22,* 705–722. http://dx.doi.org/10.1080/13854040701440493

Deetong-on, T., Puapornpong, P., Pumipichet, S., Benyakorn, S., Kitporntheranunt, M., & Kongsomboon, K. (2013). Prevalence and risk factors of mild cognitive impairment in menopausal women at HRH Princess Maha Chakri Sirindhorn Medical Center. *Thai Journal of Obstetrics and Gynaecology, 21,* 110–116.

De Jong, G., & Madamba, A. (2001). A double disadvantage? Minority group, immigrant status, and underemployment in the United States. *Social Science Quarterly, 82,* 117–130. http://dx.doi.org/10.1111/0038-4941.00011

de Jonghe, J. F. (1997). Differentiating between demented and psychiatric patients with the Dutch version of the IQCODE. *International Journal of Geriatric Psychiatry, 12,* 462–465. http://dx.doi.org/10.1002/(SICI)1099-1166(199704)12:4<462::AID-GPS510>3.0.CO;2-Q

De la Torre, G. G., Suárez-Llorens, A., Caballero, F. J., Ramallo, M. A., Randolph, C., Lleó, A., . . . Sánchez, B. (2014). Norms and reliability for the Spanish version of the Repeatable Battery for the Assessment of Neuropsychological Status (RBANS) Form A. *Journal of Clinical and Experimental Neuropsychology, 36,* 1023–1030. http://dx.doi.org/10.1080/13803395.2014.965664

Delis, D., Kramer, J., Kaplan, E., & Ober, B. (2000). *The California Verbal Learning Test—Second edition (CVLT–II).* New York, NY: The Psychological Corporation.

Del Ser, T., González-Montalvo, J. I., Martínez-Espinosa, S., Delgado-Villapalos, C., & Bermejo, F. (1997). Estimation of premorbid intelligence in Spanish people with the Word Accentuation Test and its application to the diagnosis of dementia. *Brain and Cognition, 33,* 343–356. http://dx.doi.org/10.1006/brcg.1997.0877

Demers, P., Robillard, A., Laflèche, G., Nash, F., Heyman, A., & Fillenbaum, G. (1994). Translation of clinical and neuropsychological instruments into French: The CERAD experience. *Age and Ageing, 23,* 449–451. http://dx.doi.org/10.1093/ageing/23.6.449

Diaz-Asper, C. M., Schretlen, D. J., & Pearlson, G. D. (2004). How well does IQ predict neuropsychological test performance in normal adults? *Journal of the International Neuropsychological Society, 10,* 82–90. http://dx.doi.org/10.1017/S1355617704101100

Dick, M., Teng, E., Kempler, D., Davis, D., & Taussig, I. (2002). The Cross-Cultural Neuropsychological Test Battery (CCNB): Effects of age, education, ethnicity, and cognitive status on performance. In F. Ferraro (Ed.), *Minority and cross-cultural aspects of neuropsychological assessment* (pp. 17–41). Lisse, Netherlands: Swets & Zeitlinger.

Dominguez, J., Orquiza, M., Soriano, J., Magpantay, C., Esteban, R., Corrales, M., & Ampil, E. (2013). Adaptation of the Montreal Cognitive Assessment for elderly Filipino patients. *East Asian Archives of Psychiatry, 23,* 80.

Duffy, J., Harmon, R., Ranard, D., Thao, B., & Yang, K. (2004). *The Hmong: An introduction to their history and culture*. Washington, DC: Center for Applied Linguistics, Cultural Orientation Resource Center.

Duran, E., & Duran, B. (1995). *Native American postcolonial psychology*. Albany: State University of New York Press.

Dyc, G., & Milligan, C. (2000, February). Native American visual vocabulary: Ways of thinking and living. *National Association of African American Studies & National Association of Hispanic and Latino Studies: 2000 Literature Monograph Series. Proceedings of the National Association of Native American Studies Section, Houston, TX.*

Elbulok-Charcape, M. M., Rabin, L. A., Spadaccini, A. T., & Barr, W. B. (2014). Trends in the neuropsychological assessment of ethnic/racial minorities: A survey of clinical neuropsychologists in the United States and Canada. *Cultural Diversity and Ethnic Minority Psychology, 20,* 353–361. http://dx.doi.org/10.1037/a0035023

El-Islam, F. (1982). Arabic cultural psychiatry. *Transcultural Psychiatric Research Review, 9,* 5–24.

Ennis, S. R., Ríos-Vargas, M., & Albert, N. G. (2011). *The Hispanic population: 2010*. Washington, DC: U.S. Department of Commerce, Economics and Statistics Administration, U.S. Census Bureau. Retrieved from http://www.census.gov/prod/cen2010/briefs/c2010br-04.pdf

Erickson, F., & Shultz, J. (1982). *The counselor as gatekeeper: Social interaction in interviews*. New York, NY: Academic Press.

Fallas, C., Fallas, J., Maslard, P., & Dally, S. (1992). Subclinical impairment of colour vision among workers exposed to styrene. *British Journal of Industrial Medicine, 49,* 679–682.

Fan, X., & Chen, M. (2001). Parental involvement and students' academic achievement: A meta-analysis. *Educational Psychology Review, 13,* 1–22. http://dx.doi.org/10.1023/A:1009048817385

Farahat, T. M., Abdelrasoul, G. M., Amr, M. M., Shebl, M. M., Farahat, F. M., & Anger, W. K. (2003). Neurobehavioural effects among workers occupationally exposed to organophosphorous pesticides. *Occupational and Environmental Medicine, 60,* 279–286. http://dx.doi.org/10.1136/oem.60.4.279

Farooq, S., & Fear, C. (2003). Working through interpreters. *Advances in Psychiatric Treatment, 9,* 104–109. http://dx.doi.org/10.1192/apt.01.12

Fawzi, M. M., Hashim, H. M., & Mahmoud, W. (2013). Cognitive impairment and neurological soft signs in an Egyptian sample of schizophrenia patients.

Middle East Current Psychiatry, 20, 14–21. http://dx.doi.org/10.1097/
01.XME.0000422971.41913.97

Federal Register. (2016, January 29). *Indian entities recognized and eligible to receive services from the United States Bureau of Indian Affairs.* Retrieved from https://www.federalregister.gov/articles/2016/01/29/2016-01769/indian-entities-recognized-and-eligible-to-receive-services-from-the-united-states-bureau-of-indian

Fernández, A. L., & Marcopulos, B. A. (2008). A comparison of normative data for the Trail Making Test from several countries: Equivalence of norms and considerations for interpretation. *Scandinavian Journal of Psychology, 49,* 239–246. http://dx.doi.org/10.1111/j.1467-9450.2008.00637.x

Fillenbaum, G. G., Heyman, A., Huber, M. S., Ganguli, M., & Unverzagt, F. W. (2001). Performance of elderly African American and White community residents on the CERAD Neuropsychological Battery. *Journal of the International Neuropsychological Society, 7,* 502–509. http://dx.doi.org/10.1017/S1355617701744062

Fillenbaum, G. G., Kuchibhatla, M., Henderson, V. W., Clark, C. M., & Taussig, I. M. (2007). Comparison of performance on the CERAD neuropsychological battery of Hispanic patients and cognitively normal controls at two sites. *Clinical Gerontologist, 30,* 1–22. http://dx.doi.org/10.1300/J018v30n03_01

Fillenbaum, G. G., McCurry, S. M., Kuchibhatla, M., Masaki, K. H., Borenstein, A. R., Foley, D. J., . . . White, L. (2005). Performance on the CERAD neuropsychology battery of two samples of Japanese-American elders: Norms for persons with and without dementia. *Journal of the International Neuropsychological Society, 11,* 192–201. http://dx.doi.org/10.1017/S1355617705050198

Fletcher-Janzen, E., Strickland, T., & Reynolds, C. (Eds.). (2000). *Handbook of cross-cultural neuropsychology.* New York, NY: Springer. http://dx.doi.org/10.1007/978-1-4615-4219-3

Flynn, J. (2007). *What is intelligence? Beyond the Flynn effect.* New York, NY: Cambridge University Press. http://dx.doi.org/10.1017/CBO9780511605253

Flynn, J. R. (2013). The "Flynn effect" and Flynn's paradox. *Intelligence, 41,* 851–857. http://dx.doi.org/10.1016/j.intell.2013.06.014

Freedom of Religion Act of 1977. Pub. L. 95-341, 92 Stat. 469.

Freitas, S., Simões, M. R., Alves, L., & Santana, I. (2011). Montreal Cognitive Assessment (MoCA): Normative study for the Portuguese population. *Journal of Clinical and Experimental Neuropsychology, 33,* 989–996. http://dx.doi.org/10.1080/13803395.2011.589374

Frey, M., & Detterman, D. (2004). Scholastic assessment or g? The relationship between the Scholastic Assessment Test and general cognitive ability. *Psychological Science, 15,* 373–378. http://dx.doi.org/10.1111/j.0956-7976.2004.00687.x

Fuh, J. L., Teng, E. L., Lin, K. N., Larson, E. B., Wang, S. J., Liu, C. Y., . . . Liu, H. C. (1995). The Informant Questionnaire on Cognitive Decline in the Elderly (IQCODE) as a screening tool for dementia for a predominantly illiterate Chinese population. *Neurology, 45,* 92–96. http://dx.doi.org/10.1212/WNL.45.1.92

Fujii, D. (2011). Introduction. In D. E. M. Fujii (Ed.), *The neuropsychology of Asian Americans* (pp. 1–10). New York, NY: Taylor & Francis.

Fujii, D., Umetsu, D., Schwartz, T., & Hostetter, G. (2002). Culturally sensitive strategies for practicing neuropsychology in Hawaii. *INSNET, 10*(4), 1–2.

Fujii, D., & Vang, A. K. (2011). Neuropsychology of Hmong Americans. In D. E. M. Fujii (Ed.), *The neuropsychology of Asian Americans* (pp. 71–88). New York, NY: Taylor & Francis.

Fujita, K., Maekawa, H., Ohroku, K., & Yamanaka, K. (Eds.). (2006). *Wechsler Adult Intelligence Scale* (3rd ed.). Tokyo, Japan: Nihon Bunka Kagakusha.

Fuld, P. A. (1981). *The Fuld object memory evaluation.* Wood Dale, IL: Stoelting.

Fuld, P. A., Muramoto, O., Blau, A., Westbrook, L., & Katzman, R. (1988). Cross-cultural and multi-ethnic dementia evaluation by mental status and memory testing. *Cortex, 24,* 511–519. http://dx.doi.org/10.1016/S0010-9452(88)80045-5

Gambino, C. P., Acosta, Y. D., & Grieco, E. M. (2014). *English-speaking ability of the foreign-born population in the United States: 2012.* Retrieved from https://www.census.gov.edgekey-staging.net/prod/2014pubs/acs-26.pdf

Gao, B. L. (2001). Assessment of malingering and exaggeration in patients involved in head injury litigation. *Chinese Journal of Clinical Psychology, 9,* 233–236.

Gao, B. L., Li, Z. G., & Chen, J. M. (2003). Binomial forced-choice digit recognition test in identification of dissimulation of intelligent deficit in asking compensation after traffic accident. *Chinese Mental Health Journal, 17,* 50–53.

Garber, H. L. (1988). *The Milwaukee Project: Preventing mental retardation in children at risk.* Washington, DC: American Association on Mental Retardation.

Gardner, H. (1993). *Multiple intelligences: The theory in practice.* New York, NY: Basic Books.

Garrett, M., & Pichette, E. (2000). Red as an apple: Native American acculturation and counseling with or without reservation. *Journal of Counseling & Development, 78,* 3–13. http://dx.doi.org/10.1002/j.1556-6676.2000.tb02554.x

Gasquoine, P. G. (2009). Race-norming of neuropsychological tests. *Neuropsychology Review, 19,* 250–262. http://dx.doi.org/10.1007/s11065-009-9090-5

Gasquoine, P. G., Croyle, K. L., Cavazos-Gonzalez, C., & Sandoval, O. (2007). Language of administration and neuropsychological test performance in neurologically intact Hispanic American bilingual adults. *Archives of Clinical Neuropsychology, 22,* 991–1001. http://dx.doi.org/10.1016/j.acn.2007.08.003

Gelade, G. (2008). The geography of IQ. *Intelligence, 36,* 495–501. http://dx.doi.org/10.1016/j.intell.2008.01.004

Gelfand, M. J., Raver, J. L., Nishii, L., Leslie, L. M., Lun, J., Lim, B. C., . . . Yamaguchi, S. (2011). Differences between tight and loose cultures: A 33-nation study. *Science, 332,* 1100–1104. http://dx.doi.org/10.1126/science.1197754

Georgas, J., Paraskevopoulos, I., Besevegis, E., Giannitsas, N., & Mylonas, K. (2003). Greece. In J. Georgas, L. G. Weiss, F. J. van de Vijver, & D. H. Saklofske (Eds.), *Culture and children's intelligence: Cross-cultural analysis of the WISC–III* (pp. 200–215). San Diego, CA: Academic Press.

Giger, P., & Merten, T. (2013). Swiss population-based reference data for six symptom validity tests. *Clínica y Salud, 24*(3), 153–159.

Gim Chung, R. H., Kim, B. S., & Abreu, J. M. (2004). Asian American Multidimensional Acculturation Scale: Development, factor analysis, reliability, and validity. *Cultural Diversity and Ethnic Minority Psychology, 10,* 66–80. http://dx.doi.org/10.1037/1099-9809.10.1.66

Gintiliene, G., & Girdzijauskiene, S. (2003). Austria and Switzerland. In J. Georgas, L. G. Weiss, F. J. van de Vijver, & D. H. Saklofske (Eds.), *Culture and children's intelligence: Cross-cultural analysis of the WISC–III* (pp. 161–181). San Diego, CA: Academic Press.

Glaser, R. (1963). Instructional technology and the measurement of learning outcomes: Some questions. *American Psychologist, 18,* 519–522. http://dx.doi.org/10.1037/h0049294

Glezerman, A., & Drexler, M. (2001). The Russian Adaptation of the CERAD Battery (CERAD-RA). *Archives of Clinical Neuropsychology, 16,* 826.

Goldstein, F. C., Ashley, A. V., Miller, E., Alexeeva, O., Zanders, L., & King, V. (2014). Validity of the Montreal Cognitive Assessment as a screen for mild cognitive impairment and dementia in African Americans. *Journal of Geriatric Psychiatry and Neurology, 27,* 199–203. http://dx.doi.org/10.1177/0891988714524630

Gómez, F., Zunzunegui, M., Lord, C., Alvarado, B., & García, A. (2013). Applicability of the MoCA–S test in populations with little education in Colombia. *International Journal of Geriatric Psychiatry, 28,* 813–820. http://dx.doi.org/10.1002/gps.3885

Gone, J. P. (2004). Mental health services for Native Americans in the 21st century United States. *Professional Psychology: Research and Practice, 35,* 10–18.

Gone, J. P., & Trimble, J. E. (2012). American Indian and Alaska Native mental health: Diverse perspectives on enduring disparities. *Annual Review of Clinical Psychology, 8,* 131–160. http://dx.doi.org/10.1146/annurev-clinpsy-032511-143127

Gonzales, P., Blanton, H., & Williams, K. (2002). The effects of stereotype threat and double-minority status on the test performance of Latino women. *Personality and Social Psychology Bulletin, 28,* 659–670. http://dx.doi.org/10.1177/0146167202288010

Gottfredson, L. (1997). Mainstream science on intelligence: An editorial with 52 signatories, history, and bibliography. *Intelligence, 24,* 13–23. http://dx.doi.org/10.1016/S0160-2896(97)90011-8

Gottfried, A., Gottfried, A., Bathurst, K., Guerin, D., & Parramore, M. (2003). Socioeconomic status in children's development and family environment: infancy through adolescence. In M. Bornstein & R. Bradley (Eds.), *Socioeconomic status, parenting and child development* (pp. 189–207). Mahwah, NJ: Erlbaum.

Gray, B., Hilder, J., & Stubbe, M. (2012). How to use interpreters in general practice: The development of a New Zealand toolkit. *Journal of Primary Health Care, 4,* 52–61, A1–A8.

Green, A., Garrick, T., Sheedy, D., Blake, H., Shores, A., & Harper, C. (2008). Repeatable battery for the assessment of neuropsychological status (RBANS): Preliminary Australian normative data. *Australian Journal of Psychology, 60,* 72–79. http://dx.doi.org/10.1080/00049530701656257

Green, P. (2004). *Medical Symptom Validity Test (MSVT) for Microsoft Windows: User's Manual.* Edmonton, Canada: Green's.

Green, P. (2005). *Green's Word Memory Test for Microsoft Windows: User's manual.* Edmonton, Canada: Green's.

Green, P., Lees-Haley, P., & Allen, L., III. (2003). The Word Memory Test and the validity of neuropsychological test scores. *Journal of Forensic Neuropsychology, 2*(3–4), 97–124. http://dx.doi.org/10.1300/J151v02n03_05

Green, P., Montijo, J., & Brockhaus, R. (2011). High specificity of the Word Memory Test and Medical Symptom Validity Test in groups with severe verbal memory impairment. *Applied Neuropsychology, 18,* 86–94. http://dx.doi.org/10.1080/09084282.2010.523389

Greenfield, P. (1997). You can't take it with you: Why ability assessments don't cross cultures. *American Psychologist, 52,* 1115–1124. http://dx.doi.org/10.1037/0003-066X.52.10.1115

Grégoire, J. (2003). France and French-speaking Belgium. In J. Georgas, L. Weiss, F. van de Vijver, & D. Saklofske (Eds.), *Culture and children's intelligence cross-cultural analysis of the WISC–III* (pp. 89–108). San Diego, CA: Academic Press. http://dx.doi.org/10.1016/B978-012280055-9/50008-4

Greiffenstein, M., Baker, W., & Gola, T. (1994). Validation of malingered amnesia measures with a large clinical sample. *Psychological Assessment, 6,* 218–224. http://dx.doi.org/10.1037/1040-3590.6.3.218

Greiffenstein, M. F., Baker, W. J., & Johnson-Greene, D. (2002). Actual versus self-reported scholastic achievement of litigating postconcussion and severe closed head injury claimants. *Psychological Assessment, 14,* 202–208.

Griffin-Pierce, T., Silverberg, N., Connor, D., Jim, M., Peters, J., Kaszniak, A., & Sabbagh, M. N. (2008). Challenges to the recognition and assessment of Alzheimer's disease in American Indians of the southwestern United States. *Alzheimer's & Dementia, 4,* 291–299. http://dx.doi.org/10.1016/j.jalz.2007.10.012

Grigorenko, E., Meier, E., Lipka, J., Mohatt, G., Yanez, E., & Sternberg, R. (2004). Academic and practical intelligence: A case study of the Yup'ik in Alaska.

Learning and Individual Differences, 14, 183–207. http://dx.doi.org/10.1016/j.lindif.2004.02.002

Grober, E., Sliwinsk, M., & Korey, S. (1991). Development and validation of a model for estimating premorbid verbal intelligence in the elderly. *Journal of Clinical and Experimental Neuropsychology, 13,* 933–949. http://dx.doi.org/10.1080/01688639108405109

Grothe, K. B., Dutton, G. R., Jones, G. N., Bodenlos, J., Ancona, M., & Brantley, P. J. (2005). Validation of the Beck Depression Inventory—II in a low-income African American sample of medical outpatients. *Psychological Assessment, 17,* 110–114. http://dx.doi.org/10.1037/1040-3590.17.1.110

Groves, J. A., & Engel, R. R. (2007). The German Adaptation and Standardization of the Personality Assessment Inventory (PAI). *Journal of Personality Assessment, 88,* 49–56. http://dx.doi.org/10.1080/00223890709336834

Grubb, H., & Dozier, A. (1989). Too busy to learn: A "competing behaviors" explanation of cross-cultural differences in academic ascendancy based on the cultural distance hypothesis. *Journal of Black Psychology, 16,* 23–45. http://dx.doi.org/10.1177/009579848901600104

Guàrdia-Olmos, J., Peró-Cebollero, M., Rivera, D., & Arango-Lasprilla, J. (2015). Methodology for the development of normative data for ten Spanish-language neuropsychological tests in eleven Latin American countries. *Neuro-Rehabilitation, 37,* 489–491.

Guerchet, M., Banzouzi-Ndamba, B., Mbelesso, P., Pilleron, S., Clément, J., Dartigues, J., & Preux, P. (2013). Prevalence of dementia in two countries of Central Africa: Comparison or rural and urban areas in the EPIDEMCA study. *Neuroepidemiology, 41,* 223–316.

Guo, T., & Uhm, S. Y. (2014). Society and acculturation in Asian American communities. In J. M. Davis & R. D'Amato (Eds.), *Neuropsychology of Asians and Asian Americans* (pp. 55–76). New York, NY: Springer.

Guy, L., & Miller, H. (2004). Screening for malingered psychopathology in a correctional setting: Utility of the Miller-Forensic Assessment of Symptoms Test (M-FAST). *Criminal Justice and Behavior, 31,* 695–716. http://dx.doi.org/10.1177/0093854804268754

Hahn, J. (2005). Faking bad and faking good by college students on the Korean MMPI–2. *Journal of Personality Assessment, 85,* 65–73. http://dx.doi.org/10.1207/s15327752jpa8501_06

Hair, N. L., Hanson, J. L., Wolfe, B. L., & Pollak, S. D. (2015). Association of child poverty, brain development, and academic achievement. *JAMA Pediatrics, 169,* 822–829. http://dx.doi.org/10.1001/jamapediatrics.2015.1475

Hakuta, K. (1991). What bilingual education has taught the experimental psychologist: A capsule account in honor of Joshua A. Fishman. In O. Garcia (Ed.), *Bilingual education: Focusschrit in honor of Joshua A. Fishman on the occasion of his 65th birthday* (pp. 202–212). Amsterdam, the Netherlands: John Benjamins. http://dx.doi.org/10.1075/z.fishfest1.18hak

Hall, E. (1969). *The hidden dimension*. New York, NY: Anchor Books.

Hall, E., & Hall, M. (2001). Key concepts: Underlying structures of culture. *International HRM: Managing Diversity in the Workplace, 24–40*.

Hall, K. S., Gao, S., Emsley, C. L., Ogunniyi, A. O., Morgan, O., & Hendrie, H. C. (2000). Community screening interview for dementia (CSI "D"); performance in five disparate study sites. *International Journal of Geriatric Psychiatry, 15*, 521–531. http://dx.doi.org/10.1002/1099-1166(200006)15:6<521::AID-GPS182>3.0.CO;2-F

Hall, K. S., Hendrie, H., Brittain, H., Norton, J., Rodgers, D., Prince, C., & Postl, B. (1993). The development of a dementia screening interview in two distinct languages. *International Journal of Methods in Psychiatric Research, 3*, 1–28.

Hambleton, R. K., & Patsula, L. (1999). Increasing the validity of adapted tests: Myths to be avoided and guidelines for improving test adaptation practices. *Journal of Applied Testing Technology, 1*, 1–13.

Hamdi, N., Abu-Hijleh, N., & Abu Taleb, S. (1988). Reliability and validity study of an Arabic version of Beck's Inventory for Depression. *Dirasat: Human and Social Sciences, 15*, 30–40.

Harris, J. G., Tulsky, D. S., & Schultheis, M. T. (2003). Assessment of the non-native English speaker: Assimilating history and research findings to guide clinical practice. In D. Tulsky, D. Saklofske, G. Chelune, R. Heaton, R. Ivnik, R. Bornstein, . . . Ledbetter, M. F. (Eds.), *Clinical interpretation of the WAIS–III and WMS–III* (pp. 343–390). San Diego, CA: Academic Press. http://dx.doi.org/10.1016/B978-012703570-3/50015-8

Harris, L. D., & Wasilewski, J. (1992). *These are the values we want to share*. Bernalillo, NM: Americans for Indian Opportunity.

Hauser, R. (2002). *Meritocracy, cognitive ability, and the sources of occupational success*. Center for Demography and Ecology, University of Wisconsin. Retrieved from http://www.ssc.wisc.edu/~hauser/merit_01_081502_complete.pdf

Hayama, T., Oguchi, T., & Shinkai, Y. (1999). Trial of the new psychological test MMPI-2 on the chronic schizophrenic patients: Investigation of the basic and content scales. *Kitasata Medicine, 29*, 281–297.

Hays, P. (2006). Cognitive–behavioral therapy with Alaska native people. In P. Hays & G. Iwamasa (Eds.), *Culturally responsive cognitive–behavioral therapy* (pp. 47–72). Washington, DC: American Psychological Association.

Heart, M. Y. H. B., Chase, J., Elkins, J., & Altschul, D. B. (2011). Historical trauma among indigenous peoples of the Americas: Concepts, research, and clinical considerations. *Journal of Psychoactive Drugs, 43*, 282–290. http://dx.doi.org/10.1080/02791072.2011.628913

Heaton, R., Chelune, G., Talley, J., Kay, G., & Curtiss, G. (1993). *Wisconsin Card Sorting Test manual: Revised and expanded*. Odessa, FL: Psychological Assessment Resources.

Heaton, R., Miller, S., Taylor, M., & Grant, I. (2004). *Revised comprehensive norms for an expanded Halstead–Reitan Battery: (HRB) Demographically adjusted neuropsychological norms for African American and Caucasian adults.* Odessa, FL: Psychological Assessment Resource.

Heilbronner, R. L., Sweet, J. J., Morgan, J. E., Larrabee, G. J., & Millis, S. R., & Conference Participants. (2009). American Academy of Clinical Neuropsychology Consensus Conference Statement on the neuropsychological assessment of effort, response bias, and malingering. *The Clinical Neuropsychologist, 23*, 1093–1129. http://dx.doi.org/10.1080/13854040903155063

Heilman, K. M., & Valenstein, E. (2012). *Clinical neuropsychology* (5th ed.). New York, NY: Oxford University Press.

Helms, J. E. (2002). A remedy for the Black–White test-score disparity. *American Psychologist, 57*, 303–305.

Hendrie, H. C., Hall, K. S., Pillay, N., Rodgers, D., Prince, C., Norton, J., . . . Osuntokun, B. (1993). Alzheimer's disease is rare in Cree. *International Psychogeriatrics, 5*, 5–14. http://dx.doi.org/10.1017/S1041610293001358

Hendrie, H. C., Osuntokun, B. O., Hall, K. S., Ogunniyi, A. O., Hui, S. L., Unverzagt, F. W., . . . Musick, B. S. (1995). Prevalence of Alzheimer's disease and dementia in two communities: Nigerian Africans and African Americans. *The American Journal of Psychiatry, 152*, 1485–1492. http://dx.doi.org/10.1176/ajp.152.10.1485

Henry, M., Merten, T., Wolf, S. A., & Harth, S. (2010). Nonverbal Medical Symptom Validity Test performance of elderly healthy adults and clinical neurology patients. *Journal of Clinical and Experimental Neuropsychology, 32*, 19–27. http://dx.doi.org/10.1080/13803390902791653

Hernstein, R., & Murray, C. (1994). *The bell curve.* New York, NY: Simon & Schuster.

Hilsabeck, R. C., LeCompte, D. C., Marks, A. R., & Grafman, J. (2001). The Word Completion Memory Test (WCMT): A new test to detect malingered memory deficits. *Archives of Clinical Neuropsychology, 16*, 669–678.

Hiscock, M., & Hiscock, C. K. (1989). Refining the forced-choice method for the detection of malingering. *Journal of Clinical and Experimental Neuropsychology, 11*, 967–974. http://dx.doi.org/10.1080/01688638908400949

Hiscock, M., Inch, R., & Gleason, A. (2002). Raven's progressive matrices performance in adults with traumatic brain injury. *Applied Neuropsychology, 9*, 129–138. http://dx.doi.org/10.1207/S15324826AN0903_1

Hoefer, M., Rytina, N., & Baker, B. (2012). Estimates of the unauthorized immigrant population residing in the United States: January 2011. *Population estimates.* U.S. Department of Homeland Security. Retrieved from http://www.dhs.gov/xlibrary/assets/statistics/publications/ois_ill_pe_2011.pdf

Hoeffel, E., Rastogi, S., Kim, M., & Hasan, S. (2012). *The Asian population: 2010.* Washington, DC: U.S. Department of Commerce, Economics and Statistics Administration, U.S. Census Bureau. Retrieved from https://www.census.gov/prod/cen2010/briefs/c2010br-11.pdf

Hofstede, G. (1980). *Culture's consequences: International differences in work-related values*. Beverly Hills, CA: Sage.

Holdnack, H. (2001). *Wechsler Test of Adult Reading: WTAR*. San Antonio, TX: The Psychological Corporation.

Hooisma, J., Hänninen, H., Emmen, H. H., & Kulig, B. M. (1993). Behavioral effects of exposure to organic solvents in Dutch painters. *Neurotoxicology and Teratology, 15*, 397–406. http://dx.doi.org/10.1016/0892-0362(93)90057-U

Hopp, G., Strauss, E., & Thompson, G. (1997). *VSVT, Victoria Symptom Validity Test: Version 1.0, professional manual*. Odessa, FL: Psychological Assessment Resources.

House, R. J., Hanges, P. J., Javidan, M., Dorfman, P. W., & Gupta, V. (Eds.). (2004). *Culture, leadership, and organizations: The GLOBE study of 62 societies*. Thousand Oaks, CA: Sage.

House, R. J., & Javidan, M. (2004). Overview of GLOBE. In R. J. House, P. J. Hanges, M. Javidan, P. W. Dorfman, & V. Gupta (Eds.), *Culture, leadership, and organizations: The GLOBE study of 62 societies* (pp. 9–28). Thousand Oaks, CA: Sage.

Howitt, S., Jones, M., Jusabani, A., Gray, W., Aris, E., Mugusi, F., . . . Walker, R. (2011). A cross-sectional study of quality of life in incident stroke survivors in rural northern Tanzania. *Journal of Neurology, 258*, 1422–1430.

Hsieh, S. L., & Tori, C. D. (2007). Normative data on cross-cultural neuropsychological tests obtained from Mandarin-speaking adults across the life span. *Archives of Clinical Neuropsychology, 22*, 283–296. http://dx.doi.org/10.1016/j.acn.2007.01.004

Huang, M. H. (2001). Cognitive abilities and the growth of high-IQ occupations. *Social Science Research, 30*, 529–551. http://dx.doi.org/10.1006/ssre.2001.0710

Hughes, C. P., Berg, L., Danziger, W. L., Coben, L. A., & Martin, R. L. (1982). A new clinical scale for the staging of dementia. *The British Journal of Psychiatry, 140*, 566–572. http://dx.doi.org/10.1192/bjp.140.6.566

Indian Child Welfare Act of 1978. Pub. L. 95-608, 92 Stat. 3069, codified at 25 U.S.C. §§ 1901–1963.

Indian Health Service. (2013, January). *Disparities*. Retrieved from http://www.ihs.gov/newsroom/factsheets/disparities

Indian Self-Determination and Education Assistance Act of 1975, Pub. L. 93-638.

Infoplease. (n.d.). *American Indians by the numbers: From the U.S. Census Bureau*. Retrieved from http://www.infoplease.com/spot/aihmcensus1.html

International Association for the Evaluation of Educational Achievement. (n.d.). *TIMSS and PIRLS*. Retrieved from http://www.iea.nl/

International Medical Interpreters Association. (2007). *Medical interpreting standards of practice*. Retrieved from http://www.imiaweb.org/uploads/pages/102.pdf

International Test Commission. (2010). *International test commission guidelines for translating and adapting tests*. Retrieved from http://www.intestcom.org

International Universities and Colleges. (2013). *Universities by country*. Retrieved from http://www.4icu.org

Isella, V., Villa, M. L., Frattola, L., & Appollonio, I. (2002). Screening cognitive decline in dementia: Preliminary data on the Italian version of the IQCODE. *Neurological Sciences, 23*(Suppl. 2), S79–S80. http://dx.doi.org/10.1007/s100720200079

Iverson, G. L., Lange, R. T., Brooks, B. L., & Rennison, V. L. (2010). "Good old days" bias following mild traumatic brain injury. *The Clinical Neuropsychologist, 24*, 17–37. http://dx.doi.org/10.1080/13854040903190797

Jaeggi, S. M., Buschkuehl, M., Jonides, J., & Perrig, W. J. (2008). Improving fluid intelligence with training on working memory. *Proceedings of the National Academy of Sciences of the United States of America, 105*, 6829–6833. http://dx.doi.org/10.1073/pnas.0801268105

Jana, Y. (2001). The effectiveness of the MMPI–2 in detecting malingered schizophrenia in adult female inmates in Puerto Rico who receive coaching on diagnostic-specific criteria. *Dissertation Abstracts International: Section B. The Sciences and Engineering, 62*(2-B), 1084.

Javidan, M. (2004). Performance orientation. In R. J. House, P. J. Hanges, M. Javidan, P. W. Dorfman, & V. Gupta (Eds.), *Culture, leadership, and organizations: The GLOBE study of 62 societies* (pp. 239–281). Thousand Oaks, CA: Sage.

Jencks, C., Smith, M., Acland, H., Bane, M. J., Cohen, D., Gintis, H., & Michaelson, S. (1972). *Inequality: A reassessment of the effect of family and schooling in America.* New York, NY: Basic Books.

Jensen, A. (1998). *The g factor.* Westport, CT: Praeger.

Jiménez Gómez, F. (2012). In search of a fast screening method for detecting the malingering of cognitive impairment. *European Journal of Psychology Applied to Legal Context, 4*, 135–158.

Jo, M.-Y., & Dawson, L. K. (2011). Neuropsychological assessment of Korean Americans. In D. E. M. Fujii (Ed.), *The neuropsychology of Asian Americans* (pp. 131–148). New York, NY: Taylor & Francis.

Jones, R., & Gallo, J. (2002). Education and sex differences in the mini-mental state examination effects of differential item functioning. *The Journals of Gerontology Series B: Psychological Sciences and Social Sciences, 57*, 548–558.

Jorm, A. F. (2004). The Informant Questionnaire on Cognitive Decline in the Elderly (IQCODE): A review. *International Psychogeriatrics, 16*, 275–293. http://dx.doi.org/10.1017/S1041610204000390

Jorm, A. F., & Jacomb, P. (1986). IQCODE *Informant Questionnaire on Cognitive Decline in the Elderly* (short form 16 items). Retrieved from http://www.alz.org/documents_custom/shortiqcode_english.pdf

Juarez-Cedillo, T., Sanchez-Arenas, R., Sanchez-Garcia, S., Garcia-Peña, C., Hsiung, G. Y., Sepehry, A. A., . . . Jacova, C. (2012). Prevalence of mild cognitive impairment and its subtypes in the Mexican population. *Dementia and Geriatric Cognitive Disorders, 34*, 271–281. http://dx.doi.org/10.1159/000345251

Judd, T., & Beggs, B. (2005). Cross-cultural forensic neuropsychological assessment. In K. Barrett & W. George (Eds.), *Race, Culture, Psychology & Law* (pp. 193–205). Thousand Oaks, CA: Sage. http://dx.doi.org/10.4135/9781452233536.n10

Julayanont, P., Brousseau, M., Chertkow, H., Phillips, N., & Nasreddine, Z. S. (2014). Montreal Cognitive Assessment Memory Index Score (MoCA–MIS) as a predictor of conversion from mild cognitive impairment to Alzheimer's disease. *Journal of the American Geriatrics Society, 62*, 679–684. http://dx.doi.org/10.1111/jgs.12742

Karam, G., & Itani, L. (2013). Dementia: A review from the Arab region. *Arab Journal of Psychiatry, 24*, 77–84.

Kareken, D. A., Gur, R. C., & Saykin, A. J. (1995). Reading on the Wide Range Achievement Test—Revised and parental education as predictors of IQ: Comparison with the Barona formula. *Archives of Clinical Neuropsychology, 10*, 147–157. http://dx.doi.org/10.1093/arclin/10.2.147

Karnath, H. O., Himmelbach, M., & Rorden, C. (2002). The subcortical anatomy of human spatial neglect: Putamen, caudate nucleus and pulvinar. *Brain: A Journal of Neurology, 125*, 350–360. http://dx.doi.org/10.1093/brain/awf032

Karrasch, M., Sinervä, E., Grönholm, P., Rinne, J., & Laine, M. (2005). CERAD test performances in amnestic mild cognitive impairment and Alzheimer's disease. *Acta Neurologica Scandinavica, 111*, 172–179. http://dx.doi.org/10.1111/j.1600-0404.2005.00380.x

Karunaratne, S., Hanwella, R., & de Silva, V. (2011). Validation of the Sinhala version of the Montreal Cognitive Assessment in screening for dementia. *The Ceylon Medical Journal, 56*, 147–153. http://dx.doi.org/10.4038/cmj.v56i4.3892

Kaya, Y., Aki, O. E., Can, U. A., Derle, E., Kibaroglu, S., & Barak, A. (2014). Validation of Montreal Cognitive Assessment and discriminant power of Montreal Cognitive Assessment subtests in patients with mild cognitive impairment and Alzheimer dementia in Turkish population. *Journal of Geriatric Psychiatry and Neurology, 27*, 103–109. http://dx.doi.org/10.1177/0891988714522701

Kelly, S., & Boyd-Franklin, N. (2004). African American women in client, therapist, and supervisory relationships: The parallel processes of race, culture, and family. In M. Rastogi & E. Wieling (Eds.), *The voices of color: First person accounts of ethnic minority therapists* (pp. 67–89). Thousand Oaks, CA: Sage.

Kent, M. (2007). Immigration and America's Black population. *Population Bulletin, 62*(4), 1–16.

Kenya Certificate Secondary Education. (2014). *Top 100 national schools*. Retrieved from http://www.standardmedia.co.ke/m/story.php?articleID=2000105960&story_title=KCSE-2013-TOP-100-POSITIONS-NATIONAL-SCHOOLS

Kessler, R. C., McGonagle, K. A., Zhao, S., Nelson, C. B., Hughes, M., Eshleman, S., . . . Kendler, K. S. (1994). Lifetime and 12-month prevalence of *DSM–III–R* psychiatric disorders in the United States: Results from the National Comorbidity Survey. *Archives of General Psychiatry, 51*, 8–19. http://dx.doi.org/10.1001/archpsyc.1994.03950010008002

Ketterer, H. L., Han, K., Hur, J., & Moon, K. (2010). Development and validation of culture-specific Variable Response Inconsistency and True Response Inconsistency scales for use with the Korean MMPI–2. *Psychological Assessment, 22,* 504–519. http://dx.doi.org/10.1037/a0019511

Khalil, M. S. (2010). Preliminary Arabic normative data of neuropsychological tests: The verbal and design fluency. *Journal of Clinical and Experimental Neuropsychology, 32,* 1028–1035. http://dx.doi.org/10.1080/13803391003672305

Kim, H., & Na, D. L. (1999). Brief report: Normative data on the Korean Version of the Boston Naming Test. *Journal of Clinical and Experimental Neuropsychology, 21,* 127–133. http://dx.doi.org/10.1076/jcen.21.1.127.942

Kim, J. K., & Kang, Y. (1999). Normative study of the Korean-California Verbal Learning Test (K-CVLT). *Clinical Neuropsychologist, 13,* 365–369. http://dx.doi.org/10.1076/clin.13.3.365.1740

Kim, J. S., Song, I. U., Shim, Y. S., Park, J. W., Yoo, J. Y., Kim, Y. I., & Lee, K. S. (2009). Cognitive impairment in essential tremor without dementia. *Journal of Clinical Neurology, 5,* 81–84. http://dx.doi.org/10.3988/jcn.2009.5.2.81

Kim, J. Y., Park, J. H., Lee, J. J., Huh, Y., Lee, S. B., Han, S. K., . . . Woo, J. I. (2008). Standardization of the Korean version of the Geriatric Depression Scale: Reliability, validity, and factor structure. *Psychiatry Investigation, 5,* 232–238. http://dx.doi.org/10.4306/pi.2008.5.4.232

Kisser, J. E., Wendell, C. R., Spencer, R. J., & Waldstein, S. R. (2012). Neuropsychological performance of native versus non-native English speakers. *Archives of Clinical Neuropsychology, 27,* 749–755. http://dx.doi.org/10.1093/arclin/acs082

Klimkowicz-Mrowiec, A., Dziedzic, T., Slowik, A., & Szczudlik, A. (2006). Predictors of poststroke dementia: Results of a hospital-based study in Poland. *Dementia and Geriatric Cognitive Disorders, 21,* 328–334. http://dx.doi.org/10.1159/000091788

Kluckhohn, F., & Strodtbeck, F. (1961). *Variations in value orientations.* Evanston, IL: Row, Peterson.

Koenig, K., Frey, M., & Detterman, D. (2008). ACT and general cognitive ability. *Intelligence, 36,* 153–160. http://dx.doi.org/10.1016/j.intell.2007.03.005

Konráos, S. (1996). The Icelandic translation of the MMPI–2: Adaptation and validation. In J. Butcher (Ed.), *International adaptations of the MMPI–2* (pp. 368–384). Minneapolis: University of Minnesota Press.

Koscheyev, V. S., & Leon, G. R. (1996). The Russian translation and preliminary adaptation of the MMPI–2. In J. Butcher (Ed.), *International adaptations of the MMPI–2* (pp. 385–394). Minneapolis: University of Minnesota Press.

Krch, D., Lequerica, A., Arango-Lasprilla, J. C., Rogers, H. L., DeLuca, J., & Chiaravalloti, N. D. (2015). The multidimensional influence of acculturation on digit symbol-coding and Wisconsin card sorting test in Hispanics. *The Clinical Neuropsychologist, 29,* 624–638.

Kurt, M., Karakaya, İ., Safaz, İ., & Ateş, G. (2015). Differential item functioning by education and sex in subtests of the Repeatable Battery Assessment of

Neuropsychological Status. *European Journal of Psychological Assessment, 31,* 5–11. http://dx.doi.org/10.1027/1015-5759/a000198

Kvåle, A., Ellertsen, B., & Skouen, J. S. (2001). Relationships between physical findings (GPE–78) and psychological profiles (MMPI–2) in patients with long-lasting musculoskeletal pain. *Nordic Journal of Psychiatry, 55,* 177–184. http://dx.doi.org/10.1080/08039480152036056

Kwak, K. J. (2003). South Korea. In J. Georgas, L. Weiss, F. van de Vijver, & D. Saklofske (Eds.), *Culture and children's intelligence cross-cultural analysis of the WISC–III* (pp. 227–240). San Diego, CA: Academic Press. http://dx.doi.org/10.1016/B978-012280055-9/50017-5

Laboratory of Comparative Human Cognition. (1983). Culture and cognitive development. In P. H. Mussen (Ed.), *Handbook of child psychology* (4th ed., Vol. 1, pp. 295–356). New York, NY: Wiley.

Lam, L. C., Tam, C. W., Lui, V. W., Chan, W. C., Chan, S. S., Ho, K. S., . . . Chiu, H. F. (2008). Use of clinical dementia rating in detecting early cognitive deficits in a community-based sample of Chinese older persons in Hong Kong. *Alzheimer Disease & Associated Disorders, 22,* 153–157. http://dx.doi.org/10.1097/WAD.0b013e3181631517

Larson, E. B., McCurry, S. M., Graves, A. B., Bowen, J. D., Rice, M. M., McCormick, W. C., . . . Sasaki, H. (1998). Standardization of the clinical diagnosis of the dementia syndrome and its subtypes in a cross-national study: The Ni-Hon-Sea experience. *The Journals of Gerontology: Series A. Biological Sciences and Medical Sciences, 53,* M313–M319. http://dx.doi.org/10.1093/gerona/53A.4.M313

Lau, E. (2014). Clinical interviewing and qualitative assessment with Asian heritage clients. In J. M. Davis & R. D'Amato (Eds.), *Neuropsychology of Asians and Asian Americans* (pp. 135–149). New York, NY: Springer. http://dx.doi.org/10.1007/978-1-4614-8075-4_8

Law, S., & Wolfson, C. (1995). Validation of a French version of an informant-based questionnaire as a screening test for Alzheimer's disease. *The British Journal of Psychiatry, 167,* 541–544. http://dx.doi.org/10.1192/bjp.167.4.541

Lee, D. W., Lee, J. Y., Ryu, S. G., Cho, S. J., Hong, C. H., Lee, J. H., . . . Park, S. H. (2005). Validity of the Korean version of Informant Questionnaire on the Cognitive Decline in the Elderly (IQCODE). *Journal of the Korean Geriatrics Society, 9,* 196–202.

Lee, D. Y., Lee, K. U., Lee, J. H., Kim, K. W., Jhoo, J. H., Kim, S. Y., . . . Woo, J. I. (2004). A normative study of the CERAD neuropsychological assessment battery in the Korean elderly. *Journal of the International Neuropsychological Society, 10,* 72–81. http://dx.doi.org/10.1017/S1355617704101094

Lee, E. (1997). Cross-cultural communication: Therapeutic use of interpreters. In E. Lee (Ed.), *Working with Asian Americans: A guide for clinicians* (pp. 477–489). New York, NY: Guilford Press.

Lee, J. H., Lee, K. U., Lee, D. Y., Kim, K. W., Jhoo, J. H., Kim, J. H., . . . Woo, J. I. (2002). Development of the Korean version of the Consortium to Establish a

Registry for Alzheimer's Disease Assessment Packet (CERAD–K): Clinical and neuropsychological assessment batteries. *The Journals of Gerontology: Series B. Psychological Sciences and Social Sciences, 57,* 47–53. http://dx.doi.org/10.1093/geronb/57.1.P47

Lee, J. Y., Cho, S. J., Na, D. L., Kim, S. K., Youn, J. H., Kwon, M., & Lee, J. H. (2008). Brief screening for mild cognitive impairment in elderly outpatient clinic: Validation of the Korean version of the Montreal Cognitive Assessment. *Journal of Geriatric Psychiatry and Neurology, 21,* 104–110. http://dx.doi.org/10.1177/0891988708316855

Lehrl, S., Triebig, G., & Fischer, B. (1995). Multiple choice vocabulary test MWT as a valid and short test to estimate premorbid intelligence. *Acta Neurologica Scandinavica, 91,* 335–345. http://dx.doi.org/10.1111/j.1600-0404.1995.tb07018.x

Lewin, K. (1964). *Field theory in social science: Selected theoretical papers* (D. Cartwright, Ed.). New York, NY: Harper & Row.

Lezak, M., Howieson, D., Bigler, E., & Tranel, D. (2012). *Neuropsychological assessment* (5th ed.). New York, NY: Oxford University Press.

Lichtwark, I., Starkey, N., & Barker-Collo, S. (2013). Further validation of the New Zealand Test of Adult Reading (NZART) as a measure of premorbid IQ in a New Zealand sample. *New Zealand Journal of Psychology, 42,* 75–83.

Lifshitz, M., Dwolatzky, T., & Press, Y. (2012). Validation of the Hebrew version of the MoCA test as a screening instrument for the early detection of mild cognitive impairment in elderly individuals. *Journal of Geriatric Psychiatry and Neurology, 25,* 155–161.

Lim, M. L., Collinson, S. L., Feng, L., & Ng, T. P. (2010). Cross-cultural application of the Repeatable Battery for the Assessment of Neuropsychological Status (RBANS): Performances of elderly Chinese Singaporeans. *The Clinical Neuropsychologist, 24,* 811–826. http://dx.doi.org/10.1080/13854046.2010.490789

Lim, S. M., Yoo, J., Lee, E., Kim, H. J., Shin, S., Han, G., & Ahn, H. S. (2015). Acupuncture for spasticity after stroke: A systematic review and meta-analysis of randomized controlled trials. *Evidence-Based Complementary and Alternative Medicine, 2015,* 870398. Retrieved from http://www.hindawi.com/journals/ecam/2015/870398

Lim, W. S., Chin, J. J., Lam, C. K., Lim, P. P., & Sahadevan, S. (2005). Clinical dementia rating: Experience of a multi-racial Asian population. *Alzheimer Disease & Associated Disorders, 19,* 135–142. http://dx.doi.org/10.1097/01.wad.0000174991.60709.36

Lim, Y. Y., Pietrzak, R. H., Snyder, P. J., Darby, D., & Maruff, P. (2012). Preliminary data on the effect of culture on the assessment of Alzheimer's disease-related verbal memory impairment with the International Shopping List Test. *Archives of Clinical Neuropsychology, 27,* 136–147. http://dx.doi.org/10.1093/arclin/acr102

Lim, Y. Y., Prang, K. H., Cysique, L., Pietrzak, R. H., Snyder, P. J., & Maruff, P. (2009). A method for cross-cultural adaptation of a verbal memory assessment.

Behavior Research Methods, Instruments & Computers, 41, 1190–1200. http://dx.doi.org/10.3758/BRM.41.4.1190

Liu, C. K., Lai, C. L., Tai, C. T., Lin, R. T., Yen, Y. Y., & Howng, S. L. (1998). Incidence and subtypes of dementia in southern Taiwan: Impact of socio-demographic factors. *Neurology, 50,* 1572–1579. http://dx.doi.org/10.1212/WNL.50.6.1572

Liu, K. P., Kuo, M. C., Tang, K. C., Chau, A. W., Ho, I. H., Kwok, M. P., . . . Chu, L. W. (2011). Effects of age, education and gender in the Consortium to Establish a Registry for the Alzheimer's Disease (CERAD)—Neuropsychological Assessment Battery for Cantonese-speaking Chinese elders. *International Psychogeriatrics, 23,* 1575–1581. http://dx.doi.org/10.1017/S1041610211001153

Liu, R. G., Gao, B. L., Li, Y. P., & Lu, S. (2001). Simulated malingering: A preliminary trial of Hiscock's forced-choice digit memory test. *Chinese Journal of Clinical Psychology, 9,* 173–175.

Livermore, D. (2013). *Customs of the world: Using cultural intelligence to adapt, wherever you are.* Chantilly, VA: The Great Courses.

Loewenstein, D., Duara, R., Argüelles, T., & Argüelles, S. (1995). Use of the Fuld Object-Memory Evaluation in the detection of mild dementia among Spanish and English-speaking groups. *The American Journal of Geriatric Psychiatry, 3,* 300–307. http://dx.doi.org/10.1097/00019442-199503040-00004

Lowe, D. A., & Rogers, S. A. (2011). Estimating premorbid intelligence among older adults: The utility of the AMNART. *Journal of Aging Research, 2011,* Article ID 428132. Retrieved from http://www.hindawi.com/journals/jar/2011/428132

Lu, P. H., Boone, K. B., Cozolino, L., & Mitchell, C. (2003). Effectiveness of the Rey–Osterrieth Complex Figure Test and the Meyers and Meyers recognition trial in the detection of suspect effort. *The Clinical Neuropsychologist, 17,* 426–440. http://dx.doi.org/10.1076/clin.17.3.426.18083

Luby, J., Belden, A., Botteron, K., Marrus, N., Harms, M. P., Babb, C., . . . Barch, D. (2013). The effects of poverty on childhood brain development: The mediating effect of caregiving and stressful life events. *JAMA Pediatrics, 167,* 1135–1142. http://dx.doi.org/10.1001/jamapediatrics.2013.3139

Lucca, U., Tettamanti, M., & Quadri, P. (2008). The Italian version of Consortium to Establish a Registry of Alzheimer's Disease (CERAD). *Alzheimer's & Dementia, 4,* 310–310. http://dx.doi.org/10.1016/j.jalz.2008.05.2478

Lucchini, R., Toffoletto, F., Camerino, D., Fazioli, R., Ghittori, S., Gilioli, R., . . . Alessio, L. (1995). Neurobehavioral functions in operating theatre personnel exposed to anesthetic gases. *La Medicina del Lavoro, 86,* 27–33.

Lucio, E., Duran, C., Graham, J. R., & Ben-Porath, Y. S. (2002). Identifying faking bad on the Minnesota Multiphasic Personality Inventory—Adolescent with Mexican adolescents. *Assessment, 9,* 62–69. http://dx.doi.org/10.1177/1073191102009001008

Luk, S. (2008). Overcoming language barriers in psychiatric practice: Culturally sensitive and effective use of interpreters. *Journal of Immigrant & Refugee Studies*, 6, 545–566. http://dx.doi.org/10.1080/15362940802480589

Luria, A. R. (1979). *The making of mind*. Cambridge, MA: Harvard University Press.

Lynn, E. (2006). *Race differences in intelligence: An evolutionary analysis*. Augusta, GA: Washington Summit Publishers.

Lynn, R., & Meisenberg, G. (2010). National IQs calculated and validated for 108 nations. *Intelligence, 38*, 353–360. http://dx.doi.org/10.1016/j.intell.2010.04.007

Lynn, R., & Vanhanen, T. (2002). *IQ and the wealth of nations*. Westport, CT: Praeger.

Lynn, R., & Vanhanen, T. (2006). *IQ and global inequality*. Augusta, GA: Washington Summit Books.

Lynn, R., & Vanhanen, T. (2012). National IQs: A review of their educational, cognitive, economic, political, demographic, sociological, epidemiological, geographic and climatic correlates. *Intelligence, 40*, 226–234. http://dx.doi.org/10.1016/j.intell.2011.11.004

Lyrakos, D. (2011). The development of the Greek Personality Assessment Inventory. *Psychology, 2*, 797–803.

Macartney, S., Bishaw, A., & Fontenot, K. (2013). Poverty rates for selected detailed race and Hispanic groups by state and place: 2007–2011. *American Community Survey Briefs*. Retrieved from https://www.census.gov/prod/2013pubs/acsbr11-17.pdf

Mackinnon, A., & Mulligan, R. (2005). Estimation de l'intelligence prémorbide chez les francophones [The estimation of premorbid intelligence levels in French speakers]. *L'Encéphale, 31*, 31–43. http://dx.doi.org/10.1016/S0013-7006(05)82370-X

Magierska, J., Magierski, R., Fendler, W., Kłoszewska, I., & Sobów, T. M. (2012). Clinical application of the Polish adaptation of the Montreal Cognitive Assessment (MoCA) test in screening for cognitive impairment. *Neurologia i Neurochirurgia Polska, 46*, 130–139. http://dx.doi.org/10.5114/ninp.2012.28255

Mahmud, W. M., Awang, A., Herman, I., & Mohamed, M. N. (2004). Analysis of the psychometric properties of the Malay version of Beck Depression Inventory II (BDI–II) among postpartum women in Kedah, north west of peninsular Malaysia. *The Malaysian Journal of Medical Sciences: MJMS, 11*(2), 19–25.

Mailles, A., De Broucker, T., Costanzo, P., Martinez-Almoyna, L., Vaillant, V., & Stahl, J. P., & the Steering Committee and Investigators Group. (2012). Long-term outcome of patients presenting with acute infectious encephalitis of various causes in France. *Clinical Infectious Diseases, 54*, 1455–1464. http://dx.doi.org/10.1093/cid/cis226

Maj, M., Satz, P., Janssen, R., Zaudig, M., Starace, F., D'Elia, L., . . . Sartorius, N. (1994). WHO Neuropsychiatric AIDS study, cross-sectional Phase II: Neuropsychological and neurological findings. *Archives of General Psychiatry, 51*, 51–61. http://dx.doi.org/10.1001/archpsyc.1994.03950010051007

Makeeva, O., Markova, V., Zhukova, I., Melikyan, Z., Minaycheva, L., Buikin, S., . . . Welsh-Bohmer, K. (2012). Montreal Cognitive Assessment (MoCA) population-based study of Russian elderly. *Alzheimer's & Dementia, 8*, 4(Suppl.), S773. http://dx.doi.org/10.1016/j.jalz.2013.08.108

Manly, J. J., Jacobs, D. M., Touradji, P., Small, S. A., & Stern, Y. (2002). Reading level attenuates differences in neuropsychological test performance between African American and White elders. *Journal of the International Neuropsychological Society, 8*, 341–348. http://dx.doi.org/10.1017/S1355617702813157

Manly, J. J., Miller, S. W., Heaton, R. K., Byrd, D., Reilly, J., Velasquez, R. J., . . . the HIV Neurobehavioral Research Center (HNRC) Group. (1998). The effect of African-American acculturation on neuropsychological test performance in normal and HIV-positive individuals. *Journal of the International Neuropsychological Society, 4*, 291–302.

Marcopulos, B., & Fujii, D. (2012). Neuropsychological assessment: Recent developments. In B. Marcopulos & M. Kurtz (Eds.), *Clinical neuropsychological foundations of schizophrenia* (pp. 55–80). New York, NY: Psychology Press.

Marin, G., Sabogal, F., Marin, B. V., Otero-Sabogal, R., & Perez-Stable, E. (1987). Development of a short acculturation scale for Hispanics. *Hispanic Journal of Behavioral Sciences, 9*, 183–205. http://dx.doi.org/10.1177/07399863870092005

Martinić-Popović, I., Šerić, V., & Demarin, V. (2006). Early detection of mild cognitive impairment in patients with cerebrovascular disease. *Acta Clinica Croatica, 45*, 77–85.

Martins, M., & Martins, I. P. (2010). Memory malingering: Evaluating WMT criteria. *Applied Neuropsychology, 17*, 177–182. http://dx.doi.org/10.1080/09084281003715709

Mathias, J., Bowden, S., & Barrett-Woodbridge, M. (2007). Accuracy of the Wechsler Test of Adult Reading (WTAR) and National Adult Reading Test (NART) when estimating IQ in a healthy Australian sample. *Australian Psychologist, 42*, 49–56. http://dx.doi.org/10.1080/00050060600827599

Matsuoka, K., Uno, M., Kasai, K., Koyama, K., & Kim, Y. (2006). Estimation of premorbid IQ in individuals with Alzheimer's disease using Japanese ideographic script (Kanji) compound words: Japanese version of National Adult Reading Test. *Psychiatry and Clinical Neurosciences, 60*, 332–339.

Mattson, S. N., Crocker, N., & Nguyen, T. T. (2011). Fetal alcohol spectrum disorders: Neuropsychological and behavioral features. *Neuropsychology Review, 21*, 81–101.

May, P., McCloskey, J., & Gossage, J. (2002). Fetal alcohol syndrome among American Indians: Epidemiology, issues, and research review. In P. D. Mail, S. Heurtin-Roberts, S. E. Martin, & J. Howard (Eds.), *Alcohol use among American Indians and Alaska Natives: Multiple perspectives on a complex problem* (NIAAA Monograph No. 37; pp. 321–369). Bethesda, MD: U.S. Department of Health and Human Services.

Mayer, J. D., Salovey, P., & Caruso, D. R. (2008). Emotional intelligence: New ability or eclectic traits? *American Psychologist, 63*, 503–517. http://dx.doi.org/10.1037/0003-066X.63.6.503

McBride, M. (2006). Working with Filipino American families. In G. Yeo & D. Gallagher-Thompson (Eds.), *Ethnicity and dementias* (2nd ed., pp. 189–208). New York, NY: Routledge.

McCallum, S., Bracken, B., & Wasserman, J. (2000). *Essential of nonverbal assessment*. New York, NY: Wiley.

McCurry, S. M., Gibbons, L. E., Uomoto, J. M., Thompson, M. L., Graves, A. B., Edland, S. D., . . . Larson, E. B. (2001). Neuropsychological test performance in a cognitively intact sample of older Japanese American adults. *Archives of Clinical Neuropsychology, 16*, 447–459. http://dx.doi.org/10.1093/arclin/16.5.447

McDonald, J., & Gonzalez, J. (2006). Cognitive–behavioral therapy with American Indians. In P. Hays & G. Iwamasa (Eds.), *Culturally responsive cognitive–behavioral therapy* (pp. 23–45). Washington, DC: American Psychological Association.

McGoldrick, M., Giordano, J., & Garcia-Preto, N. (2005). *Ethnicity and family therapy* (3rd ed.). New York, NY: Guilford Press.

McKeown, P. (2003). United Kingdom. In J. Georgas, L. G. Weiss, F. J. van de Vijver, & D. H. Saklofske (Eds.), *Culture and children's intelligence: Cross-cultural analysis of the WISC–III* (pp. 78–88). San Diego, CA: Academic Press. http://dx.doi.org/10.1016/B978-012280055-9/50007-2

McLoyd, V. C. (1998). Socioeconomic disadvantage and child development. *American Psychologist, 53*, 185–204. http://dx.doi.org/10.1037/0003-066X.53.2.185

Meguro, K., Ishii, H., Yamaguchi, S., Ishizaki, J., Sato, M., Hashimoto, R., . . . Sekita, Y. (2004). Prevalence and cognitive performances of clinical dementia rating 0.5 and mild cognitive impairment in Japan: The Tajiri project. *Alzheimer Disease & Associated Disorders, 18*, 3–10. http://dx.doi.org/10.1097/00002093-200401000-00002

Meisenberg, G. (2012). National IQ and economic outcomes. *Personality and Individual Differences, 53*, 103–107. http://dx.doi.org/10.1016/j.paid.2011.06.022

Meisenberg, G. (2009). Wealth, intelligence, politics and global fertility differentials. *Journal of Biosocial Science, 41*, 519–535. http://dx.doi.org/10.1017/S0021932009003344

Meldolesi, G., Picardi, A., Accivile, E., Toraldo di Francia, R., & Biondi, M. (2000). Personality and psychopathology in patients with temporomandibular joint pain-dysfunction syndrome. A controlled investigation. *Psychotherapy and Psychosomatics, 69*, 322–328. http://dx.doi.org/10.1159/000012415

Melika, L. (1987). *Wechsler Adult Intelligence Scale (WAIS)—Arabic version*. Cairo, Egypt: El-Nahda Library.

Memória, C. M., Yassuda, M. S., Nakano, E. Y., & Forlenza, O. V. (2013). Brief screening for mild cognitive impairment: Validation of the Brazilian version of the Montreal Cognitive Assessment. *International Journal of Geriatric Psychiatry, 28,* 34–40. http://dx.doi.org/10.1002/gps.3787

Merten, T., Dandachi-FitzGerald, B., Hall, V., Schmand, B., Santamaríae, P., & González-Ordi, H. (2013). Symptom validity assessment in European countries: Development and state of the art. *Clínica y Salud, 24,* 129–138. http://dx.doi.org/10.1016/S1130-5274(13)70014-8

Mesulam, M. M. (Ed.). (2000). *Principles of behavioral and cognitive neurology* (2nd ed.). New York, NY: Oxford University Press.

Migration Policy Institute. (2013). *Frequently requested statistics on immigrants and immigration in the United States.* Retrieved from http://www.migrationpolicy.org/article/frequently-requested-statistics-immigrants-and-immigration-united-states#8F

Miller, H. A. (2001). *M-FAST: Miller-Forensic Assessment of Symptoms Test professional manual.* Odessa, FL: Psychological Assessment Resources.

Miner, J. (1961). On the use of a short vocabulary test to measure general intelligence. *Journal of Educational Psychology, 52,* 157–160. http://dx.doi.org/10.1037/h0041647

Miranda, J., McConnell, R., Delgado, E., Cuadra, R., Keifer, M., Wesseling, C., . . . Lundberg, I. (2002). Tactile vibration thresholds after acute poisonings with organophosphate insecticides. *International Journal of Occupational and Environmental Health, 8,* 212–219. http://dx.doi.org/10.1179/oeh.2002.8.3.212

Mitrushina, M., Boone, K., Razani, J., & D'Elia, L. (2005). *Handbook of normative data for neuropsychological assessment* (2nd ed.). New York, NY: Oxford University Press.

Mongini, F., Ibertis, F., Barbalonga, E., & Raviola, F. (2000). MMPI–2 profiles in chronic daily headache and their relationship to anxiety levels and accompanying symptoms. *Headache, 40,* 466–472. http://dx.doi.org/10.1046/j.1526-4610.2000.00070.x

Monsen, K., & Havik, O. (2001). Psychological functioning and bodily conditions in patients with pain disorder associated with psychological factors. *British Journal of Medical Psychology, 74,* 183–195. http://dx.doi.org/10.1348/000711201160902

Montes, O., & Guyton, M. R. (2014). Performance of Hispanic inmates on the Spanish Miller Forensic Assessment of Symptoms Test (M-FAST). *Law and Human Behavior, 38,* 428–438. http://dx.doi.org/10.1037/lhb0000074

Moody, M. (2007). *Adaptive behavior in intercultural environments: The relationship between cultural intelligence factors and Big Five personality traits* (Unpublished doctoral dissertation). George Washington University, Washington DC.

Moon, A. (2006). Working with Korean American families. In G. Yeo & D. Gallagher-Thompson (Eds.), *Ethnicity and the dementias* (2nd ed., pp. 245–262). New York, NY: Taylor & Francis.

Morales, G., González-Montalvo, J., Del Ser, Q., & Bermejo, P. (1991). Validation of the S-IQCODE: the Spanish version of the informant questionnaire on cognitive decline in the elderly [in Spanish]. *Archivos de Neurobiología, 55,* 262–266.

Morey, L., & Boggs, C. (1991). *Personality assessment inventory (PAI)*. Odessa, FL: Psychological Assessment Resources.

Morris, J. C., Heyman, A., Mohs, R. C., Hughes, J. P., van Belle, G., Fillenbaum, G., . . . Clark, C. (1989). The consortium to establish a registry for Alzheimer's Disease (CERAD). Part I. Clinical and neuropsychological assessment of Alzheimer's disease. *Neurology, 39,* 1159–1165. http://dx.doi.org/10.1212/WNL.39.9.1159

Mouanoutoua, V. L., Brown, L. G., Cappelletty, G. G., & Levine, R. V. (1991). A Hmong Adaptation of the Beck Depression Inventory. *Journal of Personality Assessment, 57,* 309–322. http://dx.doi.org/10.1207/s15327752jpa5702_9

Mullen, C. M., & Fouty, H. E. (2014). Comparison of the WRAT4 reading subtest and the WTAR for estimating premorbid ability level. *Applied Neuropsychology: Adult, 21,* 69–72. http://dx.doi.org/10.1080/09084282.2012.727111

Mungas, D., Reed, B. R., Farias, S. T., & DeCarli, C. (2005). Criterion-referenced validity of a neuropsychological test battery: Equivalent performance in elderly Hispanics and non-Hispanic Whites. *Journal of the International Neuropsychological Society, 11,* 620–630. http://dx.doi.org/10.1017/S1355617705050745

Munoz-Sandoval, A., Cummins, J., Alvarado, C., & Ruef, M. (1998). *Bilingual verbal abilities tests.* Itasca, IL: Riverside.

Murphy, M. (2012). Normative CERAD-NP performance among community-dwelling older adults in Ireland. *Clinical Gerontologist, 35,* 15–26. http://dx.doi.org/10.1080/07317115.2011.626514

Muslimovic, D., Post, B., Speelman, J. D., & Schmand, B. (2005). Cognitive profile of patients with newly diagnosed Parkinson disease. *Neurology, 65,* 1239–1245. http://dx.doi.org/10.1212/01.wnl.0000180516.69442.95

Myers, J. E., Nell, V., Colvin, M., Rees, D., & Thompson, M. L. (1999). Neuropsychological function in solvent-exposed South African paint makers. *Journal of Occupational and Environmental Medicine, 41,* 1011–1018. http://dx.doi.org/10.1097/00043764-199911000-00014

Nabha, L., Duong, L., & Timpone, J. (2013). HIV-associated neurocognitive disorders: Perspective on management strategies. *Drugs, 73,* 893–905. http://dx.doi.org/10.1007/s40265-013-0059-6

Naimi, T., Cobb, N., Boyd, D., Jarman, D., Espey, D., Snesrud, P., & Chavez, P., & the Centers for Disease Control and Prevention (CDC). (2008). Alcohol-attributable deaths and years of potential life lost among American Indians and Alaska Natives—United States, 2001–2005. *MMWR, 57,* 938–941.

Nakao, M., Yamanaka, G., & Kuboki, T. (2001). Major depression and somatic symptoms in a mind/body medicine clinic. *Psychopathology, 34,* 230–235. http://dx.doi.org/10.1159/000049315

Narazaki, K., Nofuji, Y., Honda, T., Matsuo, E., Yonemoto, K., & Kumagai, S. (2013). Normative data for the Montreal Cognitive Assessment in a Japanese community-dwelling older population. *Neuroepidemiology, 40,* 23–29. http://dx.doi.org/10.1159/000339753

Nasreddine, Z. S., Phillips, N. A., Bédirian, V., Charbonneau, S., Whitehead, V., Collin, I., . . . Chertkow, H. (2005). The Montreal Cognitive Assessment, MoCA: A brief screening tool for mild cognitive impairment. *Journal of the American Geriatrics Society*, *53*, 695–699. http://dx.doi.org/10.1111/j.1532-5415.2005.53221.x

National Center for Education Statistics (2012). *National Indian Education Study 2011* (NCES 2012–466). Institute of Education Sciences, U.S. Department of Education, Washington, DC.

National Conference of Commissioners on Uniform States Laws. (1994). *Uniform Health-Care Decisions Act*. Retrieved from http://www.uniformlaws.org/shared/docs/health%20care%20decisions/uhcda_final_93.pdf

National Opinion Research Center (NORC). (n.d.). *The General Social Survey*. Retrieved from http://www3.norc.org/GSS+Website

National Virtual Translation Center. (2007). *Learning language difficulty for English speakers*. Retrieved from http://web.archive.org/web/20071014005901/http://www.nvtc.gov/lotw/months/november/learningExpectations.html

Nell, V. (2000). *Cross-cultural neuropsychological assessment: Theory and practice*. Mahwah, NJ: Erlbaum.

Ng, K. Y., van Dyne, L., & Ang, S. (2012). Cultural intelligence: A review, reflection, and recommendations for future research. In A. Ryan, F. Leong, & F. Oswald (Eds.), *Conducting multinational research: Applying organizational psychology in the workplace* (pp. 29–58). Washington, DC: American Psychological Association. http://dx.doi.org/10.1037/13743-002

Noble, K. G. (2014, May). Rich man, poor man: Socioeconomic adversity and brain development. In *Cerebrum: The Dana forum on brain science* (Vol. 2014). Retrieved from http://www.ncbi.nlm.nih.gov/pmc/articles/PMC4436198

Norris, T., Vines, P., & Hoeffel, E. (2012). *The American Indian and Alaska Native Population: 2010 Census Briefs*. Retrieved from http://www.census.gov/prod/cen2010/briefs/c2010br-10.pdf

Nygaard, H. A., Naik, M., & Geitung, J. T. (2009). The Informant Questionnaire on Cognitive Decline in the Elderly (IQCODE) is associated with informant stress. *International Journal of Geriatric Psychiatry*, *24*, 1185–1191. http://dx.doi.org/10.1002/gps.2243

Organisation for Economic Co-operation and Development. (2013). *PISA 2012 results in focus*. Retrieved from http://www.oecd.org/pisa/keyfindings/pisa-2012-results-overview.pdf

Orsini, A., & Laicardi, C. (2003). *WAIS–R e terza età* [*WAIS–R and third age*]. Florence, Italy: Organizzazioni Speciali.

Ortiz, I. E., LaRue, A., Romero, L. J., Sassaman, M. F., & Lindeman, R. D. (1997). Comparison of cultural bias in two cognitive screening instruments in elderly Hispanic patients in New Mexico. *The American Journal of Geriatric Psychiatry*, *5*, 333–338. http://dx.doi.org/10.1097/00019442-199700540-00008

Ostrosky-Solís, F. (2007). Education effects on cognitive functions: Brain reserve, compensation, or testing bias? In B. Uzzell, M. Ponton, & A. Ardila (Eds.), *International handbook of cross-cultural neuropsychology* (pp. 215–225). Mahwah, NJ: Erlbaum.

Ostrosky-Solís, F., Ardila, A., & Rosselli, M. (1997). *NEUROPSI: Evaluación neuropsicológica breve en Español. Manual, Instructivo y Protocolo de Aplicación* [NEUROPSI: A brief neuropsychological evaluation in Spanish. Manual, instructions, and application protocol]. México City, México: Bayer de México.

Owen, J., Tao, K., Imel, Z., Wampold, B., & Rodolfa, E. (2014). Addressing racial and ethnic microaggressions in therapy. *Professional Psychology: Research and Practice, 45*, 283–290. http://dx.doi.org/10.1037/a0037420

Ozel-Kizil, E. T., Turan, E. D., Yilmaz, E., Cangoz, B., & Uluc, S. (2010). Discriminant validity and reliability of the Turkish version of Informant Questionnaire on Cognitive Decline in the Elderly (IQCODE-T). *Archives of Clinical Neuropsychology, 25*, 139–145. http://dx.doi.org/10.1093/arclin/acp103

Paajanen, T., Hänninen, T., Tunnard, C., Mecocci, P., Sobow, T., Tsolaki, M., . . . Soininen, H., & the Addneuromed Consortium. (2010). CERAD neuropsychological battery total score in multinational mild cognitive impairment and control populations: The AddNeuroMed study. *Journal of Alzheimer's Disease, 22*, 1089–1097.

Paap, K. R., & Greenberg, Z. I. (2013). There is no coherent evidence for a bilingual advantage in executive processing. *Cognitive Psychology, 66*, 232–258. http://dx.doi.org/10.1016/j.cogpsych.2012.12.002

Paradis, M., & Libben, G. (1987). *The assessment of bilingual aphasia.* Hillsdale, NJ: Erlbaum. Retrieved from http://www.mcgill.ca/linguistics/research/bat

Paranawithana, C., & De Zoysa, P. (2012). Cross cultural adaptation of the Repeatable Battery for the Assessment of Neuropsychological Status to a Sinhala speaking clinical population in Sri Lanka. In *Annual Research Symposium 2012, University of Colombo.* Retrieved from http://archive.cmb.ac.lk:8080/research/handle/70130/3005

Parsons, O. A., & Nixon, S. J. (1998). Cognitive functioning in sober social drinkers: A review of the research since 1986. *Journal of Studies on Alcohol, 59*, 180–190. http://dx.doi.org/10.15288/jsa.1998.59.180

Pasi, M., Salvadori, E., Poggesi, A., Inzitari, D., & Pantoni, L. (2013). Factors predicting the Montreal Cognitive Assessment (MoCA) applicability and performances in a stroke unit. *Journal of Neurology, 260*, 1518–1526. http://dx.doi.org/10.1007/s00415-012-6819-5

Pedraza, O., Lucas, J. A., Smith, G. E., Willis, F. B., Graff-Radford, N. R., Ferman, T. J., . . . Ivnik, R. J. (2005). Mayo's older African American normative studies: Confirmatory factor analysis of a core battery. *Journal of the International Neuropsychological Society, 11*, 184–191. http://dx.doi.org/10.1017/S1355617705050204

Pedraza, O., & Mungas, D. (2008). Measurement in cross-cultural neuropsychology. *Neuropsychology Review, 18,* 184–193. http://dx.doi.org/10.1007/s11065-008-9067-9

Pena-Casanova, J., Blesa, R., Aguilar, M., Gramunt-Fombuena, N., Gomex-Anson, B., Oliva, R., . . . the NEURONORMA Study Team. (2009) Spanish Multicenter Normative Studies (NEURONORMA Project): Methods and sample characteristics. *Archives of Clinical Neuropsychology, 24,* 307–319.

Penley, J. A., Wiebe, J. S., & Nwosu, A. (2003). Psychometric properties of the Spanish Beck Depression Inventory–II in a medical sample. *Psychological Assessment, 15,* 569–577. http://dx.doi.org/10.1037/1040-3590.15.4.569

Pérez-Pareja, F., Abad, A., & Ordi, H. (2010). Fibromyalgia and chronic pain: Are there discriminating patterns by using the Minnesota Multiphasic Personality Inventory—2 (MMPI–2)? *International Journal of Clinical and Health Psychology, 10,* 41–56.

Perroco, T. R., Bustamante, S. E., Moreno, M. P., Hototian, S. R., Lopes, M. A., Azevedo, D., . . . Bottino, C. M. (2009). Performance of Brazilian long and short IQCODE on the screening of dementia in elderly people with low education. *International Psychogeriatrics, 21,* 531–538. http://dx.doi.org/10.1017/S1041610209008849

Petsanis, K., Messinis, L., Lyros, E., Papathanasiou, T., Papathanasopoulos, P., & Malegiannaki, A. (2011). Repeatable Battery for the Assessment of Neuropsychological Status (RBANS): Clinical validation in Greece. *Alzheimer's & Dementia, 7,* e45. http://dx.doi.org/10.1016/j.jalz.2011.09.190

Piaget, J. (1929). *The child's conception of the world.* London, England: Routledge & Kegan Paul.

Plomin, R., DeFries, J., Knopik, V., & Neiderhiser, J. (2013). *Behavioral genetics* (6th ed.). New York, NY: Worth.

Pongpanich, L. (1996). Use of the MMPI–2 in Thailand. In J. Butcher (Ed.), *International Adaptations of the MMPI–2* (pp. 162–174). Minneapolis: University of Minnesota Press.

Ponton, M., & Corona-LoMonaco, M. (2007). Cross-cultural issues in neuropsychology: Assessment of the Hispanic patient. In B. Uzzell, M. Ponton, & A. Ardila (Eds.), *International handbook of cross-cultural neuropsychology* (pp. 265–282). Mahwah, NJ: Erlbaum.

Poreh, A., Sultan, A., & Levin, J. (2012). The Rey Auditory Verbal Learning Test: Normative data for the Arabic-speaking population and analysis of the differential influence of demographic variables. *Psychology & Neuroscience, 5,* 57–61. http://dx.doi.org/10.3922/j.psns.2012.1.08

Postal, K., & Armstrong, K. (2013). *Feedback that sticks: The art of effectively communicating neuropsychological assessment results.* New York, NY: Oxford University Press.

Prescott, S. (1991). *The American Indian: Yesterday, today, & tomorrow. A handbook for educators*. Sacramento: Bureau of Publications, California State Department of Education.

Prince, M., Acosta, D., Ferri, C. P., Guerra, M., Huang, Y., Jacob, K., . . . Hall, K. (2011). A brief dementia screener suitable for use by non-specialists in resource poor settings—The cross-cultural derivation and validation of the brief Community Screening Instrument for Dementia. *International Journal of Geriatric Psychiatry, 26*, 899–907.

Psychological Corporation. (2001). *The Wechsler Test of Adult Reading (WTAR)*. San Antonio, TX: Author.

Quevedo, K. M., & Butcher, J. N. (2005). The use of the MMPI and MMPI–2 in Cuba: A historical overview from 1950 to the present. *International Journal of Clinical and Health Psychology, 5*, 336–347.

Rabin, L. A., Barr, W. B., & Burton, L. A. (2005). Assessment practices of clinical neuropsychologists in the United States and Canada: A survey of INS, NAN, and APA Division 40 members. *Archives of Clinical Neuropsychology, 20*, 33–65. http://dx.doi.org/10.1016/j.acn.2004.02.005

Radwan, D., Okasha, T., Elmissary, M., Sadek, H., Khalifa, A., & Abdelaziz, K. (2013). Cognitive impairment in Egyptian euthymic patients with bipolar I disorder compared with controls. *Middle East Current Psychiatry, 20*, 197–204. http://dx.doi.org/10.1097/01.XME.0000433325.69290.c9

Rahimi-Golkhandan, S., Maruff, P., Darby, D., & Wilson, P. (2012). Barriers to repeated assessment of verbal learning and memory: A comparison of international shopping list task and Rey Auditory Verbal Learning Test on build-up of proactive interference. *Archives of Clinical Neuropsychology, 27*, 790–795. http://dx.doi.org/10.1093/arclin/acs074

Rahman, T. T., El Gaafary, M. M., & Mohamed, M. (2009). Montreal Cognitive Assessment Arabic version: Reliability and validity prevalence of mild cognitive impairment among elderly attending geriatric clubs in Cairo. *Geriatrics & Gerontology International, 9*, 54–61. http://dx.doi.org/10.1111/j.1447-0594.2008.00509.x

Randolph, C. (1998). *RBANS manual: Repeatable battery for the assessment of neuropsychological status*. San Antonio, TX: The Psychological Corporation.

Ratanadilok, K. (2011). Neuropsychology in Thailand. In D. E. M. Fujii (Ed.), *The neuropsychology of Asian Americans* (pp. 301–307). New York, NY: Taylor & Francis.

Raven, J., Raven, J. C., & Court, J. H. (2003). *Manual for Raven's Progressive Matrices and Vocabulary Scales*. San Antonio, TX: Harcourt Assessment.

Raycheva, M., Mehrabian, S., & Traykov, L. (2005). Differentiation of mild cognitive impairment and Alzheimer's disease with Bulgarian version of CERAD. *Journal of the Neurological Sciences, 238*, S299. http://dx.doi.org/10.1016/S0022-510X(05)81145-1

Razani, J., Burciaga, J., Madore, M., & Wong, J. (2007). Effects of acculturation on tests of attention and information processing in an ethnically diverse group. *Archives of Clinical Neuropsychology, 22*, 333–341. http://dx.doi.org/10.1016/j.acn.2007.01.008

Razani, J., Murcia, G., Tabares, J., & Wong, J. (2007). The effects of culture on WASI test performance in ethnically diverse individuals. *The Clinical Neuropsychologist, 21*, 776–788. http://dx.doi.org/10.1080/13854040701437481

Razzak, R. A. (2013). A preliminary study on the Trail-making Test in Arabic–English bilingual young adults. *Applied Neuropsychology: Adult, 20*, 53–60. http://dx.doi.org/10.1080/09084282.2012.670163

Reban, J. (2006). Montrealský kognitivní test (MoCA): přínos k diagnostice predemencí [Montreal cognitive test (MoCA), for diagnosing pre-dementia contribution]. *Česká Geriatrická Revue, 4*, 224–229.

Reis, A., Guerreiro, M., & Petersson, K. M. (2003). A sociodemographic and neuropsychological characterization of an illiterate population. *Applied Neuropsychology, 10*, 191–204. http://dx.doi.org/10.1207/s15324826an1004_1

Rey, A. (1964). *L'examen clinique en psychologie* [The clinical examination in psychology]. Paris, France: Presses Universitaires de France.

Richman, J., Green, P., Gervais, R., Flaro, L., Merten, T., Brockhaus, R., & Ranks, D. (2006). Objective tests of symptom exaggeration in independent medical examinations. *Journal of Occupational and Environmental Medicine, 48*, 303–311. http://dx.doi.org/10.1097/01.jom.0000183482.41957.c3

Rienstra, A., Spaan, P. E. J., & Schmand, B. (2010). Validation of symptom validity tests using a "child-model" of adult cognitive impairments. *Archives of Clinical Neuropsychology, 25*, 371–382. http://dx.doi.org/10.1093/arclin/acq035

Rindermann, H. (2008). Relevance of education and intelligence at the national level for the economic welfare of people. *Intelligence, 36*, 127–142. http://dx.doi.org/10.1016/j.intell.2007.02.002

Rivera-Mindt, M., Arentoft, A., Kubo Germano, K., D'Aquila, E., Scheiner, D., Pizzirusso, M., . . . Gollan, T. H. (2008). Neuropsychological, cognitive, and theoretical considerations for evaluation of bilingual individuals. *Neuropsychology Review, 18*, 255–268. http://dx.doi.org/10.1007/s11065-008-9069-7

Rodriguez, J. J. L., Ferri, C. P., Acosta, D., Guerra, M., Huang, Y., Jacob, K. S., . . . 10/66 Dementia Research Group. (2008). Prevalence of dementia in Latin America, India, and China: A population-based cross-sectional survey. *The Lancet, 372*, 464–474. http://dx.doi.org/10.1016/S0140-6736(08)61002-8

Rogers, R., Bagby, R. M., & Dickens, S. E. (1992). *Structured Interview of Reported Symptoms (SIRS) professional manual*. Odessa, FL: Psychological Assessment Resources.

Rogers, R., Flores, J., Ustad, K., & Sewell, K. W. (1995). Initial validation of the Personality Assessment Inventory-Spanish version with clients from Mexican

American communities. *Journal of Personality Assessment, 64*, 340–348. http://dx.doi.org/10.1207/s15327752jpa6402_12

Rohde, T., & Thompson, L. A. (2007). Predicting academic achievement with cognitive ability. *Intelligence, 35*, 83–92. http://dx.doi.org/10.1016/j.intell.2006.05.004

Roldán-Tapia, L., Parrón, T., & Sánchez-Santed, F. (2005). Neuropsychological effects of long-term exposure to organophosphate pesticides. *Neurotoxicology and Teratology, 27*, 259–266. http://dx.doi.org/10.1016/j.ntt.2004.12.002

Rosen, W. G., Mohs, R. C., & Davis, K. L. (1984). A new rating scale for Alzheimer's disease. *The American Journal of Psychiatry, 141*, 1356–1364. http://dx.doi.org/10.1176/ajp.141.11.1356

Rossman, P., & Schallberger, U. (2003). Austria and Switzerland. In J. Georgas, L. G. Weiss, F. J. van de Vijver, & D. H. Saklofske (Eds.), *Culture and children's intelligence: Cross-cultural analysis of the WISC–III* (pp. 138–149). San Diego, CA: Academic Press. http://dx.doi.org/10.1016/B978-012280055-9/50011-4

Rothlein, J., Rohlman, D., Lasarev, M., Phillips, J., Muniz, J., & McCauley, L. (2006). Organophosphate pesticide exposure and neurobehavioral performance in agricultural and non-agricultural Hispanic workers. *Environmental Health Perspectives, 114*, 691–696. http://dx.doi.org/10.1289/ehp.8182

Ruschke, K., Bidar-Sielaff, S., Avery, M. B., Downing, B., Green, C. E., & Haffner, L. (2005). *National standards of practice for interpreters in health care.* Retrieved from http://www.ncihc.org/assets/documents/publications/NCIHC%20National%20Standards%20of%20Practice.pdf

Russell, J., & Batalova, J. (2012, September 27). *Refugees and asylees in the United States.* Retrieved from Migration Policy Institute website: http://www.migrationpolicy.org/article/refugees-and-asylees-united-states

Ryan, J., Paolo, A., & Dunn, G. (1995). Analysis of a WAIS–R old-age normative sample in terms of gender, years of education, and preretirement occupation. *Assessment, 2*, 225–231. http://dx.doi.org/10.1177/1073191195002003003

Sackett, P. R., Hardison, C. M., & Cullen, M. J. (2004). On interpreting stereotype threat as accounting for African American–White differences on cognitive tests. *American Psychologist, 59*, 7–13. http://dx.doi.org/10.1037/0003-066X.59.1.7

Saddik, B., Williamson, A., Nuwayhid, I., & Black, D. (2005). The effects of solvent exposure on memory and motor dexterity in working children. *Public Health Reports, 120*, 657–663.

Saklofske, D. (2003). Canada. In J. Georgas, L. G. Weiss, F. J. van de Vijver, & D. H. Saklofske (Eds.), *Culture and children's intelligence: Cross-cultural analysis of the WISC–III* (pp. 62–77). San Diego, CA: Academic Press.

Salazar, G. D., Garcia, M. P., & Puente, A. E. (2007). Clinical neuropsychology of Spanish speakers: The challenge and pitfalls of a neuropsychology of a heterogeneous population. In B. Uzzell, M. Ponton, & A. Ardila (Eds.), *International handbook of cross-cultural neuropsychology* (pp. 283–302). Mahwah, NJ: Erlbaum.

Salazar, X., Lu, P., Wen, J., & Boone, K. (2007). The use of effort tests in ethnic minorities and in non-English-speaking and English as a second language populations. In K. Boone (Ed.), *Assessment of feigned cognitive impairment: A neuropsychological perspective* (pp. 405–427). New York, NY: Guilford Press.

Salovey, P., & Mayer, J. D. (1990). Emotional intelligence. *Imagination, Cognition and Personality, 9*, 185–211. http://dx.doi.org/10.2190/DUGG-P24E-52WK-6CDG

Sánchez, G., Jimenez, F., Ampudia, A., & Merino, V. (2012). In search of a fast screening method for detecting the malingering of cognitive impairment. *The European Journal of Psychology Applied to Legal Context, 4*, 135–158.

Satcher, D. (2001). *Mental health: Culture, race, and ethnicity—A supplement to mental health: A report of the Surgeon General.* Retrieved from http://www.ncbi.nlm.nih.gov/books/NBK44243/

Savaşir, I., & Çulha, M. (1996). Development of the MMPI–2 in Turkey. In J. Butcher (Ed.), *International Adaptations of the MMPI–2* (pp. 448–460). Minneapolis: University of Minnesota Press.

Savaşir, I., & Şahin, N. (1995). *Wechsler Çocuklar İçin Zeka Ölçeği (WISC–R)* [Wechsler Intelligence Scale for Children (WISC–R)]. Ankara, Turkey: Turkish Psychological Association.

Scazufca, M., Menezes, P., Vallada, H., Crepaldi, A., Pastor-Valero, M., Coutinho, L., . . . Almeida, O. P. (2008). High prevalence of dementia among older adults from poor socioeconomic backgrounds in Sao Paulo, Brazil. *International Psychogeriatrics, 20*, 394–405.

Schiller, J. S., Lucas, J. W., Ward, B. W., & Peregoy, J. A., & the National Center for Health Statistics. (2012). Summary health statistics for U.S. adults: National Health Interview Survey, 2010. *Vital Health Statistics, 10*(252), 1–207.

Schilt, T., Koeter, M. W., Smal, J. P., Gouwetor, M. N., van den Brink, W., & Schmand, B. (2010). Long-term neuropsychological effects of ecstasy in middle-aged ecstasy/polydrug users. *Psychopharmacology, 207*, 583–591. http://dx.doi.org/10.1007/s00213-009-1688-z

Schittekatte, M., Kort, W., Resing, W., Vermeir, G., & Verhaeghe, P. (2003). Netherlands and Flemish-speaking Belgium. In J. Georgas, L. G. Weiss, F. J. van de Vijver, & D. H. Saklofske (Eds.), *Culture and children's intelligence: Cross-cultural analysis of the WISC–III* (pp. 110–121). San Diego, CA: Academic Press. http://dx.doi.org/10.1016/B978-012280055-9/50009-6

Schmader, T., Johns, M., & Forbes, C. (2008). An integrated process model of stereotype threat effects on performance. *Psychological Review, 115*, 336–356. http://dx.doi.org/10.1037/0033-295X.115.2.336

Schmand, B., Houx, P., & de Koning, I. (2004). *The Stroop Colour Word Test, the Trail Making Test, the Rivermead Behavioural Memory Test. Dutch norms.* Amsterdam, the Netherlands: Netherlands Institute of Psychologists, Section of Neuropsychology.

Schoenberg, M. R., Duff, K., Scott, J. G., Patton, D., & Adams, R. L. (2006). Prediction errors of the Oklahoma Premorbid Intelligence Estimate—3 (OPIE–3)

stratified by 13 age groups. *Archives of Clinical Neuropsychology, 21,* 469–475. http://dx.doi.org/10.1016/j.acn.2006.06.006

Schrauf, R. W., Weintraub, S., & Navarro, E. (2006). Is adaptation of the word accentuation test of premorbid intelligence necessary for use among older, Spanish-speaking immigrants in the United States? *Journal of the International Neuropsychological Society, 12,* 391–399. http://dx.doi.org/10.1017/S1355617706060462

Schretlen, D. J., Munro, C. A., Anthony, J. C., & Pearlson, G. D. (2003). Examining the range of normal intraindividual variability in neuropsychological test performance. *Journal of the International Neuropsychological Society, 9,* 864–870. http://dx.doi.org/10.1017/S1355617703960061

Schretlen, D. J., Winicki, J. M., Meyer, S. M., Testa, S. M., Pearlson, G. D., & Gordon, B. (2009). Development, psychometric properties, and validity of the Hopkins Adult Reading Test (HART). *The Clinical Neuropsychologist, 23,* 926–943. http://dx.doi.org/10.1080/13854040802603684

Seibens, J., & Julian, T. (2011). *Native North American Languages Spoken at Home in the United States and Puerto Rico: 2006–2010.* Retrieved from https://www.census.gov/prod/2011pubs/acsbr10-10.pdf

Selekler, K., Cangoz, B., & Uluc, S. (2010). Power of discrimination of Montreal Cognitive Assessment (MoCA) Scale in Turkish patients with mild cognitive impairment and Alzheimer's disease. *Turkish Journal of Geriatrics, 13,* 166–171.

Senanarong, V., Poungvarin, N., Jamjumras, P., Sriboonroung, A., Danchaivijit, C., Udomphanthuruk, S., & Cummings, J. L. (2005). Neuropsychiatric symptoms, functional impairment and executive ability in Thai patients with Alzheimer's disease. *International Psychogeriatrics, 17,* 81–90. http://dx.doi.org/10.1017/S1041610205000980

Sénéchal, M., & LeFevre, J. A. (2002). Parental involvement in the development of children's reading skill: A five-year longitudinal study. *Child Development, 73,* 445–460. http://dx.doi.org/10.1111/1467-8624.00417

Sheridan, M. A., Fox, N. A., Zeanah, C. H., McLaughlin, K. A., & Nelson, C. A., III. (2012). Variation in neural development as a result of exposure to institutionalization early in childhood. *PNAS: Proceedings of the National Academy of Sciences of the United States of America, 109,* 12927–12932. http://dx.doi.org/10.1073/pnas.1200041109

Shin, K. R., Shin, C., & Blanchette, P. L. (2001). *Health and health care of Korean American elders.* Retrieved from http://web.stanford.edu/group/ethnoger/korean.html

Shin, Y. C., Kim, E., Cheong, H. K., Cho, S., Sakong, J., Kim, K. S., . . . Kim, Y. (2007). High signal intensity on magnetic resonance imaging as a predictor of neurobehavioral performance of workers exposed to manganese. *Neurotoxicology, 28,* 257–262. http://dx.doi.org/10.1016/j.neuro.2006.03.014

Shiota, N., Krauss, S., & Clark, L. (1996). Adaptation and validation of the Japanese MMPI–2. In J. Butcher (Ed.), *International Adaptations of the MMPI–2* (pp. 67–87). Minneapolis: University of Minnesota Press.

Shoaee, F., Azkhosh, M., & Alizad, V. (2013). Health status of Iranian older people: A demographical Analysis. *Iranian Journal of Ageing, 8*(29), 60–69.

Sikaroodi, H., Yadegari, S., & Miri, S. R. (2013). Cognitive impairments in patients with cerebrovascular risk factors: A comparison of Mini-Mental Status Exam and Montreal Cognitive Assessment. *Clinical Neurology and Neurosurgery, 115,* 1276–1280. http://dx.doi.org/10.1016/j.clineuro.2012.11.026

Siri, S., Okanurak, K., Chansirikanjana, S., Kitayaporn, D., & Jorm, A. F. (2006). Modified Informant Questionnaire on Cognitive Decline in the Elderly (IQCODE) as a screening test for dementia for Thai elderly. *The Southeast Asian Journal of Tropical Medicine and Public Health, 37,* 587–594.

Sirigatti, S., & Giannini, M. (2000). Detection of faking good on the MMPI–2: Psychometric characteristics of the S scale. *Bollettino di Psicologia Applicata, 232,* 61–69.

Snowden, L., & Hines, A. (1999). A scale to assess African American acculturation. *Journal of Black Psychology, 25,* 36–47. http://dx.doi.org/10.1177/0095798499025001003

Sonnander, K., & Ramund, B. B.(2003). Sweden. In J. Georgas, L. G. Weiss, F. J. van de Vijver, & D. H. Saklofske (Eds.), *Culture and children's intelligence: Cross-cultural analysis of the WISC–III* (pp. 150–165). San Diego, CA: Academic Press.

Sosa, A., Albanese, E., Prince, M., Acosta, D., Ferri, C., Guerra, M., . . . Stewart, R. (2009). Population normative data for the 10/66 Dementia Research Group Cognitive Test Battery from Latin America, India and China: A cross-sectional survey. *BMC Neurology, 9*(48), 1–11. Retrieved from http://www.biomedcentral.com/content/pdf/1471-2377-9-48.pdf

Spinks, R., Arndt, S., Caspers, K., Yucuis, R., McKirgan, L. W., Pfalzgraf, C., & Waterman, E. (2007). School achievement strongly predicts midlife IQ. *Intelligence, 35,* 563–567. http://dx.doi.org/10.1016/j.intell.2006.10.004

Starkstein, S. E., Jorge, R. E., & Robinson, R. G. (2010). The frequency, clinical correlates, and mechanism of anosognosia after stroke. *Canadian Journal of Psychiatry, 55,* 355–361.

Starkstein, S. E., & Robinson, R. G. (1989). Affective disorders and cerebral vascular disease. *The British Journal of Psychiatry, 154,* 170–182. http://dx.doi.org/10.1192/bjp.154.2.170

Steele, C. M. (1997). A threat in the air. How stereotypes shape intellectual identity and performance. *American Psychologist, 52,* 613–629. http://dx.doi.org/10.1037/0003-066X.52.6.613

Stephens, R., Spurgeon, A., Calvert, I. A., Beach, J., Levy, L. S., Berry, H., & Harrington, J. M. (1995). Neuropsychological effects of long-term exposure to organophosphates in sheep dip. *The Lancet, 345,* 1135–1139. http://dx.doi.org/10.1016/S0140-6736(95)90976-1

Stephenson, C. L., & Halpern, D. F. (2013). Improved matrix reasoning is limited to training on tasks with a visuospatial component. *Intelligence, 41*, 341–357. http://dx.doi.org/10.1016/j.intell.2013.05.006

Sternberg, R. J. (2004). Culture and intelligence. *American Psychologist, 59*, 325–338. http://dx.doi.org/10.1037/0003-066X.59.5.325

Sternberg, R. J., Nokes, C., Geissler, P. W., Prince, R., Okatcha, F., Bundy, D., & Grigorenko, E. L. (2001). The relationship between academic and practical intelligence: A case study in Kenya. *Intelligence, 29*, 401–418. http://dx.doi.org/10.1016/S0160-2896(01)00065-4

Stevens, A., Friedel, E., Mehren, G., & Merten, T. (2008). Malingering and uncooperativeness in psychiatric and psychological assessment: Prevalence and effects in a German sample of claimants. *Psychiatry Research, 157*, 191–200.

Strassberg, D., Tilley, D., Bristone, S., & Oei, T. (1992). The MMPI and chronic pain: A cross-cultural view. *Psychological Assessment, 4*, 493–497. http://dx.doi.org/10.1037/1040-3590.4.4.493

Strauss, E., Sherman, E., & Spreen, O. (2006). *A compendium of neuropsychological tests: Administration, norms, and commentary.* New York, NY: Oxford University Press.

Strutt, A., & Scott, B. (2011). Misclassification of cognitive impairment on the MOCA with Spanish-speaking older adults. *Archives of Clinical Neuropsychology, 26*, 484.

Strutt, A. M., Scott, B. M., Lozano, V. J., Tieu, P. G., & Peery, S. (2012). Assessing sub-optimal performance with the Test of Memory Malingering in Spanish speaking patients with TBI. *Brain Injury, 26*, 853–863. http://dx.doi.org/10.3109/02699052.2012.655366

Strutt, A. M., Scott, B. M., Shrestha, S., & York, M. K. (2011). The Rey 15-Item Memory Test and Spanish-speaking older adults. *The Clinical Neuropsychologist, 25*, 1253–1265. http://dx.doi.org/10.1080/13854046.2011.609839

Su, C. Y., Chen, H. M., Kwan, A. L., Lin, Y. H., & Guo, N. W. (2007). Neuropsychological impairment after hemorrhagic stroke in basal ganglia. *Archives of Clinical Neuropsychology, 22*, 465–474. http://dx.doi.org/10.1016/j.acn.2007.01.025

Substance Abuse and Mental Health Services Administration. (2009, January). *Culture card: A guide to build cultural awareness American Indian and Alaska Native.* Retrieved from http://store.samhsa.gov/product/American-Indian-and-Alaska-Native-Culture-Card/SMA08-4354

Sue, D. (2010). Microaggressions, marginality, and oppression: An introduction. In D. W. Sue (Ed.), *Microaggressions and marginality* (pp. 3–24). Hoboken, NJ: Wiley.

Sue, D. W., Capodilupo, C. M., Torino, G. C., Bucceri, J. M., Holder, A. M., Nadal, K. L., & Esquilin, M. (2007). Racial microaggressions in everyday life: Implications for clinical practice. *American Psychologist, 62*, 271–286. http://dx.doi.org/10.1037/0003-066X.62.4.271

Sutton, C., & Broken Nose, M. (1996). American Indian families: An overview. In M. McGoldrick, J. Giordano, & J. Pearce (Eds.), *Ethnicity and family therapy* (2nd ed., pp. 31–44). New York, NY: Guilford Press.

Sweet, J. J., Meyer, D. G., Nelson, N. W., & Moberg, P. J. (2011). The TCN/AACN 2010 "salary survey:" Professional practices, beliefs, and incomes of U.S. neuropsychologists. *The Clinical Neuropsychologist, 25*, 12–61. http://dx.doi.org/10.1080/13854046.2010.544165

Tallberg, I. M., Wenneborg, K., & Almkvist, O. (2006). Reading words with irregular decoding rules: A test of premorbid cognitive function? *Scandinavian Journal of Psychology, 47*, 531–539. http://dx.doi.org/10.1111/j.1467-9450.2006.00547.x

Tannen, D. (1984). The pragmatics of cross-cultural communication. *Applied Linguistics, 5*, 189–195. http://dx.doi.org/10.1093/applin/5.3.189

Tannen, D. (1985). Cross cultural communication. In T. A. Van Dijk (Ed.), *Handbook of discourse analysis: Vol. 4. Discourse analysis in society* (pp. 203–215). London, England: Academic Press.

TEA. (1999). *WAIS–III: Escala de inteligencia de Wechsler para Adultos. Tercera versión* [WAIS–III: Wechsler Adult Intelligence Scale (3rd rev.)]. Madrid, Spain: Author.

Teacher Certification. (n.d.). *Storytelling traditions of Native Americans.* Retrieved from http://www.teachercertification.org/generalteaching/storytelling-traditions-of-native-americans.html

te Nijenhuis, J., Cho, S. H., Murphy, R., & Lee, K. H. (2012). The Flynn effect in Korea: Large gains. *Personality and Individual Differences, 53*, 147–151. http://dx.doi.org/10.1016/j.paid.2011.03.022

Te Pou. (2010). *Talking therapies for Asian people: Best and promising practice guide for mental health and addiction services.* Auckland, New Zealand: Te Pou o te Whakaaro Nui. Retrieved from http://www.tepou.co.nz/uploads/files/resource-assets/Talking-Therapies-for-Asian-People.pdf

Tewes, U. (2003). Germany. In J. Georgas, L. G. Weiss, F. J. van de Vijver, & D. H. Saklofske (Eds.), *Culture and children's intelligence: Cross-cultural analysis of the WISC–III* (pp. 122–137). San Diego, CA: Academic Press.

Thalmann, B., Urs Monsch, A., Schneitter, M., Bernasconi, F., Aebi, C., Camachova-Davet, Z., & Staehelin, H. B. (2000). The CERAD neuropsychological assessment battery (CERAD-NAB)—A minimal data set as a common tool for German-speaking Europe. *Neurobiology of Aging, 21*, 30. http://dx.doi.org/10.1016/S0197-4580(00)82810-9

Thames, A. D., Hinkin, C. H., Byrd, D. A., Bilder, R. M., Duff, K. J., Mindt, M. R., . . . Streiff, V. (2013). Effects of stereotype threat, perceived discrimination, and examiner race on neuropsychological performance: Simple as black and white? *Journal of the International Neuropsychological Society, 19*, 583–593. http://dx.doi.org/10.1017/S1355617713000076

Thissen, A. J., van Bergen, F., de Jonghe, J. F., Kessels, R. P., & Dautzenberg, P. L. (2010). Bruikbaarheid en validiteit van de Nederlandse versie van de Montreal

Cognitive Assessment (MoCA–D) bij het diagnosticeren van Mild Cognitive Impairment [Applicability and validity of the Dutch version of the Montreal Cognitive Assessment (moCA-d) in diagnosing MCI]. *Tijdschrift voor Gerontologie en Geriatrie, 41,* 231–240. http://dx.doi.org/10.1007/s12439-010-0218-0

Thomason, T. (2011). Best practices in counseling Native Americans. *Journal of Indigenous Research, 1,* article 3, 1–4. Retrieved from http://digitalcommons.usu.edu/kicjir/vol1/iss1/3

Thompson, J., Walker, R., & Silk-Walker, P. (1993). Psychiatric care of American Indians and Alaska Natives. In A. Gaw (Ed.), *Culture, ethnicity, and mental illness* (pp. 189–243). Washington, DC: American Psychiatric Press.

Thorndike, R. L. (1942). Two screening tests of verbal intelligence. *Journal of Applied Psychology, 26,* 128–135. http://dx.doi.org/10.1037/h0060053

Tombaugh, T. N. (1996). *Test of memory malingering: TOMM.* North Tonawanda, NY: Multi-Health Systems.

Touradji, P., Manly, J. J., Jacobs, D. M., & Stern, Y. (2001). Neuropsychological test performance: A study of non-Hispanic White elderly. *Journal of Clinical and Experimental Neuropsychology, 23,* 643–649. http://dx.doi.org/10.1076/jcen.23.5.643.1246

Tran, B. N. (1996). Vietnamese translation and adaptation of the MMPI–2. In J. N. Butcher (Ed.), *International Adaptations of the MMPI–2* (pp. 175–193). Minneapolis: University of Minnesota Press.

Trompenaars, F., & Hampden-Turner, C. (1997). *Riding the waves of culture: Understanding diversity in global business.* New York, NY: McGraw.

Tsai, C. F., Lee, W. J., Wang, S. J., Shia, B. C., Nasreddine, Z., & Fuh, J. L. (2012). Psychometrics of the Montreal Cognitive Assessment (MoCA) and its subscales: Validation of the Taiwanese version of the MoCA and an item response theory analysis. *International Psychogeriatrics, 24,* 651–658. http://dx.doi.org/10.1017/S1041610211002298

Tydecks, S., Merten, T., & Gubbay, J. (2006). The Word Memory Test and the One-in-Five-Test in an analogue study with Russian-speaking participants. *International Journal of Forensic Psychology, 1,* 29–37.

Ueno, K., & Nakatani, I. (2003). Japan. In J. Georgas, L. G. Weiss, F. J. van de Vijver, & D. H. Saklofske (Eds.), *Culture and children's intelligence: Cross-cultural analysis of the WISC–III* (pp. 216–226). San Diego, CA: Academic Press.

United Nations Development Programme. (n.d.). *Human development index and its components.* Retrieved from http://hdr.undp.org/en/composite/HDI

United Nations Educational, Scientific and Cultural Organization. (2012). *World atlas of gender equality in education.* Paris, France: United Nations Publishing. Retrieved from http://unesdoc.unesco.org/images/0021/002155/215522e.pdf

UNESCO. (n.d.-a). *Educational attainment of the population 25 years and older.* Retrieved from http://www.uis.unesco.org/DataCentre/Excel/LITEA/Educational%20attainment%20by%20ISCED%20level%20-%20Niveau%20de%20scolarisation%20par%20niveau%20de%20la%20CITE.xlsx

UNESCO. (n.d.-b). *Mean years of schooling*. Retrieved from http://data.uis.unesco.org/Index.aspx?queryid=242

Unverzagt, F., Hall, K., Torke, A., Rediger, J., Mercado, N., Gureje, O., . . . Hendrie, H. (1996). Effects of age, education, and gender on CERAD neuropsychological test performance in an African American sample. *Clinical Neuropsychologist, 10,* 180–190. http://dx.doi.org/10.1080/13854049608406679

Unverzagt, F. W., Morgan, O. S., Thesiger, C. H., Eldemire, D. A., Luseko, J., Pokuri, S., . . . Hendrie, H. C. (1999). Clinical utility of CERAD neuropsychological battery in elderly Jamaicans. *Journal of the International Neuropsychological Society, 5,* 255–259. http://dx.doi.org/10.1017/S1355617799003082

Uribe, F., LeVine, R., & LeVine, S. (1994). Maternal behavior in a Mexican community: The changing environments of children. In P. Greenfield & R. Cocking (Eds.), *Cross-cultural roots of minority child development* (pp. 41–54). New York, NY: Taylor & Francis.

U.S. Bureau of Labor Statistics. (n.d.). *National Longitudinal Survey of Youth*. Retrieved from http://www.bls.gov/nls/nlsy79.htm

U.S. Census Bureau. (n.d.-a). *Hispanic Americans by the numbers*. Retrieved from http://www.infoplease.com/spot/hhmcensus1.html

U.S. Census Bureau. (n.d.-b). *Selected population profile in the United States. 2009–2011 American Community Survey 3-Year Estimates: Kenya*. Retrieved from http://factfinder.census.gov/faces/tableservices/jsf/pages/productview.xhtml?src=CF

U.S. Department of Education, Institute of Education Sciences, National Center for Education Statistics. (2012). *National Indian Education Study 2011* (NCES 2012–466). Retrieved from http://nces.ed.gov/nationsreportcard/pdf/studies/2012466.pdf

U.S. Department of Education, Institute of Education Sciences, National Center for Education Statistics. (n.d.). *Trends in International Mathematics and Science Study (TIMSS) Results (2011)*. Retrieved from https://nces.ed.gov/TIMSS/results11.asp

U.S. Department of Health and Human Services. (1999). *Mental health: A report of the Surgeon General*. Rockville, MD: Author.

U.S. Department of State, Bureau of Consular Affairs. (n.d.). *U.S. Visas*. Retrieved from http://travel.state.gov/content/visas/english/immigrate.html

U.S. Department of Transportation. (2004, April). *Fatal motor vehicle crashes on Indian reservations, 1975–2002* (Technical Report DOT HS 809 727). Retrieved from http://www-nrd.nhtsa.dot.gov/Pubs/809727.pdf

Uzzell, B., Ponton, M., & Ardila, A. (Eds.). (2007). *International handbook of cross-cultural neuropsychology*. Mahwah, NJ: Erlbaum.

Valcour, V. G., Masaki, K. H., & Blanchette, P. L. (2002). The phrase: "no ifs, ands, or buts" and cognitive testing. Lessons from an Asian-American community. *Hawaii Medical Journal, 61*(4), 72–74.

van de Beek, D., Schmand, B., de Gans, J., Weisfelt, M., Vaessen, H., Dankert, J., & Vermeulen, M. (2002). Cognitive impairment in adults with good recovery after bacterial meningitis. *The Journal of Infectious Diseases, 186,* 1047–1052. http://dx.doi.org/10.1086/344229

Van Hamme, L. (1996). American Indian cultures and the classroom. *Journal of Indian Education, 35*(2), 21–36.

van Hout, M. S., Schmand, B., Wekking, E. M., & Deelman, B. G. (2006). Cognitive functioning in patients with suspected chronic toxic encephalopathy: Evidence for neuropsychological disturbances after controlling for insufficient effort. *Journal of Neurology, Neurosurgery, & Psychiatry, 77,* 296–303. http://dx.doi.org/10.1136/jnnp.2004.047167

van IJzendoorn, M. H., Juffer, F., & Poelhuis, C. W. K. (2005). Adoption and cognitive development: A meta-analytic comparison of adopted and nonadopted children's IQ and school performance. *Psychological Bulletin, 131,* 301–316. http://dx.doi.org/10.1037/0033-2909.131.2.301

Veltman, C. (1988). *The future of Spanish language in the United States.* Washington, DC: Hispanic Policy Development Project.

Vendrig, A. A., de Mey, H. R., Derksen, J. J., & van Akkerveeken, P. F. (1998). Assessment of chronic back pain patient characteristics using factor analysis of the MMPI–2: Which dimensions are actually assessed? *Pain, 76,* 179–188. http://dx.doi.org/10.1016/S0304-3959(98)00040-2

Vilar-López, R., Gómez-Río, M., Santiago-Ramajo, S., Rodríguez-Fernández, A., Puente, A. E., & Pérez-García, M. (2008). Malingering detection in a Spanish population with a known-groups design. *Archives of Clinical Neuropsychology, 23,* 365–377. http://dx.doi.org/10.1016/j.acn.2008.01.007

Vogel, V. (1970). *American Indian medicine.* Norman: University of Oklahoma Press.

Waite, L., Grayson, D., Jorm, A. F., Creasey, H., Cullen, J., Bennett, H., . . . Broe, G. A. (1999). Informant-based staging of dementia using the clinical dementia rating. *Alzheimer Disease & Associated Disorders, 13,* 34–37. http://dx.doi.org/10.1097/00002093-199903000-00005

Walker, A., Batchelor, J., Shores, E., & Jones, M. (2010). Effects of cultural background on WAIS–III and WMS–III performances after moderate–severe traumatic brain injury. *Australian Psychologist, 45,* 112–122. http://dx.doi.org/10.1080/00050060903428210

Wang, Y. L., Wu, C. W., & Wu, A. (2000). The MMPI results in patients with chronic pain. *Chinese Mental Health Journal, 14,* 321–322.

Wang, Y. P., Andrade, L. H., & Gorenstein, C. (2005). Validation of the Beck Depression Inventory for a Portuguese-speaking Chinese community in Brazil. *Brazilian Journal of Medical and Biological Research, 38,* 399–408. http://dx.doi.org/10.1590/S0100-879X2005000300011

Watkins, N., LaBarrie, T., & Appio, L. (2010). Black undergraduates' experience with perceived racial microaggressions in predominantly White colleges and universities. In D. W. Sue (Ed.), *Microaggressions and marginality: Manifestation, dynamics, and impact* (pp. 25–58). Hoboken, NJ: Wiley.

Webb, J. W., Batchelor, J., Meares, S., Taylor, A., & Marsh, N. V. (2012). Effort test failure: Toward a predictive model. *The Clinical Neuropsychologist, 26*, 1377–1396. http://dx.doi.org/10.1080/13854046.2012.728248

Wechsler, D. (1997). *WMS–III: Wechsler memory scale administration and scoring manual*. San Antonio, TX: Psychological Corporation.

Wechsler, D. (1998). *Wechsler Adult Intelligence Scale—Third UK edition: Administrative and Scoring Manual*. London, England: The Psychological Corporation.

Wechsler, D. (2000). *Manuel de l'Echelle d'intelligence de Wechsler pour Adultes—3e édition* [Wechsler Adult Intelligence Scale, Third edition manual]. Paris, France: ECPA.

Wechsler, D. (2001). *Wechsler Test of Adult Reading: WTAR*. San Antonio, TX: Psychological Corporation.

Wechsler, D. (2002). *Wechsler Intelligence Scales for Children: Manual* (3rd ed.), *Adaptação e padronização de uma amostra brasileira* [Brazilian adaptation and standardization]. São Paulo, Brazil: Casa do Psicólogo

Wechsler, D. (2004). *WISC–IV Spanish*. San Antonio, Texas: Pearson.

Wechsler, D. (2005). *Wechsler Adult Intelligence Scale* [manual] (3rd ed.). Helsinki, Finland: Psykologien Kustannus Oy.

Wechsler, D. (2008a). *Wechsler Adult Intelligence Scale* (4th ed.). San Antonio, TX: Pearson.

Wechsler, D. (2008b). *Wechsler Adult Intelligence Scale—Fourth edition (WAIS–IV), Australian and New Zealand Language Adaptation*. San Antonio, TX: NCS Pearson.

Wechsler, D. (2013). *Wechsler Memory Scale-III India*. Bangalore, India: Pearson Clinical and Talent Assessment.

Wechsler, D. (2014). *Wechsler Intelligence Scale for Children—Fourth Edition* (India) (WISC–IVINDIA). Bangalore, India: Pearson Clinical and Talent Assessment.

Weiss, R., & Rosenfeld, B. (2010). Cross-cultural validity in malingering assessment: The Dot Counting Test in a rural Indian sample. *International Journal of Forensic Mental Health, 9*, 300–307.

Wesseling, C., Keifer, M., Ahlbom, A., McConnell, R., Moon, J. D., Rosenstock, L., & Hogstedt, C. (2002). Long-term neurobehavioral effects of mild poisonings with organophosphate and n-methyl carbamate pesticides among banana workers. *International Journal of Occupational and Environmental Health, 8*, 27–34. http://dx.doi.org/10.1179/oeh.2002.8.1.27

Whitney, K. A., Mossbarger, B., Herman, S. M., & Ibarra, S. L. (2012). Is the Montreal Cognitive Assessment superior to the Mini-Mental State Examination in detecting subtle cognitive impairment among middle-aged outpatient

U.S. Military veterans? *Archives of Clinical Neuropsychology, 27*, 742–748. http://dx.doi.org/10.1093/arclin/acs060

Whyte, S. R., Cullum, C. M., Hynan, L. S., Lacritz, L. H., Rosenberg, R. N., & Weiner, M. F. (2005). Performance of elderly Native Americans and Caucasians on the CERAD neuropsychological battery. *Alzheimer Disease and Associated Disorders, 19*, 74–78. http://dx.doi.org/10.1097/01.wad.0000165508.67993.a3

Wicherts, J., Dolan, C., & van der Maas, H. (2010). A systematic literature review of the average IQ of sub-Saharan Africans. *Intelligence, 38*, 1–20. http://dx.doi.org/10.1016/j.intell.2009.05.002

Wiederholt, W., Galasko, D., & Salmon, D. (1997). Utility of the CASI and IQCODE as screening instruments for dementia in natives of Guam. *Journal of the Neurological Sciences, 150*, S89. http://dx.doi.org/10.1016/S0022-510X(97)85270-7

Wikeley, F., Bullock, K., Muschamp, Y., & Ridge, T. (2007). *Educational relationships outside school: Why access is important*. York, England: Joseph Rowntree Foundation. Retrieved from http://www.most.ie/webreports/Fatima%20reports/OST/2027-education-poverty-activitiesJRF.pdf

Wikipedia. (n.d.). *List of universities and colleges by country*. Retrieved from http://en.wikipedia.org/wiki/List_of_universities_and_colleges_by_country

Wilkinson, G., & Robertson, G. (2006). *Wide Range Achievement Test (WRAT4)*. Lutz, FL: Psychological Assessment Resources.

Wolf, S. A., Kubatschek, K., Henry, M., Harth, S., Ebert, A. D., & Wallesch, C. W. (2009). Fremdbeurteilung kognitiver Veränderungen im Alter [Informant report of cognitive changes in the elderly. A first evaluation of the German version of the IQCODE]. *Der Nervenarzt, 80*, 1176–1178, 1178–1180, 1182–1189. http://dx.doi.org/10.1007/s00115-009-2794-1

Wong, A., Xiong, Y. Y., Kwan, P. W., Chan, A. Y., Lam, W. W., Wang, K., . . . Mok, V. C. (2009). The validity, reliability and clinical utility of the Hong Kong Montreal Cognitive Assessment (HK–MoCA) in patients with cerebral small vessel disease. *Dementia and Geriatric Cognitive Disorders, 28*, 81–87. http://dx.doi.org/10.1159/000232589

Woodcock, R., & Munoz-Sandoval, A. (2005). *Bateria III*. Itasca, IL: Riverside.

World Bank. (2013). *How we classify countries*. Retrieved from http://data.worldbank.org/about/country-classifications

World Bank. (2014). *GDP per capita (current US$)*. Retrieved from http://data.worldbank.org/indicator/NY.GDP.PCAP.CD

World Health Organization. (2015). *International statistical classification of diseases and health related problems* (10th revision). Geneva, Switzerland: World Health Organization. Retrieved from http://apps.who.int/classifications/icd10/browse/2015/en

Xiong, Y. S. (2013). Recent changes and remaining challenges in Hmong Americans' educational attainment. In M. E. Pfeifer & B. K. Thao (Eds.), *State of the Hmong American community* (pp. 29–34). Washington, DC: Hmong National

Development. Retrieved from http://www.hndinc.org/cmsAdmin/uploads/dlc/HND-Census-Report-2013.pdf

Yamada, M., Sasaki, H., Kasagi, F., & Suzuki, G. (2002). The informant questionnaire on cognitive decline in the elderly (IQCODE) as a screening tool for dementia among Japanese population: The Adult Health Study subjects. *Neurobiology of Aging, 23*(Suppl.), S30.

Yamaguchi, T. (2005). *Detecting malingered memory impairment using the Rey 15-Item Memory Test and the Wechsler Digit Span subtests in a Japanese population.* UMI Dissertation Services, ProQuest Information and Learning, Ann Arbor, MI.

Yamashima, T., Yoshida, M., Kumahashi, K., Matsui, M., Koshino, Y., Higashima, M., . . . Matsushita, M. (2002). The Japanese version of RBANS (Repeatable Battery for the Assessment of Neuropsychological Status) [in Japanese]. *Brain and Nerve, 54,* 463–471.

Yang, C. C., Kao, C. J., Cheng, T. W., Yang, C. C., Wang, W. H., Yu, R. L., . . . Hua, M. S. (2012). Cross-cultural effect on suboptimal effort detection: An example of the Digit Span subtest of the WAIS–III in Taiwan. *Archives of Clinical Neuropsychology, 27,* 869–878. http://dx.doi.org/10.1093/arclin/acs081

Yassuda, M. S., Diniz, B. S., Flaks, M. K., Viola, L. F., Pereira, F. S., Nunes, P. V., & Forlenza, O. V. (2009). Neuropsychological profile of Brazilian older adults with heterogeneous educational backgrounds. *Archives of Clinical Neuropsychology, 24,* 71–79. http://dx.doi.org/10.1093/arclin/acp009

Yepthomi, T., Paul, R., Vallabhaneni, S., Kumarasamy, N., Tate, D. F., Solomon, S., & Flanigan, T. (2006). Neurocognitive consequences of HIV in southern India: A preliminary study of clade C virus. *Journal of the International Neuropsychological Society, 12,* 424–430. http://dx.doi.org/10.1017/S1355617706060516

Yeung, A., Howarth, S., Chan, R., Sonawalla, S., Nierenberg, A. A., & Fava, M. (2002). Use of the Chinese version of the Beck Depression Inventory for screening depression in primary care. *Journal of Nervous and Mental Disease, 190,* 94–99. http://dx.doi.org/10.1097/00005053-200202000-00005

Yokoyama, K., Araki, S., Murata, K., Nishikitani, M., Okumura, T., Ishimatsu, S., . . . White, R. F. (1998). Chronic neurobehavioral effects of Tokyo subway sarin poisoning in relation to posttraumatic stress disorder. *Archives of Environmental Health, 53,* 249–256. http://dx.doi.org/10.1080/00039899809605705

Yum, T. H., Park, Y. S., Oh, K. J., Kim, J. K., & Lee, Y. H. (1992). *Korean Wechsler Adult Intelligence Scale (K–WAIS) Manual.* Seoul, Korea: Hankook Guidance.

Zaroff, C., D'Amato, C., & Bender, H. A. (2014). Understanding differences in cognition across the lifespan: Comparing Eastern and Western cultures. In J. M. Davis & R. D'Amato (Eds.), *Neuropsychology of Asians and Asian Americans* (pp. 91–114). New York, NY: Springer.

Zhang, B. H., Tan, Y. L., Zhang, W. F., Wang, Z. R., Yang, G. G., Shi, C., . . . Zhou, D. F. (2009). Repeatable Battery for the Assessment of Neuropsychological Status (RBANS) as a screening test in Chinese: Reliability and validity. *Chinese Mental Health Journal, 28,* 865–869.

Zheng, L., Teng, E. L., Varma, R., Mack, W. J., Mungas, D., Lu, P. H., & Chui, H. C. (2012). Chinese-language Montreal Cognitive Assessment for Cantonese or Mandarin speakers: Age, education, and gender effects. *International Journal of Alzheimer's Disease, 2012,* Article ID 204623. http://dx.doi.org/10.1155/2012/204623

Zhou, W., Liang, Y., & Christiani, D. C. (2002). Utility of the WHO neurobehavioral core test battery in Chinese workers—a meta-analysis. *Environmental Research, 88,* 94–102. http://dx.doi.org/10.1006/enrs.2001.4322

Zoghbi, A. W., Al Jurdi, R. K., Deshmukh, P. R., Chen, C., Xiu, M. H., Tan, Y. L., . . . Zhang, X. Y. (2014). Cognitive function and suicide risk in Han Chinese inpatients with schizophrenia. *Psychiatry Research, 220,* 188–192. http://dx.doi.org/10.1016/j.psychres.2014.07.046

Zuin, D., Ortiz, H., Boromei, D., & Lopez, O. L. (2002). Motor vehicle crashes and abnormal driving behaviours in patients with dementia in Mendoza, Argentina. *European Journal of Neurology, 9,* 29–34. http://dx.doi.org/10.1046/j.1468-1331.2002.00296.x

INDEX

Behavioral changes, over time, 141–142
Behavioral observations
    cultural context for, 35
    estimating IQ with, 98
    impact of cultural differences on, 33
    impact of culture on, 36
    in reports, 205–206
Being lifestyle, 22, 23
Beliefs
    about illness, 51–54, 172–173
    in cultural context, 47–51
Bennett's developmental model of
        intercultural sensitivity, 14–18
Best performance method, 94–96
BFCR (Binomial Forced-Choice Digit
        Recognition Test), 156
Bicultural model, 46
BIE (Board of Indian Education)
        schools, 44–45
Bigler, E., 139
Bilingual Aphasia Test (BAT), 152–153
Bilingualism
    among Native Indian and Alaskan
        Natives, 45
    effect of, on neuropsychological test
        performance, 192
Bilingual Verbal Abilities Test (BVAT),
        83
Binomial Forced-Choice Digit Recogni-
        tion Test (BFCR), 156
Board of Indian Education (BIE)
        schools, 44–45
Bowden, S., 98
Brain development, and environment,
        73
Brief background history, 205
B Test, 155
BVAT (Bilingual Verbal Abilities
        Test), 83

Case formulation, 185–201
    impact of culture on, 36
    performance validity tests results,
        186–188
    potential threats to test validity,
        186–188
    in reports, 207–208
    review pertinent neuropsychological
        literature, 188–195

in sample case, 195–201
    score tests with appropriate norms,
        185–186
CDCs. *See* Culturally different clients
CDR (Clinical Dementia Rating),
        159–160
CERAD (Consortium to Establish a
        Registry for Alzheimer's Disease
        Neuropsychological Battery), 149
Charting of behavioral changes over
        time, 141–142
Chase, J., 54
Chastain, R., 93
Children, academic achievement of,
        127
Christianity, 172
Clinical Dementia Rating (CDR),
        159–160
Clinical neuropsychology, 5–6
Cognitive behavioral therapy, 13
Cognitive performance validity tests,
        154–155
Cognitive processes, 69–70
Cognitive realism, 69–70
Cognitive relativism, 70
Cognitive Screening Instrument for
        Dementia (CSI–D), 160
Coherence/cohesion, in speech, 78–79
Collaborative approach, to neuro-
        psychological testing, 49–50
Collectivism
    cultural dimensions related to, 24–25
    individualism vs., 19–21
    Native Indian and Alaskan Native
        cultures as, 48
Color Trails 1, 139–140
Comfort, with evaluation process,
        74–76
Communication
    accurate data collection impacted by,
        32–33
    as cultural consideration, 76–81
    facilitating, in cultural context,
        56–58
    limitations in, noted in reports, 30
    low- vs. high-context, 22, 23
    maximizing, 79–81
    in sample case, 173–174
    unfamiliar, in evaluation process, 74

Conceptual guidelines, 27–37
    AACN Practice Guidelines, 30
    APA ethical and multicultural
        guidelines, 28–30
    and cultural effects, 7
    impact of culture on neuro-
        psychological assessment
        process, 32–37
    *Standards for Educational and
        Psychological Testing* (AERA),
        30–32
Confucian Asia, 19, 20, 23
Confucianism, 171–172
Consecutive interpreting, 89
Consortium to Establish a Registry
        for Alzheimer's Disease Neuro-
        psychological Battery (CERAD),
        149
Construct bias, 133
Construct irrelevance, 132
Construct underrepresentation, 132
Content bias, 133
Cooperation, maximizing, 54–56
Criterion-referenced testing, 140–141
Cross-cultural neuropsychology, 5–6
CSI–D (Cognitive Screening Instrument
        for Dementia), 160
Cultural brokers
    consulting before feedback sessions,
        209
    interpreters as, 88
Cultural confusion, 65
Cultural considerations, 66–90
    acculturation, 67–68
    assessing for acculturation and
        language, 84–85
    clients' conceptualization of
        intelligence, 71–73
    communication, 76–81
    education and literacy, 68–71
    familiarity and comfort with
        evaluation process,
        74–76
    language, 81–83
    poverty and low socioeconomic
        status, 73
    preassessment questions, 66–67
    recommendations for using
        interpreters, 85–90

Cultural context, 41–58
    for behavioral observation, 35
    facilitating communication, 56–58
    macrosocietal structures, 42–47
    maximizing cooperation, 54–56
    medical conditions and beliefs about
        illness, 51–54
    problems of ethnocentric perspective
        on, 34
    recommendations within, 35
    values, beliefs, and social structures,
        47–51
Cultural dimensions
    to facilitate ethnorelative
        perspective, 18
    impact of, on neuropsychological
        assessments, 25–26
    relationship between, 24–25
    surveyed in GLOBE study,
        18–24
Culturally different clients (CDCs)
    assessment goals of, 65–66
    conceptualization of intelligence by,
        71–73
    cultural dimensions to better
        understand, 25–26
    ethical guidelines for working with,
        13–14
    evaluating education of, 70–71
    importance of rapport with, 30
    relevant supplementary information
        about adaptive functioning
        of, 141
    validity of neuropsychological tests
        for, 67–68
Culture
    and estimating premorbid function-
        ing, 95–96
    impact of, on neuropsychological
        assessment, 32–37
    impact of, on neuropsychological
        assessments, 3–4
"Culture-bound" syndromes, 33
Culture-expert interpreting, 89
Culture-relevant interpreting, 89
Cummins, J., 81

Dalai Lama, 27
Data, obtaining accurate, 32–33

SAMHSA (Substance Abuse and
    Mental Health Services
    Administration), 50
Sample cases
    case formulation in, 195–201
    evaluation in, 169–183
    feedback session in, 210–213
    as illustration of process, 8–9
    neuropsychological tests in, 161–165
    report writing for, 204–209
SAT (Scholastic Achievement Test),
    99–101
Schmader, T., 75
Schoenberg, M. R., 98–100
Scholastic Achievement Test (SAT),
    99–101
School, as transnational culture, 69
Schretlen, D. J., 139
Schwartz, T., 142
Screening batteries, 148–152
SES. *See* Socioeconomic status
Shame, in Asian cultures, 75, 80, 174
Shultz, J., 77
Siddhartha Gautama, 59
SIRS (Structured Interview of Reported
    Symptoms), 159
Small, S. A., 139
Social groups, in acculturation
    assessment, 84
Social norms
    awareness of, for clients, 79
    tight vs. loose, 23, 24
Social structures, 47–51
Socioeconomic status (SES)
    as cultural consideration, 73
    effect of, on test performance, 193
    and intelligence, 129
    of Native Indian and Alaskan
        Natives, 46
    and premorbid functioning, 122–123
Somatic performance validity tests, 157
Southern Asia, 19, 20, 23
South Korea
    Confucianism in, 172
    IQ scores for, 171
    normative data from, 195–196
Spinks, R., 98
Standardized achievement test scores,
    98–101

*Standards for Educational and Psychologi-
    cal Testing* (AERA), 30–32
Stereotype threat, 74–75, 80
Stern, Y., 139
Sternberg, R. J., 71, 145
Storytelling, as communication, 57
Stress, and test performance, 75
Structured Interview of Reported
    Symptoms (SIRS), 159
Stubbe, M., 86
Sub-Saharan Africa, 19, 20, 23
Substance Abuse and Mental Health
    Services Administration
    (SAMHSA), 50
Sue, D. W., 75–76
Summary interpreting, 89
Sun Tzu, 91
Supernatural agency, as cause of
    illness, 53

Tannen, D., 77–79
Telephone interpreters, 86
Te Pou, 174
Test equivalency, 133
Test interpretation, 30
Test of Memory Malingering (TOMM),
    156
Test selection, 132–137
    ethical guidelines involving, 29, 34
    impact of culture on, 36
    practical considerations for, 134–136
    psychometric considerations for,
        132–134
    in sample case, 176–177
    translations of tests, 136–137
Thombs, B. D., 35
Thompson, L. A., 98
Tight social norms, 23, 24
Time orientation
    monochronic vs. polychronic, 22, 23
    of Native Indian and Alaskan Native
        cultures, 48
    and performance on timed tests,
        72–73
TIMSS (Trends in International
    Mathematics and Science Study),
    95–96
TOMM (Test of Memory Malingering),
    156

ABOUT THE AUTHOR

Daryl Fujii, PhD, ABPP-CN, is a staff neuropsychologist at the Veterans Affairs Pacific Island Health Care Services Community Living Center and adjunct faculty for the Department of Psychiatry, University of Hawaii. He received his PhD from the University of Wyoming in 1991, interned at the Sepulveda Veterans Administration Medical Center, and completed a postdoctoral fellowship at the Rehabilitation Hospital of the Pacific. Dr. Fujii earned his diplomate in clinical neuropsychology from the American Board of Professional Psychology in 1999 and was elected to fellow status of the American Psychological Association in 2006. His research interests include cross-cultural neuropsychology, schizophrenia, geriatrics, secondary psychosis, and psychosis secondary to traumatic brain injury, for which he is an international forensic consultant. He has more than 50 publications, including two edited books: *The Spectrum of Psychotic Disorders: Neurobiology, Etiology, and Pathogenesis* (2007) and *The Neuropsychology of Asian Americans* (2011). Dr. Fujii is currently a co-chair of the national VA Psychology Training Committee, Multicultural Diversity Committee and chair of the VA Pacific Island Health Care Services and VA Central California Health Care System.